A Chilmark Miscellany

Van Wyck Brooks has written:
. . . .

The World of Washington Irving
The Flowering of New England
The Times of Melville and Whitman
New England: Indian Summer
Opinions of Oliver Allston
The Life of Emerson
The Ordeal of Mark Twain
The Pilgrimage of Henry James
Emerson and Others
Three Essays on America: America's
Coming-of-Age, Letters and Leadership,
The Literary Life in America
Sketches in Criticism
A Chilmark Miscellany
. . . .

Published by E. P. Dutton & Co., Inc.

A CHILMARK
MISCELLANY

By Van Wyck Brooks

1948

E. P. DUTTON *&* COMPANY, INC.

NEW YORK

AMERICAN BOOK–STRATFORD PRESS, INC., NEW YORK

CONTENTS

NOTE

Virtually all the pages in this collection have appeared in one or another of my previous books. The brief sketch of Llewelyn Powys was written as a preface for his *Earth Memories,* and a few of the *Notes from a Journal* are new.

CHILMARK, Martha's Vineyard, *June,* 1948

Notes from a Journal

NOTES
FROM A JOURNAL

A MIEL, DEFINING the critic, the "true critic" that none of us can ever hope to become, remarks, "What years of labour, what study and comparison, are needed to bring the critical judgment to maturity!" Only at fifty, he adds, can the critic "have made the rounds of all the modes of being, only by then can he have mastered all the possible shades of appreciation." Only, one might rather say, when he has lived as long as the Wandering Jew. As for the early fruit of a critic's mind, it can hardly be other than green. Losing our greenness, growing older, the danger is that we may not acquire the famous *lumen siccum* that parches and offends, as Bacon says, "most men's watery or soft natures," a light that is valuable not because it is dry, but because, being dry, it is closest to fire.

* * *

I do not believe in golden ages; and may heaven smite the praiser of times past who tries to shame the present with examples of what was never, surely, his own past. The so-called golden ages are merely times when men know how to use their powers and make more of their lives than at other times.

* * *

"I have been meditating on the great importance it is to a literary man to remain unknown till he gets his work fairly done. It can hardly be overstated." Thus Longfellow, in his

I

journal, and how right he is. If we cannot afford to take this Olympian line, if we have to seek publicity, at least let us know what we are doing. I do not envy the successful authors about whom the publicity men and reporters flock, like sharks about a raft, which, when the provisions are gone, breaks up and leaves these authors at their mercy.

*   *   *

Nothing good can come from writers who are at ease in their Zion. We should all live like Israelites at the Feast of Passover.

*   *   *

In forty years of writing, I have not gained an ounce of confidence. I begin each new book (as I have probably always begun, although I never remember it) with a sense of impotence, chaos and desperation that cannot be overstated. I always feel that I am foredoomed to failure.

Every day I begin my work with the same old feeling, that I am on trial for my life and will probably not be acquitted.

*   *   *

A little fetishism sometimes helps one. Handel and Machiavelli always composed in court dress. Buffon did the same thing. They wooed the grand style by dressing in it.

Fetishism of this kind is good for other styles too. I never used to throw away any of my old suits until I had finished another book. When I set to work on ———, I was wearing a rough grey suit of which I was particularly fond; and, before I had finished the second chapter, the suit and the book had somehow grown together in my mind. I should not have dreamed of sitting down to write in any other coat or trousers. That was the book in the middle of which I had a serious breakdown. I went on wearing the suit, hoping it would bring back my luck; and when I was able to work again the suit was in tatters. But "let back and sides go bare, go bare," would I have thrown away that suit? Not for all the treasure on Cocos

Island. I kept the suit and finished the book, and I always felt that my old grey coat had turned the trick for me.

* * *

How to dispose of one's tin cans. When one is living in the woods and writing in the morning, this is the sort of problem that provides one's afternoons with a proper focus.

Bertrand Russell is right in saying that one who wishes to do good work must expect to be bored much of the time. A state of dull vacuity is the best mental state in which to suspend one's hours of composition. When the conscious mind is over-stimulated, the unconscious mind refuses to open its door. So, at least, it is with me.

I notice in Emerson's journal that, when he was at Saint Augustine, he spent hours along the beach driving an orange with his walking-stick. Day after day, at Saint Augustine, when I was writing there, my only object was to find another coquina-shell, washed up by the tide, to take home and use for baking fish in.

* * *

When a writer begins to be successful, when he begins to soar, outwardly but especially inwardly, then, to save him from infatuation, he needs to be pelted with bitter apples.

* * *

I, as a groper, always used to feel at a disadvantage in dealing with theorists and dogmatists. Now I let them talk. For I observe that these dogmatists all fall sooner or later into the hands of greater dogmatists, either Hitler, Stalin or, in another field, the Pope.

* * *

Sainte-Beuve, in his essay on Leopardi (*Portraits contemporains,* IV), apologizes for writing of a foreign author, persuaded as he is *que la critique littéraire n'a toute sa valeur et son originalité que lorsqu'elle s'applique à des sujets dont on possède de près et de longue main le fond, les alentours et toutes les circonstances,*—"literary criticism has its full worth and originality only when it applies itself to subjects of which it possesses, through immediate contact and from a long way back, the source, the surrounding facts and all the circumstances." Certainly, Sainte-Beuve wrote about many foreign authors with surpassing grace and understanding, and yet it seems to me that he stated a principle here to which a critic may well give heed in his practice. The poet Yeats had the same thought when he wrote, "One can only reach out to the universe with a gloved hand,—that hand is one's nation, the only thing that one knows even a little about." This is my guiding thought in writing on American authors.

* * *

As against having beautiful workshops, studies, etc., one writes best in the cellar on a rainy day. I found that a rainy day in Florida,—and in California also,—wonderfully prospered the act of mental concentration. That is one reason why Ireland, England and Norway are so good for writers.

I always felt that the California sunshine had an ill effect on people's minds there. My friend M. W. gave me a case in point. The superior of the Catholic seminary at San Mateo complained that he could not get his students to work. Impossible to induce a vocation! The students were always "sitting about in the sun." That is why the Spaniards and Italians, who have lived in these warm sunny climates, and who have cared greatly for the inner life, have cultivated gloomy depths of darkness. They have known how to adjust themselves to this semi-tropical milieu. They have broken up the monotony of heat and sunshine by creating contrasts,—high and heavy walls, damp stonework, enclosures of deep shade, thickets of shrubbery, etc. Not California bungalows and Florida verandahs, but bare, stony cells, houses like Michael Angelo's at Florence, —these assist the mind to find its focus.

* * *

The Artful Dodger. Get the reputation of being a recluse. Spread it about that you are a chronic invalid. Tell them you have leprosy or rabies. You must be
> *instinctively thorough*
> *About your crevice and burrow,*

like Robert Frost and his Drumlin Woodchuck.

*   *   *

I received this morning a warranty deed entitling me to a piece of land that I have long desired and am glad to own. Yet, strangely, when I saw my name inscribed upon this deed, I felt a tremor in my bones. This deed was full of a kind of poetry. I became a grantee, with "assigns forever." The land was mine, for my "own proper use and behoof." With the "ensealing of these presents," I was "well seized of the premises." My estate was indefeasible "in fee simple." I was henceforth entitled to privileges, appurtenances and all manner of other high and mighty rights in regard to bargaining and selling, and the grantor was bound to defend me. I felt solemnly proud to associate my name with these admirable phrases, this poetry of the law that carries me back directly to the lives of my Saxon forbears in their mud-huts and manors,—for, like everyone of my name, I had forbears in both. Well I know what all these phrases represented in terms of toil and sweat and self-respect for untold generations of these forbears, what struggles and triumphs they stood for and what a large portion of history in this country and England. And yet I felt a tremor in my bones.

My instinct does not claim property, however I may rejoice in it. I have another kind of estate to which it is inimical. All men are tamed nomads, born to wander after adventure, and this is especially true in the case of writers. They are, and must be, sojourners on this earth, and they dread the trap of property, the trap of possessions. "Sell all thou hast" is their motto. True writers in their hearts are like Arabs and soldiers. Tolstoy stood for them all when he ran away at the end of his life, preferring to die anywhere on the open road. How well I understand my friend the sailor-novelist, who cannot bear to see a garden planted round his house. He sees every shoot as a nail that holds him in place. His rolling fields remind him of the waves, and he longs to be off again.

* * *

I understand too the painter Rothenstein's saying, "It is in the atmosphere of poetry and among men of large vision and magnanimous natures that I have been most happy and comfortable." How delightful is the company of generous people, who overlook trifles and keep their minds instinctively fixed on whatever is good and positive in the world about them. People of small calibre are always carping. They are bent on showing their own superiority, their knowledge or their prowess or good breeding. But magnanimous people have no vanity, they have no jealousy, they have no reserves, and they feed on the true and the solid wherever they find it. And, what is more, they find it everywhere.

* * *

I feel about my work as President Eliot felt about Harvard: "Things seem to be going fairly well, now that a spirit of pessimism prevails in all departments."

* * *

George Gissing was one of the writers who thrive on their irritations. "Every man," he says somewhere, "has his intellectual desire; mine is to escape life as I know it, and dream myself back into that old world which was the imaginative delight of my boyhood." It was this world, the Mediterranean world of the past, that gave him a scale by which to measure the scenes that surrounded him in London; and in the last years of his life he set out to seek the traces of it in the Magna Græcia of which he wrote in *By the Ionian Sea*. What was it then that kept him for so many years confined in his City of Dreadful Night?—for he felt about London much as Jar Thomson felt. Not poverty alone. He hated London, with all the instincts of the born recluse. He was offended by crowds, he shrank from casual encounters, he disliked the "tongue of Whitechapel" and the "blaring lust of life." "Every day," he said, "gives me a deeper loathing of city life. If I cannot escape from it to die amid green fields, my end will be wretched indeed." Yet virtually his whole life was passed in cities; even when he came to America, he made no effort to seek the countryside,—he spent all his time in Chicago and Boston,—and, of his twenty-two novels, twenty-one deal, at least largely, with London. Thus we can see that his instinct of artistic self-preservation was constantly at war with all his normal tastes.

Is it not a fact that novelists usually thrive best on their irritations? Hawthorne throve in the dust and wind of Salem. Flaubert, Stendhal, Sinclair Lewis, Dreiser are other cases in point; and do not Henry James's early novels show that this was also true for him? As long as he dealt with native Americans, who irritated him all the time, everything went well with James. Perhaps the less we satisfy our tastes, the more they serve to give us a scale and a measure.

* * *

My friend H., who fought in the Spanish-American War, described to me once a moment which he witnessed in the life of Stephen Crane. They were together at the battle of Guantanamo, where Crane was acting as a correspondent. An unusually vicious fire was in progress, directed by the Spaniards against an earthwork behind which the American troops were huddled. Suddenly Crane, who was incapable of bravado, let himself quietly over the redoubt, lighted a cigarette, stood for a few moments with his arms at his sides, while the bullets hissed past him into the mud, then as quietly climbed back over the redoubt and strolled away. It was impossible, H. said, to question the insouciance of this act: Crane's bearing was that of a somnambulist. He appeared to be, as it were, detached from himself, possessed by an irresistible impulse to register, in his body, and without regard to the safety of his body, certain sensations. The curiosity of the artist, who wishes to know, was so completely in the ascendant as to inhibit the fundamental instincts of the man.

For to the pure artist, as countless incidents show, physical existence is not an end but a means, something that has value not because it *is,* but rather because, having it, one can feel and express it. Think of the painters one has known, penniless, half-fed, ill-clothed, unwarmed, working all day in feverish ecstasy at unsalable pictures. Why should the human animal, born to inherit a gracious world, subject himself to these tortures?—for the painters in question would have murdered anyone who suggested a compromise with the market. Could Stephen Crane have explained why he exposed himself to the Spanish bullets?—and would have exposed himself, with a similar purpose, to the Spanish Inquisition? Let Nietzsche answer for him: "What an endless amount of distress, privation, bad weather, sickness, depression, isolation we have to endure! Yet, after all, we manage to put up with all this, born as we are to a subterranean, struggling existence; every now and then we emerge into the light, we live once more through our golden hour of victory."

As for Crane himself, who saw everything, heard, tasted, felt with the exquisite aptitude of a convalescent, of one who is recovering from an illness (from which he never recovered), so sensitive that the tremor of a butterfly's wing was not too slight to escape him,—as for Crane, who had none of that desire to "see life" which is felt by those who have little capacity for it, his ruling passion was yet a kind of curiosity. The recurring theme in his stories, in *The Red Badge of Courage,* in *Active Service,* in *The Open Boat,* is that of the sensations of a man in peril of death. For some reason, the deepest part of his nature had elected the theme for him, and no doubt to have experienced the sensation in its sudden fullness he would have risked death not once but a dozen times.

* * *

What I like about my village. Plenty of good solitude, and plenty of the kind of interruptions that do not soothe the social man but challenge all his prepossessions.

In New York, I should die of stimulus.

In Boston, I should be soothed to death.

Yes, I know what would happen. I should go the way of all the gadflies,—like our well-known Z., the satirist, when, in the simplicity of his heart, he took to playing billiards every evening with his jolly neighbours on Long Island. The sting of his talent atrophied. How could he find fault with all those good fellows? He ceased to be able to find fault with all the abuses they stood for.

* * *

People who are too agreeable and cultivated lull one insensibly into a kind of fatuity. One gets into a fools' paradise. Except in very small doses, "good society" is not good for writers. This is because they need to be misunderstood, they require something harsh in the air about them.

Children and writers feel the need of grit and sand, of something astringent in the moral atmosphere, that causes them to define themselves and their aims, as one needs salt in one's diet, as the teeth require both alkali and acids.

As much as to understanding, children are entitled to misunderstanding. Not the brutal variety, but the bland variety. After the primitive needs have received attention, they should be confronted with a blank wall of incomprehension. It is by reacting against this that they define themselves, become aware of themselves and their intentions.

The same thing is true of writers and artists, and this is one reason why England has been so fertile in geniuses. The stolid egoism of the English household is the milieu for poets. Americans are too sympathetic to provide a good medium for the development of individuality. They are always talking about and trying to meet its problems, and by this very process they inhibit its growth. The process merely produces self-conscious hobbledehoys, the geniuses of the family circle who never come to anything.

Everyone, in fact, needs incomprehension, and even oceans of it. This is especially true of writers and artists. It is only when we are misunderstood by others that we really understand ourselves.

The infallible way to produce uniformity is to cultivate individuality, which, in its proper growth, is always a by-product. The great age of American genius, the generation before the Civil War,—certainly not yet equalled in this respect by any succeeding generation,—was an age of rigid social discipline. Michelet said he grew up like a blade of grass between two paving-stones. So did Thoreau, Emerson and Hawthorne. So did Emily Dickinson and Winslow Homer. It is true that Poe and Melville encountered too much incomprehension. The last straw breaks the camel's back, but at least a large proportion of the other straws serve to develop its muscles.

*   *   *

Gibbon observes that the ancient Germans, when they were summoned to a public meeting, would lag behind the appointed time in order to show their independence. This trait was still more marked, according to Parkman, among the American Indians of Pontiac's time.

Similarly, my friend X. and other editorial potentates rattle their papers on their desks for ten or twenty minutes, before they admit their suppliants, in order to show how important and busy they are. Henceforth, I shall think of editors as ancient Germans.

*   *   *

Today I received another of those questionnaires that are sent out to Tom, Dick and Harry, asking for my views on socialism and communism and "how the American author ought to stand" regarding this, that and the other matter. I fully agree that authors should "take sides," and I always do so; but I ignore or decline these invitations to develop my views at length. It is not that I have not strong feelings on all these subjects; but may heaven preserve me from expressing them beyond the point of a Yes or No until the spirit calls me to do so in the normal course of my writing. Well said Nietzsche, "How happy are we, we finders of knowledge, provided that we know how to keep silent long enough." If there is anything "the American author ought" to do, it is to keep the steam in his own boiler. If, storing away their opinions, writers allowed them to roll up interest in their minds, their legitimate writings would have a weight which they sadly lack at present.

* * *

I sympathize with my youthful neighbour, who is struggling to inject a little order, a little taste and style,—a little readability, in short—into a mass of manuscript that is supposed to be a book. A great lawyer thinks he has written this book, and he proposes to sign it. These legal luminaries, these magnates, these presidents of corporations, these very important men who are always pressing buttons have notions of their own in regard to writing. They imagine that all they have to do, to commit their thoughts to immortality, is to command a squadron of secretaries to look this, that and the other up, and then, in some hour of ease, with their spoils assembled about them, and a box of the best cigars on the desk before them, dictate to Miss Daphne or Miss Hebe. And they are always surprised to find that no one will read their writings. So many *whereases* and *wherefores* have crept into their manuscript that, although Miss Daphne strives to conceal the fact, she would rather walk home to Brooklyn in a March blizzard than read a page of the great man's lucubrations. Then the same result always follows. The great man turns for help to some youthful writer and offers him a chauffeur's wages if he will take the manuscript in hand and make it worthy of his signature.

These very important men do not know that literature is a learned profession, ten times more difficult than law. They do not know that there are some problems which cannot be solved by pressing a button, that literary taste and skill are the reward of years of humble effort. And in this they resemble certain writers who are also very important, if one judges them by a similar standard,—the degrees and decorations they have received and the confidence with which they address the public in their interviews and radio-speeches. One knows of authors who hire young men and women to do their drudgery for them. But God is not mocked in regard to them, nor is the critic deceived. This was not the way that Gibbon worked, or Prescott or Parkman, who used the secretarial crutch only because they were halt and blind. A real writer feels about his work as a healthy mother feels about her baby. His instinct revolts against the incubator and every mechanical substitute for brooding. The writer who does not brood, in every sense of the word, the writer who is not his own drudge, who does not earn his notes by loving investigation, pays a heavy forfeit. His prose lacks depth, tone and texture, and nothing can compensate for this.

I add that no good writer has ever liked drudgery, and Prescott and Parkman,—and Motley too,—found research repulsive. The tension created by this repulsion is characteristic of first-rate minds.

*   *   *

I like painters. They are just like writers, without the nonsense. Of course, they have their own nonsense, but I don't have to bother about that.

Why do artists of every kind gravitate to painters? It is because they are apt to be simple and happy. As Virgil Thomson says, in *The State of Music,* "The Seeing Eye has no opinions" and "The painter's whole morality consists in keeping his brushes clean and getting up in the morning." Therefore painters are "a pleasant lot, cheerful and healthy." It is natural that the rest of us, writers, musicians and what not, who are so often morbid, are drawn to painters.

*   *   *

Why do I wish to avoid such men as X., who abound among artists and writers? They are the men with a foot in each sphere, the sphere of the mind and the sphere of the mundane. They have a superstitious regard for those who have both feet in the sphere of the mind, after which they hanker, but, if they had to make a choice, if they had to plant both feet on one side of the line, they would take the side of the mundane, not with the integrity of worldly people, but because they lack the strength for the other side. This tormented double-mindedness subtly poisons the air about them. I know how to deal with the frankly worldly, but the effort to contribute to the self-respect of people who feel they have lapsed from the other world and lack the will to recover it, or even seek it, is not good for anyone. Healthy people are those who make clear decisions. The half-artists, soft within, affect me like stretches of marshland. You never know, in their company, where to place your foot, for fear of hurting their feelings, and you begin to doubt your own ground. They *give* at every point, and, meeting no resistance, your muscles become an illusion to yourself. It does not do to linger after nightfall in swamps of this kind. One is sure to catch malaria.

* * *

Most modern art-lovers are discontented modish people who seize upon art for quite extraneous reasons. The lovers of art and literature are as few as ever, and they do not include many who are always talking of art and literature,—even professional critics,—and who claim an exclusive right to do so. Real lovers are not exclusive in this fashion, though they sometimes find it difficult to include the exclusive.

The modern artist takes as axiomatic the notion, no concession to the public taste, i.e., the taste of the gross public; but the age in which he assumed this motto has been the age in which he made most concessions to the *élite* public. Conscious of the larger herd, the artist nowadays never belonged so much to a lesser herd. One hardly knows a painter who dares not to be influenced by Derain or Picasso, or Orozco, or Matisse. Painters feel they *ought* to paint in the manner of this artist or that, as writers feel they ought to write in the manner of Kafka or Henry James. Never was the vogue so dominant in fields where it should not be dominant, i.e., in fields other than that of dress, where fashion has a function. Our age of alleged independence shows far less independence than the Victorian age, in which originality was almost the rule; and this is a result of urban life, which insensibly draws everyone into a herd. The desire not to be of the herd is in itself a herd-desire. It is a recognition of the herd of which the original man is incapable.

The artists formed the *élite* herd in self-defence, in order to separate from the gross herd. But just as, in the immediate past, the enemy was the gross herd, so the *élite* herd is the enemy of the artist of the future.

*   *   *

One is a long time finding out how different others are from oneself, and what wildly improbable lives, from one's own point of view, can still be happy lives. I, who could be happy in a tub, or on St. Simeon's pillar, if certain other things were right with me, think all the other folks are queer. And I continue to think them queer and am only relieved to know that they like their queerness.

*   *   *

Our age of psychology is not an age of interest in human nature. Think of the excited wonder with which the novels of Dickens and Balzac were written, a wonder that vibrates in their pages. This is the trait that also gives life to the great portraits of Ingres, Beechey and Gilbert Stuart, as of Velasquez and Rembrandt. No matter how good our novels and portraits may be, in every other respect, they lack this relish for charac-ter which has stamped all the enduring novels and portraits. Our novelists turn their characters inside out, and sometimes describe them inimitably, but can one imagine a writer of our time laughing and weeping over his characters, living their lives and sharing their feelings as Victor Hugo and Thackeray lived the lives of their men and women?

This excited wonder over human nature was one of the marks of the Victorian age, as of all the ages of energy. Is there a portrait-photographer living who has an eye for character that is comparable to David Octavius Hill's? Stieglitz had an eye for certain types, but he was more interested in other matters. The aim and the effect of most of our portrait-photographers is to make their sitters conform to a preconceived type,—they all emerge from the camera as captains of industry or as pretty women, when they are not decorative arrangements. Well spoke Emerson, writing to Carlyle, about his "thirsty eyes," his "portrait-eating, portrait-painting eyes." All the great novelists and portrait-painters, Carlyle and Taine among them, have "eaten" their characters in this way.

In his *Origins of Modern Sculpture*, W. R. Valentiner observes that modern portraits are less good than the old ones because the age of individualism has come to an end. Along with individualism, the interest in portraiture has faded,—and what I call the feeling for character also. How else can one explain T. S. Eliot's remark that "Nothing seems odder about that age (the Victorian) than the respect which its eminent people felt for one another"? What is "odd" about respect for character, which everyone admits the eminent Victorians had? There are even some modern novelists who do not pretend to care for character. Thus D H. Lawrence said, in a letter of 1914, "You mustn't look in my novel for the old stable ego of the character . . . Somehow, that which is physic—non-human—in humanity is more interesting to me than the old-fashioned human element, which causes one to conceive a character in a certain moral scheme and make him consistent." Aldous Huxley comments upon this, "For ordinary practical purposes we conceive human beings as creatures with characters. But analysis of their behaviour can be carried so far, that they cease to have character and reveal themselves as collections of psychological atoms." It is just as it is with diamonds, which are also composed of atoms, which in turn are composed of electrons and protons. As Huxley says, most of us are more interested in diamonds than we are in the elements that make them up. And it is surely the "old-fashioned human element" for which, as human beings, we look in novels.

In no respect does it appear more clearly that ours is not an age of energy than in this indifference to character. The seventeenth century, like the nineteenth, was an age of energy. That is why Queen Elizabeth forbade even a single shadow in her portrait.

Psychology is one thing, and it is the dominant thing today. Perception and feeling are something else,—have not the Germans proved it? It was they who invented psychology and, with the Austrians, psychoanalysis. But did they not lose two world wars largely because they knew nothing of human nature? If they had understood the never-say-die disposition that has always governed the English and American mind, they would not have joined battle with it, so stupidly, twice. The Germans have proved how remote psychology is from perception and feeling,—the qualities that have always been dominant in the great ages.

*   *   *

The method of psychoanalysis, in the writing of biographies, has a very limited value, and I believe that, having once passed, it will not be used again. If one could accept for biography the dictum of George Brandes, that, while the romantic intellect is interested in the significance of things, the modern intellect is interested only in their causes, then one could say that the day of the Plutarchs has passed and that Freud is the master of the future. In reality, what concerns the biographer, whether "romantic" or not, is always the significance of things. Psychoanalysis serves the psychologist in the biographer by placing him in possession of certain facts which he cannot obtain so easily by other methods. But these facts are no more useful than other facts, and all a biographer's facts are useless until he has reconceived them in the light of his intuitive faculty, with its feeling for reality and proportion. This is a different mental organ from the intelligence, which actually paralyses its operation. It is not the causes that matter in biography, it is the character itself, which belongs to the moral and aesthetic sphere, a sphere that is quite apart from the sphere of causation. The attempt to turn biography into a science is as futile as it is with history.

* * *

The old Shaker house at Harvard village. It was interesting to note the perfection of the manuscript books copied by the brothers, as the monks copied MSS in the Middle Ages. One was a New Testament, written in a round clear hand in a large folio volume. It was a rule of the community that if a copyist made a blot or an error he was obliged to discard the sheet and write it over again from the beginning.

The Shakers, and their American monastic life, devoted to weaving, carving, rug-making, etc. This is only one of the life-patterns of which we have lost sight in the general compulsion to make money in the shortest available fashion. People's imaginations have been so dulled by industrialism that they cannot respond to these patterns any longer. A century ago, the popular mind was filled with the biblical patterns, the patterns presented by Plutarch, etc., so that all the classical modes of living were latent in people's minds and had only to be touched into action by some inspired leader. It was this preliminary work accomplished by popular custom that made possible the influence of Jefferson, Garrison and Thoreau.

What strikes me among all the relics of our older time is the vivid reality of these life-patterns that have passed utterly out of men's minds.

* * *

What determines the value of a civilization? There is only one criterion, according to Leopardi,—the amount of the singularity one finds among the people of the country. To put this in other words, character exists when people are interested in it and tolerate it. Character is the basis of civilization. Variety of character is the life of civilization.

It is this variety of character that has passed away along with the life-patterns that I have just mentioned. There was a time when our population was full of singularity. In old New England, as in the West and the South, the nobler types were commoner than they are at present, but also, and this is to be observed, the queer fellows, the odd fish, the cracker-barrel sages and the like,—the village atheists, even the town drunkards,—had a sort of privilege, as they had in Russia. They might have been considered reprobates, but they were encouraged as amusing, if not worthy of respect. People seemed to realize that some of these men were geniuses, *in posse* if not *in esse*. Towards all such persons, in recent times, the general attitude is one of impatience, and they have almost died out, along with the Shakers and other sects that once gave such variety to the human landscape. This indicates,—to follow Leopardi,—a definite retrogression in our civilization.

*   *   *

Poor Mrs. Y. flutters in, crying for help, as usual. She reminds me of one of those little birds, astray on the ocean, that light on a passing steamer, preen their feathers and wildly dart about, and vanish again, most certainly to perish, unless some other ship happens along.

*   *   *

In London once, B. and I went to an Industrial Exhibition with an attaché of the Chinese embassy, the latter, with his drooping moustache, wearing the largest and roundest of spectacles and a bright red button on his cap. Said B., calling his attention to the X-ray machine, "You can see all the bones in the body." Our Chinese companion studied the photographs. "Ah," he replied, after a pause, tapping B.'s arm, "you can see all the bones, but you cannot see the heart." And this was all he could be induced to say about the Occidental magic of machinery.

* * *

I like Rudolph Ruzicka's story about his Boston friend who, when he comes to New York, and settles in the great New York hotel, opens his parcels and puts away in a drawer together every scrap of wrapping-paper and every fragment of string,—so they will not be "lonely" until he can take them back to Boston.

* * *

We are developing, in our circle, a Howells character in the person of Mrs. W., who has so many scruples and so many emotional problems, real to her yet utterly fantastic, that she makes life a problem for everyone else. Of course, as with so many of Howells's people, these problems are unconscious attempts to fill a sadly empty life. They create the drama that human nature requires, for, like nature itself, human nature abhors a vacuum and insists upon creating drama out of nothing if it has nothing else to feed upon. American life is riddled with this furtive drama. I like people who speak their minds, and I think life ought to be thoroughly ventilated; but, if American life had been ventilated, what would have become of Howells?

* * *

We wonder why the lives of the saints are so fabulous, why worthies of the dark ages appear so distorted in history. But what happens in our own enlightened age? Wait till you lose by death some eminent friend, and then go about in the circles he frequented and try to piece together the legend of his life. You will find that he survives in the minds of his associates as both a sentimentalist and a cynic, a crimson revolutionist and a sky-high tory, a simpleton, a snob and a bourgeois, a man of bold ideas and a teacher's pet. All these at once, and all revealing what?—the little serpents and the little doves that every circle of friends cherishes in its bosom. Rare is the rectitude of the realistic eye, quite as rare in our age of light as it was in the ages of darkness. Did we not see Henry Cabot Lodge construct before our eyes the myth of Theodore Roosevelt as the classic statesman, who never swerved from principle and never acted on any but second thoughts? One can live in the centre of the world, in a complicated web of social relations, and remain as invisible as a grasshopper in a spring meadow.

* * *

A man who has the courage of his platitudes is always a successful man. The instructed man is ashamed to pronounce in an orphic manner what everybody knows, and from his silence people think that he is making fun of them. They like a man who expresses their own superficial thoughts in a manner that appears to be profound. This enables them to feel that they are themselves profound.

* * *

I am always impressed by people who give themselves out as persons of large importance. At least, in this regard, the serpent of doubt entered my garden only when I had reached years of discretion. Judging by the mask and gown, the beetling brow, the gesture of command, I used to imagine that I had encountered a dozen Dantes and Beethovens.

In later years, I found that genius and virtue more often clothe themselves in hodden grey than in the splendid feathers of macaws and peacocks. Corneille looked like a cattle-dealer, and Descartes might have been taken for an honest Dutch merchant, as Balzac says in *Les Illusions Perdues*,—while visitors to La Brède, meeting Montesquieu in a cotton nightcap, carrying a rake on his shoulder, mistook him for a gardener. They followed in this the law of protective coloration, which is based upon another law, that of the conservation of energy. It takes a great deal of energy to maintain an appearance of greatness, more than the really great are able to spare.

* * *

An evening with three eminent men of law. They began to speak of literature, in all amiability, and then what a pulling out of chestnuts, fossilized for ages in the legal mind, half the familiar quotations in Bartlett, chiefly from Pope, and the question rose, Who wrote Junius? It was evident that one and all were talking as they thought lawyers ought to talk, that they were following the well-known pattern of the learned judge unbending. What children are these great men, so exactly living up to the parts that conventional public opinion expects them to play.

In *Fors Clavigera*, Ruskin relents towards lawyers enough to admit them to a "dignified almshouse," because they are picturesque,—"for the sake of their wigs." I should preserve them for another reason, also one that springs from a love of the past. For as long as lawyers exist, Bartlett's "familiar quotations" will never be unfamiliar.

*   *   *

She makes me feel like a syringa-blossom, she being the humming-bird. I can feel her little brain revolve and vibrate, whirring at such a rate that it makes me dizzy, while the proboscis fathoms me, all to extract a drop of honey.

*   *   *

She has seen everything and met everybody, and she cannot understand why I do not wish to see her. She has all the latest news from behind the scenes. She has just spent an evening at the White House, and Hitler has told her all his secrets. She has such remarkable things to say, as that Hitler in his heart loves the Jews, that Mussolini has only the kindest intentions, and that the next war is going to start from a difference of opinion in the Andes. It is all new and exciting, and everything is different from what one supposed, just as reality always is. And yet I am not consumed with a passion to meet her.

But has she really seen things, or has she perhaps seen nothing? How these awfully knowing people abound! The lady neglects to consider one fact, which is that the value of reflections depends upon the quality of the mirror. A looking-glass walking down the road was Stendhal's definition of a story-teller, and the world at present is full of looking-glasses. Then why is the world so unfamiliar with its own features? It is because most of the looking-glasses come from Mr. Woolworth's basement.

*   *   *

You do not know, I do not know. This is the only attitude to assume in the presence of the "knowing" political prophets. I soon saw at Washington, in 1940, that most of the officials did not know what was going to happen, in Germany or Italy or Japan, and that those who really knew the most knew that they did not know. It was all a matter of "feeling," and the people who "feel," in regard to these events, are very seldom those who are "in the know." The only invincible ignorance is knowingness, which always deceives the simple. When, for a dozen years, we have watched our favourite political prophet, whoever he may be, predicting revolutions that do not occur, and failing to predict revolutions that do,—as I saw in the case of my own chosen prophet, a very knowing man, whom I took for gospel years ago,—we end by ceasing to read them. The feeling life is the only life that matters, and, when it comes to the movements of peoples, it is the old women who know, not the brilliant publicists, with their bright and shining information. That is why Napoleon resorted to the sooth-sayers, as the German and Austrian emperors, in the first world-war, consulted Madame Sylvia, if that was her name.

I do not refer to the commentators, Sheean, Swing, Shirer, who have added a third dimension to political reporting. These journalists of our time, moreover, who care for social justice, are a most admirable development of this generation. What a contrast to the older correspondents, who were so often mainly soldiers of fortune. Nor am I attacking the intelligence, except when it is used improperly. Its proper use is to solve solvable

questions, on a basis of known data. But the great questions of
life can seldom be approached in this fashion; and those who
pursue life in a straight line, as if it were a game of chess, pay
a heavy price for their nonchalance. They lose the use of their
perceptions, which are chiefly active when the intelligence is in
abeyance. For the feeling men, the brooding men, life is a tragi-
comedy, not a game. Men of this type are always guessing.
The intelligent men disdain to guess. They base their predictions on evidence. But as the elements of the evidence are
largely emotional elements, their predictions are usually wrong,
while the guesses of the others are often right. One can be
weather-wise about human questions, as well as about the crops
and the snowstorms.

* * *

J. C. tells me about the brilliant young men at Princeton,
and I remember T.'s account of the young men of his day.
They were all going to reform the country, and now they are
clipping coupons in their fathers' offices. "These matters are
delightfully uncertain," as Hawthorne says, in *The House of
the Seven Gables*. "At almost every step in life, we meet with
young men of just about Holgrave's age, for whom we antici-
pate wonderful things, but of whom, even after much and care-
ful enquiry, we never happen to hear another word. The
effervescence of youth and passion, and the fresh gloss of the
intellect and imagination, endow them with a false brilliancy,
which makes fools of themselves and other people. Like certain
chintzes, calicos and ginghams, they show finely in their first
newness, but cannot stand the sun and rain, and assume a very
sober aspect after washing-day."

* * *

Eugène Delacroix, in his journal, says of his young friend
Riesener, "He is lost. He is beginning to say, 'It's too late now,'
like all the lazy men who have forever been saying with assurance, 'I have plenty of time.' "

* * *

Do not flatter yourself that by mere inertia you can sink to the lower depths. In order to sink, as well as to rise, a well-organized person has to work, for he has to violate all manner of instincts which it is easier to satisfy. The line of least resistance is to float on a dead level, like a large inexpensive cake of soap.

*   *   *

To "have a good time" is the sole object of life for untold thousands of our countrypeople. I sympathize with this ideal in people who are born for it, but I think they are rare. However, I know a few who have a real vocation for it. Nature intended them to have a good time, and one feels they ought to have it; and, when they fail to have it, when circumstances turn against them, one feels a desolation in the general air. It is just as K. says about the Negroes, who enjoy their clothes and finery so much. When I see a young Negro in a brand new spring suit, with a bright new necktie and a flower in his buttonhole, I feel as if every one of them should have an annual dividend to carry out this obvious intention of nature. But Negroes, in this particular, are especially blest,—they outnumber other people as ten to one. In general, I believe in supporting all vocations, knowing how rare and special they are. The vocation for a "good time" is just as rare as any other.

*   *   *

Earnest people are often people who habitually look on the serious side of things that have no serious side.

*   *   *

How few people are able to praise without appearing to patronize, even when they sincerely admire.

*   *   *

Nothing is sadder than the consequences of having worldly standards without worldly means.

*   *   *

Cant is moral assumption without moral feeling.

* * *

Nothing is so soothing to our self-esteem as to find our bad traits in our forbears. It seems to absolve us from them.

* * *

It is only the instructed soul who represents the present. The crowd is the soul of the future in the body of the past.

* * *

Epigrams are truly like coins. There are very few whose image and superscription are not obliterated if we carry them long enough in our mental pockets.

* * *

"America is an extraordinarily ghostless country." Thus my Irish friend,—a lover of ghosts,—who compares us with England and his country. He means that America has a great deal of exposed surface, and this is the novelty for Europeans. They are not interested in our nooks and crannies, where the ghosts abound, because these are too much like their own. They come here for new impressions, and our exposed surface gives them a dazzling array of these. Our "ghostlessness" is as striking to them as the ghostly is to Americans in Ireland and England. Nothing ever takes them to Poughkeepsie or Portsmouth or Charleston, or the pre-urban surroundings of the past generations. But Kipling found more of the ghostly in Vermont, when he spent three years there, than he ever found in England; and I fancy there are more ghosts in the South, between Savannah and Memphis, than there are in any similar area in Europe. From Hawthorne to Henry James, from Mary E. Wilkins to William Faulkner, our story-tellers' world has been peopled with ghosts.

* * *

I distrust Santayana's "Epicurean contentment" with a world

run by cardinals and engineers. For is not this the moral of Mario van der Weyer, the hero of *The Last Puritan,* his novel? I say the hero, for which is the hero, Oliver or this other young man to whom in his Epilogue Santayana says, "Any future worth having will spring from men like you"? Of course, Santayana never understood this country; and does not *The Last Puritan* tell us why?

Consider this picture of Emerson's house in Concord: "To feed Oliver's idealism they stopped on their way back at Concord . . . They looked at the dreadful little house in which Emerson lived, and at his cold little sitting-room; and then they looked at each other. *Could such great things leave such mean traces?"* But, surely, this "dreadful little house" has a simple grace and charm; and was not Emerson free there to live in the mind?

Suppose one turned the tables and imagined the Italian thinkers in the Rome that Santayana likes so much. No doubt, their dwellings are of "white marble," like Santayana's talent, and one could not call these dreadful; but, in their world of cardinals and engineers, what has become of their freedom to live in the mind? Should we not therefore be obliged to say, fifty years hence, *Could such mean things leave such great traces?*

I am prejudiced perhaps in favour of Emerson's house. But one would expect a thinker to prefer the tub of Diogenes to the Mussolinian Rome of Santayana.

* * *

I usually find Englishmen refreshing because they are direct, unequivocal, outspoken. Beside their conversation, too much of our American conversation is indirect, over-abounding in tact, equivocal, diplomatic, as if one were always having to consider people's feelings, always thinking twice, fearing to step on someone's toes. It is all circumlocution and beating about the bush. One would think Americans never knew where they stood. Englishmen almost always suggest veracity and courage;

Americans too often suggest mendacity and fear. There is a long story behind these two attitudes. We are the victims of many circumstances which we have not mastered. One of these is the mixture of races who have little in common at the bottom of their minds. They are unable to meet without equivocation and are always putting forth tentacles to feel one another out. This plays the devil with people's minds.

*   *   *

Americans in general are no great shakes at conversation, and one of the reasons for this, I think, is that we are too sympathetic. All conversation among sympathetic people tends to adjust itself to the weakest link in the chain. If one person is self-conscious, they all tend to become self-conscious. If he has a woolly mind, the conversation becomes woolly. I have seen a whole table demoralized by one poor lamb whose secret wish was merely to be somewhere else.

*   *   *

How generally uniform are American minds.

Percival Lowell, in *Chöson*, speaks of an old Korean mapmaker who left America out of his map of the world. But he mentioned some French sailors who were said to have seen it. "On reaching it, they found it to be one vast level wilderness. The only sounds of life which they heard in this great wilderness were the cries of some parrots in the distance."

I seem to remember hearing these cries myself.

*   *   *

Much of the weakness of the American mind is due to our ingrained habit of taking our bases lightly and shifting them easily,—moving our habitations, resorting to divorce,—instead of committing ourselves for good and all to one fixed base and set of relations. Our history is a kaleidoscope of creeds and no-creeds, and the habit of pioneering and changing homesteads,— "tents of a day,"—at every obstacle or at every prospect of better fortune elsewhere, the habit of the permanently transitory, all this has taken from us the stability of mind, the continuity of environment that one should have in order to produce great things. How familiar in my childhood was the sight of a dwelling, mounted on beams and drawn by horses, uprooted from its original situation, in process of being dragged through the streets to better its position somewhere else. Half the streets of my childhood were periodically blocked by these foolish structures,—sometimes even churches,—endeavouring thus to get up in the world.

As John Jay Chapman said, "The constant change of habitat of men in this country, and our jumble of nationalities, is like the tossing of the Persian princes in a blanket; it makes men aliens and non-conductors; they die for lack of rest in one another." And let me add two phrases of Charles Horton Cooley, like Chapman another unappreciated American sage: "A discontinuous life breaks the fibre of our minds and makes shoddy of our thoughts. A haphazard society will generate unstable men."

The secret of living is not to shift one's base, in any respect whatever, except under a force of circumstances that amounts to a moral compulsion.

* * *

Wool-gathering is the great American intellectual vice, stewing and day-dreaming for lack of direction. Few of us get under way before we are middle-aged. In Europe there is more of the tradition of command, and of self-command as both a cause and effect of this.

* * *

"Alas, at thirty-five to be still preparing for something!" Thus Dmitri Rudin. How many times, within the last twenty-four hours, has this apostrophe been addressed to the American air. It is one of the tragedies of our writing life that so many of our writers begin too late, when their mental bones, so to speak, are set in impossible patterns and they cannot find their true orientation. Observe what Flaubert wrote at the age of thirteen: "I see with indignation that the censorship of the press is to be established again, and the liberty of the press abolished . . . It is of his conscience that the man of letters is now being robbed, of his artist's conscience." There are few American writers under thirty as conscious of their vocation as this shows Flaubert to have been at the age of Huckleberry Finn.

* * *

When I was in England, at the sanitarium, and we used to cut down trees,—or cut them up,—I always by preference used an axe when all the Englishmen used saws. The doctor, observing this, remarked that all his American patients had always used axes, even when the saw was more effective, and he asked me why it was. It is a hundred years,—as I am surprised to find, thinking it over,—since any of my forbears has really lived in the country; and it is more than a hundred years since any of them used an axe, as a means of livelihood, or in the building of a homestead, or for any essential purpose. And yet is this not plainly a case of inherited aptitude? Every American of the old stock has a pioneer backwoodsman somewhere near the base of his family tree; and I was amused by a passage in Tocqueville's travel-diary (recently discovered): "The country-dwelling Americans spend half their lives cutting trees, and their children learn at an early age to use the axe against the trees, their enemies." We Americans are axemen by instinct. We all have a Leather-Stocking under our skins.

* * *

Thinking over the difference between the Civil War and the first world-war, as also between the North and the South, I compare Charles Francis Adams and Walter Page as ambassadors to England. Adams was the statesman, Page was not. What do I mean by this, and what was the reason? Adams was the public man by instinct, the impersonal spokesman of his country. Page was always the private man, swayed by his personal feelings, as modern men are apt to be and as Southern men are apt to be. (Of course, the old Southerners were quite different, and for a very good reason. They were statesmen in grain, even more than the Northerners were.) Imagine Adams governed by an affection for Lord John Russell, as Page was governed by his affection for Sir Edward Grey! And yet undoubtedly Adams knew Russell better than Page knew Grey.

*   *   *

The Tough New England Strain. I predict that on the last day of this planet, when the sun hangs cold in the sky, only two men will be left to face it. One will be a Chinaman, and if you ask the other he will say, "O yes, I was born at Cohasset."

*   *   *

On my afternoon walks in winter, I always receive the same impression from the effect of the sunlight on the farmhouse window-panes. It is the winter light of four or five o'clock, and it produces in me an indefinable sense of desolation,—like the whistle of the railway trains in wide empty spaces of sea-coast or prairie. I am stricken at once with a lonely feeling, as if I were abandoned in the void between the worlds. Byron must have had this feeling when he wrote some of the passages in *Cain* and *Manfred*. Charles Burchfield catches this effect of light on the window-panes of the forsaken houses that he paints in so many of his water-colours.

I find a word that describes this sensation, under the same conditions, in one of the old Vermont ballads:

> *Till when at length he reached the cabin,*
> *Black and desolate it stood;*
> *Cold the hearth and windows* ralist
> *In their stillest solitude.*

This word, with its indescribable associations, reminds me of the Polish word "żal," of which Liszt makes so much in his life of Chopin.

*   *   *

R. B. has been telling me of an Indian foot-path he used to see as a boy, along the Delaware river, near Trenton. It was clearly marked, although hidden by the underbrush, and the local woodsman who showed him where to find it had traced this path miles northward until it joined the old Mohawk trail. Nothing catches more at one's imagination than these ancient paths, which are apparently never obliterated,—like the path round Walden Pond in Concord, "worn by the feet of Indian hunters," as Thoreau says. In Concord, there is another path, along the ridge by the Boston road, which Hawthorne wore with his feet, during his last brooding years, 1860–1864, and which was still clearly marked eighty years later. Prescott wore a similar path at Lynn, where he had a summer villa. There was a cherry-tree beside the house, and he plodded round and round this tree for hours every day. He could not, in his blindness, venture further, and the shade of the cherry-tree protected his eyes. The traces of this path remained for years.

There was a path like this in our garden in California, which had not been used for a hundred years. It was worn by the Franciscan monks of the mission, and was said to have led to a spring. In England, at various times, I have seen the traces of two disused Roman roads, one from Shooter's Hill, the other from one of the Sussex downs. They were invisible on the plain, even if one happened to walk along them, but easily seen from above, although they were covered with waving grain. Or am I mistaken in thinking that the Sussex road was a Roman road? It may have been the one that Kipling speaks of,—

> See you the dimpled track that runs
> All hollow through the wheat?
> O that was where they hauled the guns
> That smote King Philip's fleet.

However it may have been, Elizabethan or Roman, the plough, during all these hundreds of years, had stirred only the earth on the surface. The subsoil had remained so packed by the traffic of those far-off days that the grain in the ruts still grew in a different fashion from the surrounding grain. Mary Austin told me it was the same way with the pioneer trails over the Western deserts, that a road, once beaten, however long disused, was never quite blotted out.

* * *

President Eliot had a personal grandeur that one might fail to find the equal of, in a long life passed in a dozen countries. It was a grandeur of bearing, voice and presence which, in its perfect simplicity, explained why republican Rome felt that it was better than the empire. But he was practical, O how practical. The only words of his that I remember, from the only speech of his that I remember,—his address to the freshman class when I was in college,—are the words "serviceable fellowship," which I think he meant us to regard as the great prize and object of college life. These words shocked me at the time, and it was because they shocked me that I recall them; for it had never occurred to me that "fellowship" could be "serviceable," far less that one should make it so. The phrase has stuck in my mind, for thirty years, as a very strange sort of fishbone to have been inserted there by this "gigantic schoolmaster," as John Jay Chapman happily called him.

* * *

I saw Theodore Roosevelt once or twice. He came to a tea at the *Advocate* sanctum when I was in college. It was my first experience of animal magnetism raised to the proportions of the jungle, for one could feel his presence approaching down the corridor, before he came in sight, "like echoes whispering where great armies be." Another guest was there, the English author, W. H. Mallock, who had written *The New Republic*. Roosevelt, hearing his name, grasped his hand; and then, although the meeting was quite impromptu, he poured forth a flood of comment on Mallock's views and books, every one of which he seemed to have read. It was like Niagara falling on a fern. The little old man was stunned with confusion and pleasure. Since then, I have never had a doubt that Theodore Roosevelt, whatever else he was, was a portent, if not a man of genius.

* * *

Twice I saw Swinburne in the flesh, performing an act, moreover, that he celebrated in a score of rondels of his own composition,—not to mention various odes, ballades and sonnets, —an act at which, as the seasons went round, day in and day out, any man in London might have assisted. What was the act?—playing with the toes of a baby. Every day in the year, at eleven in the morning, Swinburne clicked the gate of The Pines behind him and marched up Putney Hill and across Wimbledon Common and sat him down at a public-house with a bottle of Shakespeare's "brown October." And it was on Putney Hill that the act occurred, two, three or four minutes after eleven.

Was it an unworthy instinct that led me to play the spy and saunter along the pavement across the street, pretending I did not know that I was within twenty yards of the greatest poet living in the world? (For I so thought him then.) I heard the door of The Pines open and shut; with the tail of my eye I saw the little figure coming down the path. He swung the gate, made a sharp turn to the left and then began his progress up the hill.

What an odd little apparition—like a tin soldier. Who could have believed that he could have been so tiny and so shiny, so exactly as if he had just come out of a box? The prodigious head, with the reddish nose and the white and yellow beard, was crowned by a turban, a big white turban with a brim, and the neat little military figure, stiff and straight, with the great circular watch-chain, rose out of varnished boots that twinkled as he walked. In his gait he suggested a mechanical toy, and his arms swung with the precision of a miniature grenadier on parade. One seemed to see Watts-Dunton in the background, winding him up for the day.

Then one foresaw that the act was about to happen. Down the hill moved a perambulator, propelled by a nurse in a long blue cape with streamers. It was evident that she was prepared for the ceremony. She stopped, she waited, and presently the poet was abreast of her. Suddenly he turned to the right and bent from the middle. Up came the forearm, down went the hand; then the prodigious head plunged, and nose, beard, turban, brim and all were lost among the billows. To the chant of the birds, in the eye of the morning sun, Algernon Charles Swinburne, naughty poet of secrecy and shade, perverse lover of how many a perverse and evil-flowering feminine ghost, had caught and kissed the toes of the baby. And who could doubt that, marching on, he plotted another rondel on that same theme, to be written down as he sat in the public-house over the bottle of "glorious British beer"?

* * *

How much a simple phrase, rightly remembered, can mean. My dear old friend in England, S. E., went to school with a son of Matthew Arnold and visited the Arnolds on one of his vacations. He remembered how the great man entered the room, and, lifting his left hand, waved it in the direction of the awe-struck boys, saying, in a sweetly deprecating sing-song voice, "You may sit down." As much of Arnold lingers in this picture as there was of conduct in his theory of life, not that I disagree with the theory of conduct.

There also comes back to me a phrase uttered by Charles Eliot Norton on one of his "Dante evenings" at Shady Hill, perhaps when the sherry was being passed, with the little silver basket of caraway cakes. It was to the effect that the picture of heaven in the Book of Revelation,—with its excess of precious stones,—was such as might have been conceived "by a New York woman." What a phrase was that for expressing how Boston and Cambridge felt about the gaudy New York splendours that had vulgarized their beloved Newport.

Still a third phrase comes back, in a reminiscence of my

childhood. It evokes a house of the eighteen-sixties, of which I used to hear much, where Horace Greeley was lunching on one of his political journeys. "You can be fixing me some" was the phrase, in reply to a question of his hostess, whether he would have a little salad,—uttered no doubt with one of his hands in the butter and his honest pumpkin face shining over all.

*   *   *

I hope for a socialized world, but I do not think it will come any quicker if we misinterpret human motives. How much of the man is the economic man? All of the man, said Marx,—which explains why Americans are not Marxists. When people have attained the economic level that millions have attained in this country, they see life not in terms of economic necessity but in terms of a game. It is the sport of the thing, very largely, that draws Americans into business, just as, in the eighteenth century, men were drawn into gallantry, or, in the seventeenth, into war. The chance, the gamble, the hazard, this is the determining motive, as often as not. Don John of Austria and Casanova are more universal types in our business world than the miser in his counting-house, who is also playing his game with gold; and to say that the working-man wishes to be a capitalist,—and that he does so wish is the despair of the Marxists,—is to say that he too wishes to share in this game.

The vast free minorities of the Western world, of which we are the greatest residuum, are shot through and through with this conception, the heritage of the age of chivalry and the age of exploration; and the fact that communism succeeds in Russia is largely the consequence of another fact, that the Russians as a whole do not share in this heritage of the wager. They did not know our age of chivalry, they did not know our age of exploration. The great objection to Utopia, a socialized and reasonable world, in the eyes of our *moyen homme sensuel,* is that it would be dull; and this belief is shared by everybody who is above the level of destitution except the small minority of writers and artists who know that they would always find life exciting. Security means much to me, as to every man of imagination; for security permits the man of imagination to live undividedly the life he loves. Therefore most writers are socialists by instinct. They have everything to gain from a happy world, a world without war or competition, a world without riches or poverty, a world without prejudice or hatred, in which the inner life can develop freely. But security, as it appears, for the average man, means an eternity of dullness, and only the old desire it. Except in times of financial depression, the poor boys long for the hazard as much as the rich boys; and because they long for the hazard, they will not fight for security. For the possibility of wealth means romance and adventure. It is the great wager of the average man, who has no inner life, no imagination, as dreams of knight-errantry, conquest, exploration or glory were the great wagers of other times. And yet this great game of American business cannot be expected to go on forever. The taste for it represents, no doubt, a kind of arrested development,—like the similar taste for sport, in Veblen's view,— and, besides, it has thrown us out of step with the rest of a world that is entering another phase of civilization.

* * *

Whatever their conscious beliefs may be, Americans are instinctive free-willers. They may think they are determinists, but, when this is the case, they always turn out to be fatalists, and that is quite a different matter. William James made this clear in his *Principles of Psychology*: "The fatalistic argument is really no argument for simple determinism. There runs through it the sense of a force which might make things otherwise from one moment to another, if it were only strong enough to breast the tide. A person who feels the *impotence* of free effort in this way has the acutest notion of what is meant by it, and of its possible independent power. How else could he be so conscious of its absence and of that of its effects? But genuine determinism occupies a totally different ground; not the *impotence* but the *unthinkability* of free will is what it affirms."

In this sense, I say that all American fatalism assumes and demands free will. It springs from a kind of disappointment, and this is the characteristic American mood from Mark Twain and Henry Adams to John Dos Passos and William Faulkner. Our world has not lived up to its assumptions, and the single man feels helpless before the mass. Hence these tears, or this hard-boiled denial of the right to weep. But this does not argue that free will does not exist; it merely affirms that the will is not effective. It pays the highest tribute to the will, for it says that life is meaningless and empty precisely because of this nega-tion. How many Americans are there, living or dead, for whom the will has not been the core of life, either in its operation or in its suspension?

The only unthinkable thing, for American minds, is that the will should not exist; and that is the reason why, when it is not effective, its impotence seems to Americans so overwhelm-ing. One could never imagine an Asiatic writing as Dos Passos and Faulkner write. It takes long generations of disappoint-ment, hundreds and thousands of years of disillusion to produce the deterministic frame of mind. Or perhaps the true determin-ist is one who has never known expectations. Fatalism presup-poses hope, and any child can be a fatalist. Take away his kite or his train of cars, or lock him up in a closet, and he sees life stretching before him as an endless desert or prison. We have lost so many kites and trains of cars, in our recent American history, we have had to exchange so many nurseries for closets, that we have ceased to think of ourselves as the children for whom the world was one big vacant lot.

* * *

I like definitions. I like the firm fresh crystalline thinking of the great writers, those who do not share what Saintsbury called "the vulgar fear of the commonplace and obvious." I have an imperfect sympathy with our well-known poet who is so afraid of uttering a *cliché*, of saying something that someone has said before, that he never finishes a sentence. (It is true that to make the obvious not commonplace one has to be a Tolstoy.)

* * *

Always begin with elements. Restate elements. They are the least considered in ages of sophistry like ours. All the elements need to be restated. It is always surprising to find how confused people are in regard to them. Define; always give definitions, and always insist on the primary meanings of words.

* * *

Theories,—how Renoir and Degas abhorred them! Artists should abhor them, except in regard to technical questions, and I say that critics should abhor them too. I have no theories and wish to have none. They are all grey, as Goethe said, and I love the "green golden bough of life."

Nor, while I like incidental definitions, do I like total definitions of literature, the function of criticism, etc. Neither formula nor treatise could ever comprise so vast a subject. But I like suggestions of definitions, such as Pater's, in *Appreciations*,— "It is on the quality of the matter it informs or controls, its compass, its variety, its alliance to great ends, or the depth of the note of revolt, or the largeness of hope in it, that the greatness of literary art depends, as *The Divine Comedy, Paradise Lost, Les Misérables*, the English Bible are great art,"—which of course consigns Pater to the second class.

* * *

I never get anything out of abstract discussions. They never rouse my mind. Whatever they might give, I get from a novel of Balzac better. A good novel at once heats my mind and sets the source of all my perceptions flowing. A Balzac "interior" recalls all my interiors; his *ville de province*, my own; his town, my town; his types, my types,—and all the bells begin to ring in my buried city.

* * *

As a critic, one should be wary of terms that end in *ism*,—Classicism, Romanticism, Naturalism and the like. All these terms must go back to the button-moulder, for they are played out. A critic in our time must mint new coins. If he cannot do this, he must explain in what sense he uses the old ones.

These pigeon-holes are not for imaginative minds; and all such classifications, which form the stock in trade of so many critics, are of recent origin, and a not very creditable origin at that. One should reconceive the states of mind and the tones of feeling that lie behind these labels. Every real writer partakes of the nature of all these categories and is partly romantic, partly naturalistic, classical, humanistic and all the rest.

* * *

I have no choice whatever in the matter of my thoughts. I think what my constitution obliges me to think,—in other words, what I *do* think, what comes up from inside and forms itself in words without any interposition of my will. How absurd to tell me then what I *ought* to think, or that I should think as I thought when I was thirty! As well tell me that I ought to have wings, or blond hair, or green eyes, or that I should be four or seven feet tall. And yet these well-wishers pride themselves on their perception, their knowledge of psychoanalysis and all the rest.

* * *

There has been a sounding-board behind European writers that has carried their voices across the ocean, while American writers, facing the other way, have until recently faced a keen east wind.

* * *

A. E. once quoted to me in a letter a phrase from the Bhagavad-Gita, "Let the motive for action be in the action itself and not in the event." That a man's opinions may have consequences, that literature itself has consequences of a very important kind, is naturally perhaps the first of a critic's convictions, but he must feel that a writer should disregard them. For Renan was right when he said, "To be able to think freely, one must feel that what one writes will have no consequences."

* * *

In criticism, no faint praise. Take from the author everything that is not his by right, take it as a surgeon takes away every last cell of morbid tissue, with a strict and relentless knife; then cauterize the wound and help the victim to his feet again and send him away with both hands filled with flowers.

An author whose tissue is so morbid that he cannot survive the ordeal should not be subjected to it. He should be allowed to die in peace.

* * *

Criticism exists to determine values, to cherish them, define them and maintain them. That is the reason why criticism is central in civilization. Our criticism is too high-pitched. It is always in the position of Philip drunk, who cannot stay drunk forever and is always waking up with a morning headache. Its midnight enthusiasms look very bleak and drear in the rays of another sunrise, bleaker than they ought to be or would be if they were midday enthusiasms, or judgments formed in dark and cloudy weather. This high pitch does not pay. What caused the prodigious success of *The Education of Henry Adams?* As much as anything else, its tone of understatement. This ingrained New England tone, applied to our history, in a world that was no longer used to hearing from New England, caused a sensation in contrast to the hullabaloo of the criticism to which the public is accustomed.

* * *

Good as our best reviewers are, and they are very good in comparison with the reviewers of twenty years ago,—I do not say fifty, for that is another matter,—they are still strangely the reverse of learned. When they are not too eager to score, to strike while the iron is hot, they show a shocking lack of general reading. The field of their consciousness and reference is infinitesimally narrow. The same fixed names occur again and again in everything they write of current books, a few conscientious references to Aristotle, or some other classic author who happens to be in vogue, because some French or English author has brought him to their attention, a little patter of popular names,—Donne, Kierkegaard or Kafka,—and Stendhal or Baudelaire at the end of every vista. This literary cosmogony that begins with Baudelaire is a singular thing. Still, it is better than the cosmogony of thirty years ago, which often began with Oscar Wilde. But what a descent in learning from the days of George Ripley, who wrote about books in *The Tribune* in the days of our grandsires.

It is true that in readability our reviewing has improved. Many of the reviews in the weeklies are remarkably good. But most of the reviewers sail without a keel. As they seem to be able to hold in their minds only a handful of recent discoveries, they are constantly discovering for themselves things that other people have always known; and then most of their movements are herd-movements, like those of the rest of the population. They are always "going over in a body" to some new major prophet, who may indeed be a major prophet, Freud, Marx, Spengler, Pareto or Dr. Reich. The shortness of their memories is only matched by the facility of their transformations. Thus, at the present time, a few old fogies still speak up for Shaw and Wells, who represent the past before the deluge. But Shaw and Wells were talked about to death; and I foresee that, in another five years, the shades of Kierkegaard and Kafka will not have where to lay their heads. If one runs through a bound volume of one of the weeklies, one learns what mutability means in a world that has lost its memory.

It is probably right that living authors (with a few revived authors) should fill the foreground of a reviewer's mind. But if one reads these reviews five years later, one is surprised to find how remote they seem. This is because the subjects have not been related to the general stream of critical tradition. The authors have not been read as wholes or brought into connection with other wholes. The reviewers have lived so much in the present that they have not even seen the present, and, having no sense of the past, they have no sense of the future.

One can sum up in a phrase the weakness of our reviewers, and of our critics in general. They can only parry direct attacks. They cannot stand up against flank attacks, still less attacks from the rear.

* * *

The Function of Criticism. "The rocky, dry, fallow ground says, 'I can produce nothing, nothing will grow; yet I see the sun and feel the rain as much as you do.'—'Aye,' replies the corn-field, 'but they have plucked away my stones and turned up my surface and let in the water-courses; and now the sun and the air, the heat and the snow all serve me.' "—Emerson's Journals.

* * *

No one is fit to judge a book until he has rounded Cape Horn in a sailing vessel, until he has bumped into two or three icebergs, until he has been lost in the sands of the desert, until he has spent a few years in the House of the Dead.

* * *

In view of the mistakes he is always making, a critic should wear sackcloth as his everyday garment.

* * *

In *The Future in America*, H. G. Wells remarked: "I am curiously not interested in things, and curiously interested in the consequences of things." This reminds me of George Brandes's remark,—the romantic mind asks for the significance of things, while the modern mind asks for their causes. I draw from these two phrases a general deduction. As between Wells and Brandes, the modern mind cares only for causes and consequences, not for things themselves and the significance of things. The latter concern only the "romantic mind."

Well, then, I say we must restore the romantic mind, if this is its definition. We must restore the sense of things, the sense of their significance, along with their consequences and their causes. If things have no "significance," things are hollow; and, if things are hollow, are not their causes and consequences meaningless also?

*   *   *

Why this morbid suspicion of the popular? Why do they see it as a menace? Because the popular, as we know it, is often a vulgarization of the primary, and it has the primary in it, which they have not.

In a recent article Joseph Wood Krutch explained on some such ground as this the popularity of the detective-story. Is this not due to the fact, he asked, that the detective-story preserves certain primary virtues of fiction that "serious" novelists have all but abandoned? For instance, it exemplifies the dictum of Aristotle that the "fable" is the most important element in a work of fiction. Then it must hold one's interest constantly or it wholly fails. How far, in fact, can literature stray from the centre of the human field? That is a question which critics can no longer ignore.

*   *   *

The spread of science has made us feel that we ought to be "broad-minded" and strive to understand every point of view, however it may repel our natural tastes. It is more important that we should maintain the right of our natural tastes, at whatever cost in "narrow-mindedness." There are large areas of modern speculation, of thought, feeling and writing, in which the proper response is to say nothing but to kick, as Dr. Johnson did, against the first object that comes in one's way. Kicking is an eloquent argument that may have a world of thought behind it. Every man of good sense knows when not to argue and has his mind made up on a thousand matters that are not discussible for him. In fact, without a closed mind one cannot have an open mind. One becomes a house without doors or windows, and I should not call that an open house.

* * *

There are writers who, as writers, ought to die, and the only way to contribute to this end is not to mention them.

* * *

An effect of cosmopolitanism,—it makes fashion the lawgiver. Deracinated people have no standards aside from the standard of fashion, for they are out of touch with the bases of life. They have few or no ties that create responsibility and give one a scale for measuring values. Fashion is the only law for all these floating people. Besides, as the aesthetic of social relations, fashion is attractive to artists, and all the more to artists who are also floating. This infects artists with an awe of fashion. One saw this awe of fashion even in the poet Yeats, whose anthology of modern English poetry was almost ruined by it. He included several bad poems that were not to his own taste because of his respect for literary fashion.

* * *

Fashionable writers depend on immediate returns. They have to keep their goods in the shop-window. They have to cash their drafts at once, for fashion allows only short credits. The real writers are like real swells who can afford to be simple and to disregard the times.

* * *

Does history repeat itself? Hear the words of Leopardi on his native town: "As to Recanati," he writes to one of his friends, "I answer that I will leave it, escape from it, hurry away from it, as soon as ever I can. But when can I? That is what I cannot tell you. Meanwhile, be assured that my intention is not to stay here, where I see no one beyond our household, and where I should die of frenzy, of life-weariness, of hypochondria, if one could die of these ills . . . It is all very well to say, Plutarch and Alfieri loved Chæronea and Asti. Loved them and left them. In this fashion I also will love my native place when I am far away from it. Here literature is a word unknown. The names of Parini, Alfieri, Monti, and of Tasso and Ariosto, and all the others, need a commentary."

Is that not what our own writers say of the Gopher Prairies of their childhood? Leopardi's only wish was to escape to Rome, where he supposed that everything was going to be different. And this was the Rome where, in 1831, Stendhal, I note, was bored to death "for want of the opportunity to exchange ideas with anyone."

Out of the frying-pan, into the fire. See also what Flaubert says of Paris, and what our friends say of New York: "Do you know in this Paris, which is so great, one single house in which literature is talked about? And when it is incidentally approached it is always in its subordinate and exterior aspects, the question of success, morality, utility, etc. It seems to me that I am becoming a fossil, a being without any relation to the creation that surrounds me."

*   *   *

Reading Halvdan Koht's *Life of Ibsen,* I am greatly struck, as many times before, by the parallel between the Norwegian literary movement and the century-old American effort to create an independent literature (now undoubtedly achieved). In the West, where they are starting all over again, where each of the newer states is having its coming-of-age, they should forget London and Paris and study these parallel national and regional movements, Ibsen's Norway, Dostoievsky's Russia and the Irish revival. Ibsen's milieu constantly suggests America—the white clapboard wooden houses, the small-town society and the ethical centre of the Norwegian mind. I have only to close my eyes, while reading him, to feel that I am living in Salem or Portsmouth, or, as often, in some Main Street of the Middle West. There is no literary life like Ibsen's for showing an

American writer how to observe his world, and how to universalize himself,—for Ibsen's mind was formed in the stress of Norway before he went abroad. Western writers should forget the "mysteries of Paris." They should study Ibsen's struggle against the aestheticism of which, as an artist, he felt the pull, while knowing it was opposed to his natural genius.

We have everything to learn from the Norwegians, who are so closely related to us. It took a Norwegian writer, Ole Rölvaag, to tell us, in human terms, the real meaning of pioneering. It took another Norwegian, Thorstein Veblen, to explain the consequences of it in economic terms.

* * *

In a regional area one can find everything if one has had a taste of the world and if one has developed a sense of proportion. If, moreover, it is the area of one's deepest feeling, there is nothing like having one's vital connections concentrated within it. Except in the case of the strongest talents, the attempt to embrace the whole of America tends to make one's emotional life sketchy, thin and vague.

* * *

It is the rule that writers flourish best in the oldest part of any country. So New England will never be deserted, nor will the South be. Just so, regionalism flourishes best,—other things being equal,—in the oldest part of the given region.

* * *

We should speak less of sophistication and much more of innocence, I mean the necessity of innocence of which D. H. Lawrence spoke: "How to regain the naive or innocent soul—how to make it the man within man—your 'societal'; and at the same time keep the cognitive mode for defences and adjustments and 'work'!" We cannot tell how far we are capable of this until we have ceased to preach knowingness. What painters call the "innocence of the eye" belongs to the writer too;

and how right Amiel was in requiring naivety of a story-teller, saying, "The novelist must be ingenuous, at least when his pen is in his hand." He means the fresh heart that can be surprised by things, that gift of "looking at the world with eyes wide open in wonder," as Ortega y Gasset puts it. The greatest writers have all had this, and many of our writers have it, Sherwood Anderson, Willa Cather, Thomas Wolfe. This was Whitman's enormous gift, as it was Tolstoy's also. It is the spring of all clear perception. Think of Blake's innocence, both of mind and character. The universal man-of-the-world ideal, which tends to dominate our modern writers, is altogether foreign to the artist's nature.

* * *

The world recognizes but one cause as worthy of man's devotion, the cause that cannot fail, whether it has man's devotion or not. Let us have nothing but ideals, but woe to the ideal that is not already thrice realized and armoured in triple brass.

As truisms need no proofs, so the reigning fact needs no advocates. It advocates itself twenty-four hours every day. The intellectual man, if he follows his instincts, will always throw what weight he has on the side of "lost causes, and forsaken beliefs, and unpopular names, and impossible loyalties."

* * *

The little tailor in Grimm got the best of the giants by convincing them that he had killed seven at a stroke. One might suppose from the seriousness with which the mighty organs of popular opinion combat the vicious tendencies of the radical critics that our great lumbering civilization is as pathetically helpless as these giants. But the fairy-tale in question was a "wish-fulfillment" on the part of its peasant author. In real life, tailors are nothing but tailors, and critics are only critics. Change may come, and revolution, but upon the things that are dear to the world the sun never sets.

* * *

Arnold Bennett speaks somewhere, in a characteristic phrase, of "the subtle ether which the truly civilized diner demands." These "civilized diners,"—how much we hear about them! Why do I dislike this current popular use of the harmless word "civilized," in the sense of *savoir vivre*? It is not because I dislike *savoir vivre*, but because it is used to indicate the acme of what one desires from life, and I feel that this should be something less accessible. Those who care so much for *savoir vivre* must have had little experience of this state of being, a fact that no doubt explains the use of the term "civilized." It is a phrase that has come into use at a time when large areas of the population are in process of rising socially and when that which is taken for granted on the upper levels has become an attainable object for those who have been below. The newly arrived exaggerate its value. After five thousand years of civilization, one must be very unexacting to preen oneself on an art that so many have inherited, as they have inherited their hands and feet.

Regarding this passion for the "civilized," Willa Cather says shrewdly, in her story, *Paul's Case*: "Perhaps it was because, in Paul's world, the natural nearly always wore the guise of ugliness, that a certain element of artificiality seemed to him necessary in beauty. Perhaps it was because his experience of life elsewhere was so full of Sabbath-school picnics, petty economies, wholesale advice as to how to succeed in life, and the unescapable odours of cooking, that he found this existence so alluring, these smartly-clad men and women so attractive."

This explains the "civilized diners," whom one ought to regard as pathetic. The phrase is so tiresome because it insists on a value that mature people take for granted. Besides, worldly people who are also wise have always known what place in the scheme of things their worldly accomplishments rightly occupy. They have worn their hair-shirts, like Philip the Second. They have offered their libations to the gods, for they know on what tenuous terms their good fortune exists. They have recognized, in other words, other values than their own, though they may not live by these values.

If one must have worldly people, I prefer those who are well-seasoned. But I have small interest in worldly people, even from the point of view of manners. There are unworldly people who do everything better.

In regard to all such matters, Coleridge has laid down the law for writers: "The world in which I exist is another world indeed, but not to come."

*   *   *

A Well-Connected Man. I once knew a man, well-connected in New York, who bore the name of a great Spanish painter. I asked him if he was related to the Spanish painter. "O yes," he said, "he was a distant cousin, but he belonged to the peasant branch of the family."

*   *   *

Is it possible that sharks and rattlesnakes have nightmares in their sleep, in which they have to feel they are something else, and then wake up again to the delicious realization that they still have their jaws and rattles?

*   *   *

I believe in force, but only against the strong; irony, but against the arrogant.

Soften the callosities; but, if the creature is a pachyderm, do not spare the whips and scorpions.

*   *   *

I like Ryder's saying, after he had been working for eighteen years on a landscape, "The sky is getting interesting."

*   *   *

The characteristic American style suggests a plethora of stimulus. It is spiced and "pepped" to a degree that reminds

one of the abnormal flush of the consumptive patient. And, in
fact, these writers burn themselves out. They write to be overheard in the noise of the subway or to score in a crowded room
where everyone is chattering. Their foot is always on the loud
pedal, and of course they soon become tiresome. Hence the
holocaust of American writers that takes place every few years,
when the last "younger generation" is kicked upstairs or out
and a new younger generation appears at the door.

The style that lasts, the good style that has resources behind
it, almost never resorts to the loud pedal. It unconsciously avoids
the clever phrase, unless the phrase is more than clever, together
with every sort of emphasis, and is therefore never tiresome.
Most of the characteristic modern styles, in music and painting
as well as writing, take for granted the "law of acceleration"
that Henry Adams described; but, as the great composers prevail in the end, over the composers of the moment, in the midst
of an accelerated world, so it is with writers. The type of American writers who have prevailed, over and through the "jazz
age," are those for whom the age has existed but not the jazz in
the age. Those who have accepted the "law of acceleration"
have perished by this law. They obeyed the rule of the subway, "Step lively." They who were so afraid to see the door
slammed in their faces have seen the door slammed on their
backs.

* * *

It is the fashion to decry taste as a superficial thing, but taste
is more important than some people think. Many a time I have
heard a good reader, one of the sort that writers ought to cherish, say of some author of the moment, "Of course, he has
plenty of ideas, but he has such bad taste." In other words, "I
cannot and will not read him." If some of our writers were only
aware of the handicap under which they labour, they would
take this question seriously and try to learn the laws which they
offend. We have dozens of talented writers who are wholly in
the dark in regard to their failure to receive recognition. They
are in the position of the girl of whom the advertisers make so

much, who cannot understand why it is that the young men do not flock about her. They are always aggrieved, and they never learn.

We can impugn our friends for every fault, and they will take it good-naturedly. But let us for a moment impugn their taste, and their self-esteem is up in arms. In real life the friends of the girl in the advertisements seldom take her aside and whisper the awful secret in her ear. The advertising men are not so squeamish, nor should criticism be. Our criticism, almost wholly concerned with ideas, and with more technical questions, makes too little of taste. But although, without taste, a writer may win the great public, he will never win the little public that gives the great prizes, but only to those who speak its language.

* * *

I am struck by the arrogance of this author. He offers me his book, not personally but through his publisher, and slaps me in the face for reading it. He is ill-advised. Authors have often complained of the public, the "many-headed beast," but they have been shrewd enough to convey to the person who reads them that he too has suffered from the beast. The author of this book conveys no such feeling, so flattering to the reader's self-esteem. He remains in a minority of one, and this is a dangerous position. One can be a private minority simply by holding one's peace, but when one becomes a public minority one must have a caucus and a vote. This author, like every author, if his ideas are to be considered, depends to some extent on his electors. What does he represent *in them,* which they can feel sure that he represents? He can attack the majority as much as he likes, but when he attacks his own minority the minority in question feels inclined to vote for someone else.

Great writers are often solitary, but in a different fashion. They are alone with the Alone. This author is a minority-party who does not follow the rules of parties. He is in serious danger of losing the next election.

* * *

The poet Cowper remarked that he could not imagine a man writing without the idea of being read. This is a point of common sense, and we cannot ignore it in face of the writers of our day who seem to be so anxious not to communicate their thoughts. In their desire, which is natural enough, not to cooperate with a vulgarized public, they exclude even the judicious public, to their own great loss. For surely the good will of the judicious public is one of the prerequisites of good writing; and a writer who ignores this fact, for whatever reason, finds himself, as Melville put it, "bombinating *in vacuo.*" So necessary is this coöperation that Vernon Lee well described writing as "the craft of manipulating the contents of the reader's mind."

The good writer of prose stands to his reader in the relation of an interlocutor. He must therefore be a master of the social virtues. The response of the reader completes the work of literary art, and writing loses its sociality, and therewith its completeness, when the writer cannot feel this response from without. It is no accident that the French, the most social of races, are also the greatest masters of prose; and, considering the chaos of our society, it is natural that our writers should be so generally wanting in the social virtues. It is natural that we should lack the serenity and clarity, not to mention the tact, discrimination and grace, with which one becomes endowed only through the habitual presence of exacting but sympathetic listeners. All the more reason then to seek for these listeners and to cultivate the social virtues;—and what can be said for writers who cultivate the opposite and wish, at all costs, to bar us out? And why do they wish it, for that matter? Why do they wish to throw dust in our eyes? Because their personalities are so insufficient that they cannot afford to expose them. If they were intelligible, we should soon see how small they are. "How many authors," says André Gide, "have no personality that would not be lost in the mass of humanity on the day when they consented to use *who's* and *which's* as everybody else does?" These writers are of the kind which, as Gil Blas said, only deceive their own generation, and yet they are permitted to talk one another into fame. They have a way of referring to one another as if not to know of them were to inhabit perpetual night.

*   *   *

These novelists are such children. They are story-tellers, at bottom, whose true place is the nursery; and, if they depart too far from this primitive function, they may become valuable as something else but they are not good novelists. I sympathize with Renan's complaint, "The mistake the novelists make is in thinking that people have the time to read them."

It is true, if we do not read them we do not know the world we live in, well as we may know life. But novelists must take their law from the saints and sages, as Dickens and Thackeray took their law from Carlyle, as Tolstoy took his from the Gospel. When they become a law unto themselves, as modern novelists are prone to do, we feel that they do not know their place.

*   *   *

For style, I like Nietzsche's saying, "Everything divine runs on light feet."

But I like many styles, including the florid. My friend T., talking on the street-corner, scornfully pointed to the gutter. He said that all the authors of the nineteenth century belonged there. Away with Dickens, George Eliot, Ruskin and De Quincey! Too many flourishes, too many words,—they were all blubber. (Though it goes without saying that he retained the fashionable admiration for Melville and James, who were perhaps the wordiest of all.) Well, I say that floridity represents emotional fullness, albeit an excess and abuse of fullness; and emotional fullness is a great virtue.

*   *   *

Mannerism is the sign of a second-rate mind; pride in mannerism is the sign of a third-rate mind.

*   *   *

I have never loved the standardizer of our spelling, the utilitarian Connecticut Yankee Noah Webster, though I know he acted in the interest of our independence. I never liked his thin and calculated rigours, and I could never forgive him for removing from our language so much of its inherited succulence and fullness.

*   *   *

No one should ever publish a book until he has read it aloud to a woman. A letter from Madame Roland, written about 1790, gives me a good reason for thinking this: "Do you know that Massachusetts is a very barbarous name? And that a man of fashion was never known to utter such a word when saying soft things to the fair sex? I have heard of a lady who was so shocked at the sound of Transylvania, which was quite new to her, that she desired the impertinent speaker to leave the room."

I protest on behalf of Massachusetts, but the principle stands. (And even regarding Massachusetts, the French still have their rights. Léon Bazalgette, who said he could not bear this word, but who was obliged to use it, called it *Le Mass*.) Women are the arbiters of words, and we should listen to them because they live close to the meanings of words. Men become infatuated with words themselves. Women are closer to the general life, the source of good style, while men tend to live the particular life, the source of bad style. So women will never allow you to say "obfuscate" when "bewilder" will do just as well; and they shiver at words like "historicity" and will not be comforted if you use them.

Is not this the reason why French prose is so generally good, and why German prose would be better if the Germans respected women more? The badness of German prose is a judgment on the Germans for their lack of respect for women.

*   *   *

It is difficult to understand living writers because they are involved in our own problems, which we cannot solve for ourselves.

*   *   *

What we call insincerity is the expression of thoughts that do not go to the bottom of our own minds.

* * *

Irony is the mortar with which one fills the space between the partial and the universal.

* * *

It is not that the French are not profound, but they all express themselves so well that we are led to take their geese for swans.

* * *

Fabre's books on insects,—why are they so fascinating? Because of the ghastly sidelights they throw on human life, the relief into which they cast our own instincts and habits, comparable to that of the theatre.

* * *

A generation lasts thirty years, or five, as we say in America. Who form the next generation? Not those who bask complacently in this, although they must have one foot in it in order to make the transition.

* * *

"The women lived it, the men wrote about it," Rudolph Ruzicka said of the German romantic movement. This is true of all movements.

* * *

"Nowadays everything grows old in a few hours; reputation fades, a work passes away in a moment. Everybody writes; nobody reads seriously." I record this in 1936, but it was written in 1836, just a hundred years ago (by Chateaubriand, in *Sketches of English Literature*).

* * *

"Democracy in economics, aristocracy in thought." I like this phrase of A. E. My political creed is based on the assumption that everybody ought to be given a chance. My literary creed is based on the assumption that few will ever take the chance.

* * *

Some writers have a tendentious importance that is quite aside from any intrinsic importance. I can think of two living writers, one of whom cannot write and the other has nothing to say, yet who, in the history of our time, will have their place, for they represent tendencies of feeling, characteristic of the time, which the more important writers have not expressed at all.

* * *

"The Genteel Tradition." This phrase has had too long a run. It has been stretched in so many directions that it is as useless as an old elastic. One cannot bear too heavily on suggestive phrases, and one grows heartily sick of such phrases as this when they have been used three times. Besides, the writers who use this phrase confound the genteel with the noble. They will be calling Marcus Aurelius genteel next.

* * *

The Psychology of the Literary "Cult." The devotees of an author,—I mean the kind of author who has devotees, such as Oscar Wilde or Henry James,—differ from those who admire him in the ordinary way. They differ in this, that they always possess the defects of their idol. By means of this idol they worship themselves and find excuses for their own shortcomings.

* * *

A seed-catalogue,—Stumpp and Walter's,—says that if you wish to develop new and beautiful varieties, you must save the weak seedlings. The strongest seedlings are pretty certain to run true to type.

* * *

The phrase "the younger generation" is one that should

never be used. All generations are alike when they are
"younger," beginning with the one to which I belonged; and
all the "older" generations have said the same things about
them. What could one add to the comment of Pliny the
Younger, when he had become the "older"?--it fairly describes
my generation when we were twenty-one: "Which of them
pays submission as an inferior to age or authority? These young
gentlemen begin life as sages; they know everything from the
outset; and there is no one they revere or imitate, for they are
themselves the only models which they are disposed to follow."
—*Letters*, VIII, 23.

* * *

With all that can and will be said of Kipling,—and much
will be said, for he was a great writer,—we cannot forget that,
in his biblical argot, he invented the thieves' slang of imperial-
ism.

* * *

Stevenson always writes as if he were talking with a woman
who admires him. It is this that gives him his air of conscious
heroism.

* * *

According to Coleridge, it is no decisive mark of genius that
a man should write well concerning himself. This cannot be
ignored in any discussion of the many autobiographical novelists of our time.

* * *

A writer is important not by the amount of territory he enters
or claims, but by the amount he colonizes. Tolstoy and Balzac
fill all the space they occupy. They do not merely lie, like Milton's Satan, full many a rood prone on the flood.

* * *

This writer reminds me of the Pasha's remark, in Kinglake's
Eothen, marvelling over the ways of the Europeans, "Whirr!
Whirr! All by wheels! Whiz! Whiz! All by steam!"

* * *

It was easy for Thoreau to like winter. All the winter colours that depress other people, the so-called drab and dreary colours, the browns and iron greys, suggested to him the moral traits that constituted his conception of beauty.

Thoreau has become with time a world-classic. Henry James said of him, echoing Lowell, "He is worse than provincial, he is parochial"; but we have seen his essays paraded before all mankind as the *vade mecum* of Gandhi, the greatest spiritual leader of our time. If there was, however, in Thoreau's nature an element of the really parochial, which still irritates me, was this not the result of an excellent cause? It was due to an over-determination that met the facts of his place and moment. He had to resist the migratory tendencies of other Americans,—the drag westward of the pioneering impulse and the drag towards Europe of the cultivated classes. He knew how hostile these impulses were to the personal growth he lived for; and, feeling this, he could not take Concord for granted. He was driven to insist upon it a little too much.

* * *

In Cambridge, in the Concord of *Little Women,* throughout the New England of the "golden day," children were everywhere present, both heard and seen. All the New England writers understood them and wrote about them, sometimes with exquisite feeling. *Uncle Tom's Cabin* was composed, under the lamp, on a table surrounded by children conning their lessons, in a hum of earnest voices asking questions. Hawthorne's stories were as full of children as ever the summer woods were filled with birds, and Whittier's shy affections and Holmes's salty humours were addressed as often as not to boys and girls. In later times, when boys and girls were "problems," and most of their fathers and mothers were also problems, when the old cultural forms had broken down, and literature was produced by childless rebels,—or largely so produced,—against the abuses of the older culture in the hour of its rigidity and decay, when the nation had lost much of its faith and even so much of its will to live that "race-suicide" was a pressing question, one found it difficult to return in fancy to Longfellow's "children's hour," when life flowed so freely between the generations. This ever-present consciousness of children, in minds so unconscious of themselves, spoke for a culture at its highest tide, a community that believed in itself, serenely sure of itself and sure of its future, eager to perpetuate its forms.

* * *

The wonderful sermon of the New Bedford preacher in Melville's *Moby-Dick* was a drama, as it were, of Jonah in modern dress,—the prophet had left his hatbox and his carpetbag behind him. For the rest, did not Father Mapple's sermon suggest the picture of Jonah and the whale that was painted by Albert P. Ryder, who was born in New Bedford? One saw there too the "tormented deep," the steep gullies, the raging flood, the rush of the mighty whale cleaving the seas, just as the old picture in the Spouter Inn, with its vague "masses of shades and shadows," besmoked and defaced, suggested another Ryder. The "black mass of something hovering" in the centre of the picture that appeared to be a foundering Cape Horner in a midnight gale, together with the "indefinite sublimity" that haunted the picture, belonged as much to Ryder as it belonged to Melville.

* * *

Melville, with his taste for what he called "oldness in things," liked Hawthorne's flavour and body, suggesting old wine, as he loved the antique note of Jeremy Taylor and Sir Thomas Browne, whom he had bought in old folios on a visit to London. In one of his letters he praised what he called "old-age-ifying youth in books," as one of the two great arts that were yet to be discovered, and in writing *Redburn* he had tried to extract and reproduce on his own page the antiquated style of an obsolete Liverpool guide-book. The seventeenth-century flavour of many a page of *Moby-Dick* was the fruit of a taste as consciously cherished and developed as the taste of certain American painters from William Page to Duveneck for the so-called "brown sauce" of the Munich school. These painters also wished to achieve the amber patina of age, the sombre harmonious richness of so many old masters, attempting to reach this normal effect of the gradual oxidation of the oil by constantly using bitumen as an undertone and glaze. In cultivating the antique style of the writers whom he loved, Melville used literary bitumen in a similar fashion.

* * *

We have had more than enough of what Wyndham Lewis called the "cult of the savage and the child." The cult of *Huckleberry Finn* is the cult of both; yet, according to Mencken, this is our only classic, and Hemingway says, "It's the best book we have. All American writing comes from that."

I think I understand Huck Finn, and I love the poetry amid which he sits enthroned like an unkempt cherub on a summer cloud. Moreover, I know how he feels,—when, for instance, I have been in an air-conditioned library, where I cannot smoke or even cough, then I long for the rags and the salubrious barrel. I resent this life at "the widow's," where one has to wash and comb one's hair, all so "cramped up and smothery," and I long for the raft, where one feels so comfortable and so easy and free. I long to light out for the territory, where there are no Aunt Sallies to civilize me; and I almost understand how Mencken can say that his discovery of *Huckleberry Finn* was the most stupendous event of his life.

But I reflect that life on the raft would not be so good if someone had not civilized the Mississippi or made it only picturesquely bad. If it had been the resort of savages and panthers only, Huck would not have felt so free and easy. Huck Finn's freedom was only possible because the way had been cleared for him by men who had worked for his freedom.

Huckleberry Finn is unique as a book of boys, for boys, by a boy. But, if it were our only classic, would it not be sad that a

boy should be our Faust and our Don Quixote? Especially when
we have had a Leather-Stocking?

*   *   *

Mark Twain was equally notable for badness of judgment
and goodness of heart. He ridiculed the notion that our Indians
had any poetry in them, and he could never deride sufficiently
the "Fenimore Cooper Indians."

Of course, he had the frontiersman's prejudice against them.
This prejudice destroyed his good judgment, for, regarding the
poetry of the Indians, Fenimore Cooper was ten times closer to
the truth than Mark Twain.

But Mark Twain was too tender-hearted to maintain for long
a grudge against any variety of under-dog. It was a Piute Indian he had known in Tulare County who was present to
receive Captain Stormfield when he visited heaven.

*   *   *

Both Cooper and Howells, in their generations, observed that
the Americans were the most homogeneous people in the world.
Howells went on to say that "in another generation or two,
perhaps it will be wholly different"; and nowadays only the
oldest Americans can recall a time when the word "homogeneous" really applied to our people. I have been scouted as an
ignoramus for suggesting that this was ever true.

But even the old Far West was strikingly homogeneous, and
one needs to recall only one story to prove it. I mean the oft-
repeated story of Horace Greeley and Hank Monk, the famous
stage-driver of the Sierras who was "always on time" at any cost.
Mark Twain said he had heard this story four hundred and
eighty-one times, at Julesburg on the Platte, at Fort Bridger
from a Colorado man, from a wandering Mormon beyond Salt
Lake, etc. Drivers told it, conductors, inn-keepers, chance passengers, lone Indians. Bayard Taylor told it, Artemus Ward referred to it and Joaquin Miller made it the subject of a poem
and a play. What could better show the homogeneity,—along

with the diversity and chaos,—of the far-spreading Far Western life of the time? Writers, travellers and settlers alike repeated the story in a similar spirit over an area as large as Central Europe.

*   *   *

The Gargantuan fantasies of Rabelais have something in common with our own Western myths of David Crockett. All our tall tales were natural growths of a world that had burst its bonds, a young mind that had cast the skin of ancestral conventions and social forms and exulted in a freedom that knew no limit. In this sense the frontier really had something in common with Rabelais, who spoke for a lusty France that was trying its strength after the long constriction of the Middle Ages. The early mythology of the Hindus was gigantesque for other reasons that were germane as well. Sagur had sixty thousand sons, all of them born in a pumpkin, the army of Nanda comprised ten billions of soldiers, and a mountain range dividing two of the kingdoms was no less than six hundred thousand miles in height. Like the Western tales, these monstrous fictions were allied in some way to the physical features of the country, the vast rivers, plains that were boundlessly fertile and animals of wondrous variety, fierceness and size.

*   *   *

"Time-Provincialism." Half the energy of Americans in the last two generations has been spent in trying to escape from provinciality. They have done their best to ape some dimly conceived aristocracy; they have struggled to place themselves at Matthew Arnold's "centre." But provinciality of place is not the only provinciality. There is also "time-provincialism," in Professor Whitehead's phrase. ("Men can be provincial in time as well as in place.") Those who have jumped out of Mencken's "boobery" have jumped into this frying-pan. They feel that they are obliged to keep up with some hypothetical "minute," as if to be "up to the minute," the "last minute," were more important than any of the great realities of life and

death. Is not this what Ezra Pound means by "awareness-to-the-present"?

In other times people were just as eager to keep up with Dickens and Thackeray, or with Smollett and Sterne. But they never lost touch with the past and the minds of their forbears. This gave them equipoise and a standard of value; and did they understand their times less well? Of course, they understood their times far better.

*   *   *

Literature, properly speaking, has three dimensions, but, instead of describing these as length, breadth and thickness, I should call them breadth, depth and elevation. Most great writers have had these three dimensions, but few of our modern writers have more than two. Thus Dreiser and O'Neill have breadth and depth, but no elevation. Sinclair Lewis and Mencken have breadth, but no elevation and little depth. Willa Cather has little breadth, but some depth and much elevation. Frost and E. A. Robinson, who are both deep and elevated, have still less breadth than Willa Cather. So it goes. The rarest dimension in our literature at present is elevation, which three generations ago was the chief dimension possessed by several writers. Thus the American mind swings to extremes. The time has come round for elevation, and I hope it will not be abused.

*   *   *

How odd it is that people have come to connect the classics with privilege, that the classics are regarded as "snobbish." One recent writer pretends, for instance, that because the word "classic" was used by the Romans to mean "classy,"—appertaining to the work of men who were property-owners,—it has not come to mean in two thousand years something wholly different, which alone counts for us. The only book I inherited from one of my grandfathers was a well-conned copy of Plutarch, which he had read as a farmer's boy; and this was rather the rule than the exception in our old American life of the country.

Our modern wooden wagon-wheel was invented by a New Jersey farmer, who had found an exact description of it in Homer. It was Thomas Jefferson who recorded this fact, when the invention was claimed for an Englishman, and he proved that it was true. (With equal truth, he added that the American farmers were "the only farmers who can read Homer," inasmuch as most European farmers were peasants.)

So the classics will never seem "classy" to me; and democracy in fact was conceived in an aura of the classics, as much in America as in France. The American revolutionists and the French revolutionists met on the common ground of the Greeks and the Romans; and even long years later in France, at the time of the Restoration, it was the liberals and radicals who stood by the classics (just as our Abolitionists stood by them). The royalists were all for liberty in literature, while those who stood for liberty in life upheld the strictest forms in literature. They maintained the classical forms and the classical themes, for the classical themes defended liberty, and the classical forms were the most effective. Was not this what Lucien de Rubempré found when he arrived in Paris?

Sentimental democrats may disregard the classics, but those for whom democracy is based on certain principles will find them where Thomas Paine found them.

Scenes

SCENES

NEW ENGLAND IN 1815

I. THE BOSTON OF GILBERT STUART

A T THE time of the Peace of Ghent, which brought to a close the War of 1812, Gilbert Stuart, the portrait-painter, was an old inhabitant of Boston. He had lived in the town,—for it was still a town, not to become a city for almost a decade,—nine good years. The son of a Rhode Island snuff-grinder, he had made his way up in the world of art until nobody questioned his eminence. He was famous in London and Dublin, where he had been a rival of Lawrence and Beechey. In all American circles, his word was law. No one dared to praise an American poet until the *Edinburgh Review* had done so, but Stuart was the arbiter in painting. In his careless way, he had neglected to answer the letter from the Academy of Florence asking for a portrait of himself. He did not need these testimonials. In the capital of New England, whither he had come to live and die, everyone praised and admired him. Even John Adams, the patriarch of Quincy, who said he would not give sixpence for a Raphael, yielded to the spell of the genial artist. The old man had rejoiced, with a Puritan's fervour, that the age of painting and sculpture had not arrived to corrupt his beloved country. But Gilbert Stuart's witty anecdotes charmed away his prejudices. After his first sitting, he exclaimed that he would be glad to sit to Stuart from one year's end to another.

Times had undoubtedly changed in the Christian Sparta, as John Adams's cousin, Samuel Adams, had called the town of Boston. Gilbert Stuart, who was a notable wag, liked to begin his anecdotes by saying, "When I lived in the Athens of America." Everyone knew what he meant by the phrase: he was referring to Philadelphia. And every Bostonian knew that he was mistaken. William Penn's town had taken the lead in all these matters of enlightenment,—thanks to a good Bostonian, Benjamin Franklin; but that was in days past. The real American Athens was the Christian Sparta. At least, it was advancing towards this position, with large and rapid strides; and Stuart knew it. He was only indulging a taste for mischief. In England, when people had asked him where he was born, he had said, by way of explaining Narragansett, "six miles from Pottawoone and ten miles from Poppasquash." His sitters were little the wiser when he added that he had spent his early years at Newport, where, in some of the old merchants' houses, he had seen portraits by Van Dyck and Kneller, real or supposititious; and if he liked to tease the men of Boston, who suffered from no lack of self-esteem, it was not because he found them dull. He laughed at blue laws and blue noses, but so did many of his Boston sitters, those who had not lost their tory ways and some of those who belonged to the younger circles. For the dominant Boston nose was far from blue: it was a Roman rose, flanked by a full-blown complexion. Stuart, with his lordly style, his fresh, ruddy face and downright manners,—not to mention his taste for the best Madeira, which he poured from a half-gallon ewer, throwing off tumblers like cider in haying-time,—was quite at home with the great East India merchants, whose ships had sometimes carried the Madeira twice round the Cape, to give it a good rocking. They liked the hearty freedom of a man who, when one of his sitters fell asleep, painted him with ass's ears. They liked a man who, if he used snuff, used half a pound of it a day. They liked his high spirits and his flowing talk, as well as the claret he seemed to mix with his paint. And they liked the uncanny skill with which he dived into their own thoughts,—for they were proud of their thoughts, —and made them live and speak on his eloquent canvas.

This was the golden age of portrait-painting. It was an age

of public men. It was an age of family pride, nowhere more marked than in Boston. It was an age of modest wealth, which the recent war had checked but not extinguished. For three generations, since the days of Smibert, Boston had supported its portrait-painters, and Gilbert Stuart was another Copley. It was true that the town had little feeling for art. Stuart was to die as obscure and poor as any tippling poet in the gutter. The Boston people did not cherish him,—much as they enjoyed his company,—because they were proud that one of the world's artists had chosen to live in Boston. They cherished him because he so greatly added to their own pride in themselves; and when they finally buried him in the Common, near the famous Julien of the "soup," they did not even mark his grave. Boston was torpid in aesthetic matters. Stuart had refused to exhibit his pictures because they had been hung so badly. Boston was congenitally obtuse in all that concerned the senses, except Madeira; and this was still to be true a century later, when, with little more aesthetic feeling, the town possessed so much aesthetic knowledge. It was always to look on the plastic arts, instinctively, as a clever woman said, in the days when New Yorkers liked to tease Bostonians, merely as branches of literature. There was something cold and dry in its perceptions. But the very elements in its social life that nourished the portrait-painters,—the family pride, the wealth, the public spirit,—were obviously creating a situation that fostered all its natural faculties. The merchant-patricians, like those of Holland and Flanders, in times gone by, wished to perpetuate their names and glorify their capital not only in the elegance of their mansions but also in churches, parks and public buildings, in professorial chairs at Harvard College, in schools and asylums and hospitals. Such were the desires and thoughts that Stuart caught in the faces of his sitters.

All the omens favoured these intentions. The recent war had cleared the atmosphere. For twenty years after the Revolution, Boston had been poor and apprehensive. The nation was torn with sectional dissensions. Everyone feared the interference of

England. Napoleon was abroad like a wolf in the night. But Waterloo and Commodore Perry had quieted these anxieties. England had ceased to be a menace. The abhorrent career of Napoleon had broken the old connection with France. Europe had become engrossed in problems that had little meaning across the ocean. America, united and free at last, with all its problems solved, as it seemed at the moment, faced a future that was almost dazzling. The "era of good feeling" was beginning, and circumstances had been kind to Boston. The war, which had largely destroyed the commerce of the smaller New England ports, had had no lasting effect on the capital. Strong enough, in fact, to survive the crisis, it prospered with the ruin of so many rivals; and it was attracting more and more the younger merchants of the rural regions who had taken advantage of the decline of shipping, during the years of war, and the boycott of English goods that followed the war, to build up a manufacturing system and supply the American people with native products. Factory-towns were rising on every hand, in eastern Massachusetts and New Hampshire,—Lawrence, Lowell, Fitchburg, Manchester, Lynn. Every village with a waterfall set up a textile-mill or a paper-mill, a shoe-factory or an iron-foundry; and as Boston remained the financial centre, as well for manufacturing as for shipping, the mercantile fortunes of the inland counties were joined with those of the magnates of the seaboard.

Boston was rich, in short, as never before; and, having the means, the leading citizens could not imagine why their little town should not be the finest in the world. No one challenged this prepossession. New England was an isolated region, and Boston had some right to its self-esteem. It had taken the lead in the Revolution, with the statesmen of Virginia, and played a large part in both the wars in which the United States had defeated England. The boast of the Boston poet, "We have the guns, we have the ships," was justified by the British themselves. All their commentators had asserted that the American cruisers were the best and that the Yankee rifle in Yankee hands had set a new standard of marksmanship. No one could guess what happy fortunes lay before the valiant young republic, and Boston hoped for a special dispensation. The old dream of a Puritan commonwealth, a true city of God, lingered in the New England mind, and it seemed as if the appointed hour had come. Cotton Mather had foretold this hour. Jonathan Edwards, on his lonely rides over the forest hills of leafy Stockbridge, had seen the millennium approaching. Bishop Berkeley, on his farm at Newport, had prophesied the golden age. The hard conditions of life in earlier days had yielded to more propitious circumstances. The time was surely ripe; and what wealth was unable to compass might be left to piety and reason. The Boston people had only themselves to blame, or so, at least, they felt, if the kingdom of heaven, a sober New England kingdom,—not built of the gaudy materials that vulgarized the Book of Revelation,—was not, at last, at hand.

They meant to do their best. The Lowells, the Cabots, the Appletons, the Jacksons, the "codfish aristocracy" and the "Essex Junto,"—the members of which had wished to break the Union, in favour of their New England separatism,—the Perkinses, Higginsons, Cushings, the brothers Lawrence, who had made their fortunes on the sea, along with the Hong merchants of the Flowery Kingdom, or from the whirring of their wheels and spindles, united in a passion for the *genius loci*. Some of them suggested in their faces, faithfully painted by Stuart, the florid merchants of colonial times, their grandsires and uncles, in velvet cap and flowered robe, flushed with wine and generosity. Others recalled the Puritan cast, the lean, shrewd, nervous Yankee type, cautious, with a turn for metaphysics, dried by the American atmosphere. All of them lived and moved, walked and spoke as if their little town was a holy city and Rome, Paris and London were their suburbs. For this there were certain reasons. Boston was only a regional capital, but a Boston man could say to himself, quite truly, that it was much more a capital than either New York or Philadelphia; for the people were more homogeneous. A visitor from New York, observing

the crowd in the streets, exclaimed, "Why, all these people are
of one race. They behave like members of one family, whereas
with us a crowd is an assembly of all the nations upon earth."
As one of the results of this homogeneity, the institutions of
the town and country had a greater similarity than in other
regions,—a fact that was full of meaning for the future. It
favoured the growth of the region in all its parts. For, while
Boston attracted the master-minds and took them away from
the smaller towns, it rendered them more active and efficient;
and, precisely because of this concentration of powers, it was
able to send forth influences that were beneficial to the rural
districts. It was able to do so and it wished to do so, more and
more as the century advanced. The older patrician families,
those that had come over in the "Arbella," and those of whom
it was said that, at the time of the Deluge, they had a boat to
themselves, possessed a sense of responsibility that sometimes
seemed acute. The eminent men who had come from the country, or from the smaller ports and county-seats, and who mingled on equal terms with the patricians, were loyal to their
rustic antecedents. One and all felt, as the Boston orators were
always saying, in the old "cradle of liberty," Faneuil Hall, that
they were the heirs of the Revolution. They were determined
to carry out, in every sphere in which their interests lay, their
duties as American citizens. They meant to make Boston a
model town. They meant to make New England a model
region.

Boston was another Edinburgh, with marked variations of
its own. It resembled Edinburgh in many ways, as New England resembled Scotland. The bitter climate and the hard soil,
the ice, the granite and the Calvinism, yielding to more gracious
forms of faith, the common schools, the thrifty farmer-folk, the
coast-line, with its ports and sailors' customs, the abundant
lakes and mountains, the geological aspects of the region, all
suggested the land of Sir Walter Scott, as well as the adjacent
land of Wordsworth, whose bareness and simplicity, together
with his loftiness and depth,—proofs, as Hazlitt said, that his

work was written in a mountainous country,—commended him
to the young New England mind; and if, in this mind, there
was something cold and hard that recalled the ice and the
granite, there were reserves of feeling and perception that
were to find expression in the years to come. A well-known
English traveller remarked of Boston, "I could scarcely believe
I was not in Scotland." One found there, as in Edinburgh, the
same wealth, similarly earned, the same regard for manners
and decorum, the same respect for learning, the same religious
point of view, alike in its antecedents and in its liberal modifications, the same scrupulous conscientiousness, the same
punctiliousness and the same pride, even the same prudence.
One found the same exactions in matters of taste, the same
aristocratic prepossessions and the same democratic feeling un-
derneath them. The golden calf the Bostonians worshipped was
a mere pygmy, as Dickens said, a generation later, beside the
giant effigies one found in the other American cities.

Not that the Boston people were other-worldly, for all their
messianic expectations, except as compared with the profane
New Yorkers. Some of them lived in magnificent style. Many
of them were accomplished in the art of living. The Cushing
house in Summer Street was surrounded with a wall of Chinese porcelain. Peacocks strutted about the garden. The
Chinese servants wore their native dress. The older folk, sedate,
a little complacent, dwelling in the solid garden-houses that
stood about the Common, each with its flagged walk and
spacious court-yard, filled with fragrant shrubs, shaded by its
overarching elms, were genial and pleasure-loving, as a rule.
Here and there one found a Sybarite. Harrison Gray Otis, at
the age of eighty, after forty years of gout, breakfasted every
morning on *pâté de foie gras*. Every afternoon, at the Otis
house, ten gallons of punch evaporated out of the Lowestoft
bowl that was placed on the landing. One of the Perkins
brothers, challenged by a rigorous pastor, who had come out
for total abstinence, doubled his children's ration of Madeira.
Even the young girls, in some of these houses, where they

maintained the royalist traditions and sometimes toasted "the King," under the rose, read *Tom Jones,* Smollett and *Tristram Shandy,* as if they had never heard of a Pilgrim Father. In every house one found the standard authors, Hume, Gibbon, Shakespeare, Milton, Dryden, Addison, the *Arabian Nights, Don Quixote,* Sir William Temple's works in folio, a set of Hogarth's original plates, perhaps, or two or three first editions of Pope, books that were worthy of their calf bindings, on shelves that might have been carved by Grinling Gibbons, surmounted by marble busts. The children were brought up on Maria Edgeworth and the writings of Mrs. Barbauld and Fanny Burney. Sons who came home from abroad with too many airs were greeted with an almost crushing composure. The Boston people were willing to learn, but only if one recognized how much they knew already. Their minds were closed on certain lines, and they did not like "originality." But, as a generation that knew the world, they were prepared to humour their sons and daughters.

There were many strains in the Boston mind, a warm and chivalrous tory strain, a passionate strain of rebelliousness, a strain of religious fervour, a marked and even general disposition,—despite the sybaritic Mr. Otis, who, for the rest, was public-spirited,—to sacrifice at other than mundane altars. The town abounded in quixotic souls, "unmanageable" Adamses, younger sons who refused the social uniform, visionaries, *exaltés,* non-conformists. The future was to provide them with their causes. It was true that these idealists, who spoke for "impossible loyalties," found Beacon Hill a mountain of ice. Principle was a reality in Boston. Conscience was a large reality. Everyone knew the story of the merchant who, when one of his ships was overdue, found that he was more anxious about his thoughts than about the money he was losing. Was it possible, he asked himself, that he had really grown to love his money more for itself than for its noble uses? To settle the point in his own mind, he reckoned the value of the ship and cargo and gave the sum to his favourite charity. The story was

typical of the Boston merchants who, within a space of thirty
years, from 1810 to 1840, established thirty benevolent institutions. And yet there were those who said that Boston had a
double intellect and only half a heart. The prevailing mind was
cautious, excessively formal, singularly obsessed with its own
importance, bigoted in its fear of political change. The mother
of "Athenæum" Shaw enjoined upon him, during his early
travels, the virtues of silence, secrecy and circumspection, quoting the counsel of an experienced father, that one should keep
one's countenance open but one's thoughts close. The Puritans
had learned this art in their days of persecution, and a trading
community had found it useful. Moreover, the prevailing mind
was legalistic. Burke,—with Dr. Johnson, its favourite author,—
noted that more than half of the first edition of Blackstone's
Commentaries found its way to America. A large proportion
had remained in Boston, where it served as an arsenal of logic
against the Jacobins and their bob-tailed crew. For Boston was
controlled by an oligarchy, an unofficial caste of leading men
for whom a "republic" and a "democracy" had next to nothing
in common. Hamiltonian Federalists to a man, Whigs after
the fall of Federalism, they found that the doctrines of
Burke and Johnson admirably supported their property-inter-
ests. For the rest, they had "looked at France," as Fisher Ames
had advised them to do, and witnessed the results of a red revolution,—anarchy, infidelity, just as Burke had prophesied, with
a lord of misrule, Napoleon, as the end of all things.

Stability at any price! They had had too many wars and
altercations. The first French Republic had gone to the dogs.
They could not believe that their own would fare much better.
In days of disunity and debt, it was a natural assumption
that power ought to go with property. The theory had a special justification in days when *not* to have property, if one
wished it, was almost a certain sign of shiftlessness. "Where are
your poor?" said Lafayette, when, a few years later, he scruti-
nized the crowds in the Boston streets. The slum was a thing of
the future, and most of the rich men had acquired their wealth

by the superior exercise of traits that almost every Yankee shared and applauded. Besides, if their minds were closed in political matters, they were more than liberal in religion. They took a lenient view of human nature. Few traces of puritanism were left among them. Most of them had seen the world, as supercargoes, merchants, statesmen, students. They had fought with Tripolitan pirates, visited Canton, India and Egypt, bought skins in Canada and sold them in China, carried ice from Labrador to Java, taken the grand tour to Rome and Naples and had themselves measured by London tailors, who continued to make their clothes when they had shrunk within the measurements. The fact that the clothes were made in London was more important than that they did not fit. If their views were not loose, like their clothes, at least they were enlarged, as people said. They no longer looked on their fellow-beings with the eyes of Puritan deacons. Indeed, the human nature they found about them, far from being totally depraved, seemed, in the light of these wider circumstances, compared with Chinese coolies and Italian beggars, singularly innocent and good. Who had measured its capacity? Boston boys believed in themselves. They grew up alert and self-reliant, battling with the east winds, coasting over the frozen snow, convinced that they were able to "lick creation." How could they accept the ancestral doctrine of the worthlessness of human efforts and motives? How could they hear themselves described as "vipers"? Were Boston boys "little fallen wretches," even worse than vipers? They were more ready to think that, having succeeded in so many things, they could succeed in everything. In short, they believed in perfectibility.

This change in their religious point of view, gradual, scarcely perceptible at first, signified an emotional revolution as marked as the events of '76. Absorbed as they were in politics and trade, the Boston folk were hardly aware that the old faith had vanished from their horizon. Twenty years before, the well-known wit, Robert Treat Paine, had cursed the "vandal spirit of puritanism,"—a levity of the fashionable circles, savouring of the colonial governor's court, that had grown to be a common-place. In 1809, the most popular preacher in Boston, referring to the creed of the Pilgrim Fathers,—Calvinism, with its "revolting forms,"—spoke of Milton's eyes as having been "quenched in the service of a vulgar and usurping faction." A mild and tolerant Unitarianism, torpid, utilitarian, rationalistic, had been set up as the State Church. Known far and wide as the "Boston religion," it still possessed a frail dogmatic structure, of which it was only conscious when it was challenged. The ministers were graceful rhetoricians. Calling themselves Arminians or Arians, sometimes Moderate Calvinists, they still believed in the supernatural; and, having "disproved" the Trinitarian doctrine, with most of the other doctrines of their forbears, they clung to the Christian miracles, as the proper evidences of the faith.

Negative and pallid as it was, the new religion sprang from an atmosphere that was favourable to the flowering of the mind. The ministers, learned, cultivated men, lovers of music and eloquence, had introduced the literary sermon. Their models were Bossuet and Massillon. They had abandoned the older pulpit methods, the texts, the arguments and the commentaries. Their sermons were glowing essays, dealing with the interests of daily life. Joseph Stevens Buckminster, the melodious preacher, the "Chrysostom of America," as he was called, who had read his Greek Testament at five, had prophesied the birth of a great school of American letters. Poets and historians, he had said, in one of his discourses at Harvard College, were soon to appear, to direct American taste and mould the genius of the young republic, men of whom posterity was to stand in awe. "You, my young friends," he had exclaimed, "are destined to witness the dawn of our Augustan age, and to contribute to its glory,"— a very different note from Fisher Ames's, the spokesman of the previous decade, who had never missed a chance to say that the American genius was foredoomed to fail. Buckminster's successor, William Ellery Channing, the great ethical leader of the future, equally sanguine, was more critical. The impassioned little saint with the burning heart, whose intellect was the conscience of New England, felt that the hour had struck for American thinkers. Mind, mind required all one's care! In his youth he had had a sudden illumination, a vision of human nature, which seemed to him a godhead in the making. He ceaselessly preached the gospel of self-improvement. "We want great minds," he said, "to be formed among us. We want the human intellect to do its utmost here."

Boston corresponded to Plato's city, a population that was not too large to hear the voice of a single orator. The people were prepared for these stirring sermons. With Faneuil Hall as their Acropolis, they were accustomed to public speaking, and oratory had filled them with exalted thoughts. At school they learned to recite the swelling strains of the *Life of William Tell*: "Friends of liberty, sons of sensibility, ye who know how to die for your independence!" Bombast, in a sense, but they believed it. Their fathers and uncles had fought in a similar cause, swept along by a tide of eloquence. Moreover, Plutarch was their second Bible, together with Pope's Homer. Deep in their hearts they cherished the conviction that they could emulate these heroic models and reproduce the deeds of history. The sons of William Emerson, for instance, the former minister of the First Church, who had founded the Philosophical Society, were born with these convictions in their blood, and one of them, a boy of twelve named Ralph, a chubby little spouter of Scott and Campbell, who had recently trundled his hoop about the Common, where he pastured the family cow, was to express them later in his essays. The Emerson boys, "born to be educated,"—the object of a Boston childhood seemed to be to prepare for the Latin School,—were typical of a ministerial household, heirs of a long line of divines and scholars, one of whom had prayed every evening that none of his descendants might ever be rich. Their mother, like all the devout New England matrons, enjoyed her morning hour of meditation. Their aunt, the minister's sister, Mary Moody Emerson of Concord, who despised the new religion, poor, low, thin as she thought

it was, dwelt in the fiery depths of a Calvinism which, although
she only half believed it, filled her with a sombre poetry. She
prophesied that her nephews were to be called of men Rabbis
and Fathers. Ralph already had a mind of his own. He carried
the *Pensées* of Pascal to church, to read during the sermon. At
night, in his cold upper chamber, covered with woollen
blankets to the chin, he read his precious Dialogues of Plato.
He associated Plato, ever after, with the smell of wool.

Under its placid surface, Boston tingled with a new ambition. Half the boys expected to go to sea. They hovered about
the ships and the wharves, scenting the salt air, the ropes and
the tar, listening to tales of Chinese pirates, greeting some
cousin, home from Spanish Manila, in white trousers and
jacket of sky-blue silk, marvelling over an older brother who,
for a lark, on his way back from Cairo, had travelled the length
of Italy, in his carriage, dressed as an Oriental potentate. As
many others dreamed of a life of letters. Here and there, some
poor young man, who could not go to the Latin School, bought
his own Andrews and Stoddard's grammar, from which every
proper Boston boy supposed the Latin language had been derived, and spent his nights over a commonplace-book, copying
his favourite passages from Gibbon. Learning was endemic
in the Boston mind, as befitted a town whose first inhabitant,
the Cambridge scholar Blackstone,—who had built his thatched
cottage, with a garden and spring, on the site of Louisburg
Square,—had brought his library with him. There had been
books on the slope of Beacon Hill when the wolves still howled
on the summit. There had always been some Boston man who
could address in Arabic or Persian a merchant or diplomat from
the land of Xerxes; and now that the war was over, and the
nation seemed to be on a solid footing, the intellectual life
grew apace. The clever Frenchmen, with their godless notions,
had made all thought suspicious for a while. The Boston people preferred to settle questions by thumping the table, or by
whacks and blows, in the manner of Dr. Johnson. But subtlety
had grown with confidence. The argand lamp, improved by

Jefferson, had furthered the habit of reading. It was observed
at once that dinner-parties, formerly lighted by candles, ceased
to be as brilliant as of old. Those who had excelled in talking
took to their books and writing-desks. It was true that this intellectual life was timid, cautious and derivative. In short, it
was still colonial, forty years after Bunker Hill. English culture
had a right of way that no one thought of challenging, and
every Boston boy was taught to regard Pope and Burke as un-
approachable. The literary government of Europe was a more
potent yoke than the political government had been. But the
ferment of the rising generation might be expected to break it.

As if to provide the future with a proper setting, the Boston
people had rebuilt the town. The architect, Charles Bulfinch,
the son of a doctor, had appeared with providential promptness.
A man of sensibility, he had been moved to tears, on a tour of
Europe, when he had entered St. Peter's at Rome. He had been
obliged to teach himself. Among so many carpenters and builders, skilful, well-trained craftsmen, schooled in the styles of
Wren and Inigo Jones, there was not an architect in Boston
when he returned in 1787; and, search as one might, high
and low, one could not find a book on architecture. Bulfinch,
who had bought some books in Europe and found his taste and
talent in demand, soon developed a style,—an outgrowth of the
prevailing style, more delicate than the colonial Georgian, quite
without the English massiveness,—that caught the temper of
the Boston people. It was modestly elegant, somewhat prim,
but dignified and simple. He had built the first theatre in the
town, as far back as 1793, where all Boston rejoiced in *The
School for Scandal*, disguised as a "moral lecture." He had
built the admirable State-house, which was to serve as a model
for so many others. He had filled Boston with his works, houses
and blocks of houses, crescents, churches, which, with their
grace and propriety, struck the note of an epoch, an outward
and visible sign that the new Boston mind had crystallized and
found its appropriate form. Various institutions of learning
followed in rapid succession, a Library of Law in 1806, a

Theological Library in 1807,—in the same year, the Boston
Athenæum. Modelled on the Liverpool Athenæum, this was
largely the work of Buckminster, who had spent most of his
little fortune buying books in Paris. He had sent three thousand
volumes home, sets of the British essayists and poets, the *Botanical Magazine,* topographical works on Greece and Rome that
brought the classical world before one's eyes, works in unknown realms, Roscoe's *Lorenzo de' Medici,* Duppa's *Life of
Michael Angelo,* Italian and Spanish dictionaries. The first
wistaria vine, the first mimosa was scarcely more of a novelty
in Boston than some of these intellectual plants and vines that
were to scatter their seeds across New England.

Two other institutions, the Handel and Haydn Society and
the *North American Review*—founded, both, in 1815—marked
the coming-of-age of the Boston mind. For music and for letters, these were of the future. The culture of the immediate
past and present found expression through another organ. For
several years there had existed, from 1803 to the outbreak of
the war, a club devoted to literary interests. The Anthology
Society, as it was called, numbered among its members Buckminster, Channing, William Emerson, Dr. Gardiner, the rector
of Trinity Church, William Tudor, the merchant, President
Kirkland of Harvard, John Lowell and other well-known men.
The members met one evening every week to discuss the manuscripts for their magazine, the *Monthly Anthology,* over a
modest supper of widgeons and teal, brants or a mongrel goose,
with a little good claret. There was too little intercourse, they
felt, among Americans who cared for letters. They even hoped
that their review, the first of its kind in the country, which
had succeeded many feebler efforts, might foster the growth of
a national literature.

The members were not professional men of letters, a species
that was still unknown in Boston. Moreover, their expectations
were not excessive, or much beyond the pleasures of their task.
William Emerson was the editor. William Tudor, who had

established the club, had made a small fortune, with his brother, shipping ice, cut from their pond at Saugus, to Martinique and South America. Indeed, the Tudors introduced, throughout the equatorial world, even as far as Calcutta, the custom of using ice in table-drinks. Dr. Gardiner, an Episcopalian, conducted a little school in his spacious study, instructing a chosen handful in Latin and Greek, following the methods of his master, the great English scholar, Samuel Parr. Among the other contributors or members, some of them correspondents from a distance, were the rising Portsmouth lawyer, Daniel Webster, who had not yet moved to Boston, the Reverend Aaron Bancroft, who lived in Worcester, a theologian of the older school, the father of a son who was soon to be famous, Joseph Story of Salem, the notable jurist, the greatest writer on the law since Blackstone, as the Lord Chief Justice of England called him later, and various younger men of ample promise, Alexander Everett and George Ticknor. Judge Story, a classmate of Dr. Channing, had published a poem, *The Power of Solitude,* suggested by the writings of Zimmermann. Although he had taken a "lawyer's farewell of the muse," he often entertained himself in court by making his notes of arguments in verse.

The magazine, though somewhat staid in manner, decidedly starched and impersonal, was yet an enterprise that promised much, in days when "Who wrote Junius?" was still an exciting topic of conversation. In style it resembled the British reviews, not yet irradiated by Lamb and Hazlitt,—the English Unitarian minister's son who had spent three years, as a boy, in Massachusetts, who had seen Boston before he saw London and never forgot the Yankee barberry-bushes. Far from calling a spade a spade, it always called a name an appellation. Behind these traits of Johnsonese, moreover, might have been discerned the self-distrust that marks the colonial mind, a mind that has no centre of its own and clings to the well-tried ways of the mother-country after the mother-country has thrown them off. It abounded in Addisonian bric-a-brac, playful bits on toast and cranberry sauce, worthy of a Grandison's hours of ease, accounts of visits to Dr. Johnson's birthplace, continuations of Collins's *Ode to the Passions*, reviews of *The Gamesters: or Ruins of Innocence*, Beresford's *The Miseries of Human Life* and *A Wreath for the Rev. Daniel Dow*. It defended Pope against all comers, especially Coleridge's nonsense. Even in Boston there were lawyers who thought its tone was pompous and said that Dr. Gardiner was a snob. This was a little severe. The magazine was well-informed. It reviewed the museums, the theatres, the social assemblies, and criticized the state of Harvard College. It noticed the important publications, Washington Irving's *Knickerbocker*, Aaron Bancroft's *Washington*, Madame de Staël's *Corinne*, Wilson's *American Ornithology*. It published intelligent essays on Erasmus, the Carelessness of Dryden, Sir Walter Scott, whose poems stirred the Boston breast and who was supposed to be writing the Waverley novels. "Who writes the Waverley novels?" was almost as thrilling a question as "Who wrote Junius?" It attacked Blair's *Grave*, for the mortuary vein was running out. It printed papers on Italian painters, Luca Giordano, the Caracci, and even a version of the *Shakuntala*, the first Hindu work to appear in the country. It deplored the backward state of American letters, the servile imitation of England, the fruits of a superficial education. Whatever the future might produce, the writers of the review showed that the Boston of Gilbert Stuart had roused itself out of its ancient slumbers.

Some of these writers, in fact, prefigured the future. Buckminster professed the daring notion that there was a higher poetry than the "mere language of reason." He had himself taken as much delight in the ragged splendours of a western sunset, rich, disorderly, indistinct in shape, as in the seven colours of the rainbow, properly disposed in a semicircle, as if a good Bostonian had arranged them. This was quite absurd, Dr. Gardiner said. Heaven could only tell what it betokened, in a world that persisted in moving and changing its mind.

All about Boston, to the north, west and south, there still
dwelt, in these days of Gilbert Stuart, many a veteran of the
Revolution, protagonists, master-minds and lesser worthies. In
Cambridge, in Concord, up and down the coast, in every port
and village, one found survivors of the stirring hour, with their
firelocks over their chimney-pieces. They recalled the brave
days of the Roman republic, when the chief men of the State
stayed on their farms, awaiting some summons for a public
council to call them from their villas to the Senate.

At Pepperell, near the New Hampshire line, Colonel William Prescott had his farm, which he held by its original Indian title. The hero of Bunker Hill, like Cincinnatus, had taken
up the plough again where he had left it standing in the furrow.
Passing through Dorchester southward, or driving through the
quiet lanes of Brookline, where the great East India merchants
had their villas, with spreading lawns and airy parlours, filled
with plaster casts and Italian paintings, and summer-houses in
the Chinese style, one came at last to Quincy, where John
Adams lived. There, like Thomas Jefferson at Monticello, with
whom he had resumed his correspondence, on all his ancient
terms of good will,—since all passion was spent now,—the
patriarch cheerfully sat for the painters and sculptors and
studied the greater art of growing old. Once a year, together
with his Bible, he read and pondered Cicero's *De Senectute*.
He liked to talk with his friends on subjects suggested by his
reading, such as the merits of Alexander the Great; and, as
the years passed, he waited calmly for a better world, where
he expected to meet all the great and good who had gone before him.

Close by, his kinsfolk, the Quincy family, dwelt. Josiah
Quincy, now in the prime of life, the ancient doge of later
times whose mind had been formed in the stress of the previous
age, also spent his leisure hours, those he could spare from

active politics, either in Boston or Washington, or from the
toils of his farm, reading his three editions of Cicero, one for
the shelf, one for the table and one, in twenty volumes, for
the pocket, along with his Plutarch and his well-conned
Horace. For generations, on their ancestral acres, where, with
his six servants, the first American forbear of the family had
raised his honoured roof-tree, the Quincys had lived as magistrates and squires, loving their field-sports as they loved their
country and poring over the Tusculan Disputations: for Cicero,
the defender of liberty, stirred a responsive chord in the Quincy
bosom, Cicero, the instructor of every profession, the friend of
every age! If the present master of the house, a house as
ample as those of the Brookline merchants, overflowing with
cousins and friends and public men of half a dozen countries,
—if the present Josiah Quincy was not himself a man of the
Revolution, he might, equally well, have been his father, whose
life he had seen mirrored in Pope's Homer. He was the happy
warrior who, for a long generation to come, was to fight for all
the Revolution had stood for. He was the man of life unblem-
ished who, like the Romans, in his inmost heart, had built
twin temples to virtue and honour, so joined that one could
enter the temple of honour only by passing first through the
temple of virtue. He knew and loved the ancients, as Harvard
knew them, not so much because he cared for learning as for
their noble patterns of behaviour.

The happiest moments of the Adams household, few as they
were at present, snatched from the busiest life that America
knew, were those that John Quincy Adams, the rising hope
of the old President's heart, was able to spend with his aging
father and mother. Already in train for the White House,
minister to England, Secretary of State, almost a popular hero,
like Andrew Jackson, thanks to his work in concluding the
recent war, he, too, was a man of the Revolution. At eight, he
had watched the Battle of Bunker Hill; at nine, he had served
as a little post-rider; at fourteen, he had entered public life as
secretary to the minister to Russia. He had known Washington,

Franklin, Jefferson, Jay, as a younger member of their constellation, and had followed a proud, unmanageable course that had won him the hatred of his own party and the gratitude of the nation. Against the interests of his Federalist friends, for whom money counted more than country, he had fought for Jefferson's Embargo, as later, in the teeth of the cotton-interests, he was to fight the slave-power. For the selfish claims of his class and breed he cared no more than he cared for his own popularity; and yet, by the force of his intellect and will, he had carved for himself a career that every common politician envied. It was a career that his father understood and Abigail Adams rejoiced in, for he had never compromised his faith that statesmanship was the noblest of human callings. And if, at times, his methods were those of the hedgehog, at Quincy the quills were always folded in.

There, in the peaceful homestead, where later generations of Adamses were to sit in the old President's chair, in the quiet upstairs study, and write their memoirs and their histories, father and son, at these propitious moments, discussed the great problems of their country. John Quincy Adams, now turning fifty, short, stout and bald, less florid than his father,—for the English type was gradually dying out,—had passed his earliest years there, and there, in later years, still fighting, in the House at Washington, for justice, for improvement, justice for the Negroes, justice for the outraged Indians, for science, for the Smithsonian Institution, with both feet planted on the Rock of Ages,—there he was to pass his long vacations, always writing, writing, with ink-spots on his fingers, notes on Plutarch, notes on the Book of Leviticus, speeches, essays, poems, nodding in his chair, wandering about the garden and the ragged orchard, with hatchet and saw in hand, pruning his pear and cherry-trees, hoeing and plucking weeds, bending over his plants in their pots and boxes or using his wife's best tumblers to cover the caterpillars that were supposed to turn into butterflies but—as his grandsons noticed—never did so. At Quincy, as a little boy, with his thoughts filled with birds' eggs and trifles, he had begun his famous Diary, enjoined thereto by his austere papa, so that he might later be able to note the stages by which he had advanced in taste, knowledge and judgment. There he had read his fairy-tales and revelled in the *Arabian Nights* and Shakespeare. In all the furious years he had passed in Holland, Prussia, Russia, France and England, as well as in Boston and Washington, since, as a boy, he had gone to school in Paris, in Amsterdam and Leyden, the charm of his life had been literature. Rising at four or five, lighting his fire and candle, reading his Bible first, with English, French and German commentaries, reading his Homer and his Latin authors, without whom he could not have endured existence, reading Evelyn's *Sylva* for his garden, reading all the new books on science, bent on his own improvement, bent on the improvement of his children before he undertook to improve his country, he had mastered Dutch and Russian as well as the tongues that other people knew. And the summit of his ambition was to write, to serve his country, at its feeblest point, by some enduring work of literature.

One work he was to write that served his country, the celebrated *Report on Weights and Measures*. But this was not the work he had in mind. Nor was the Pepysian Diary, incomparable in American letters, the living portrait of his wilful mind, with malice towards all, with charity for none, least of all himself. He had written a volume of *Letters on Silesia* that showed what gifts he had for observation. His *Lectures on Rhetoric and Oratory*, delivered at Harvard College in 1806, revealed his powers of organized reflection. He had heard the greatest orators of the previous age, Fox, Pitt and Burke, as well as their American contemporaries, and Harvard was prepared to hear the doctrine, sanctioned by Cicero and Demosthenes, that, while liberty was the parent of eloquence, eloquence was the stay of liberty. It was a doctrine that Harvard wished to hear, in an age when the art of the pulpit, the art of the forum, the art of the judge and the lawyer, soon to be followed by that of the lecture-platform,—all one art, in its several branches,—was the only literary art that performed a vital function; and Adams, with his experience and his learning, his gifts of perspicuity and order, was certainly the most competent instructor the college could have found. His lectures served as a text-book for the rising generation of public speakers. But this was not the writing he had dreamed of, and dreamed of still, when, on a Christmas morning, he read Pope's *Messiah* to his household, or when he noted that an actor's letter, asking for his analysis of *Othello*, pleased him more than all his political honours. Like his own grandson, Henry Adams, who, longing to think like Benvenuto, knew that his instinct was "blighted from babyhood," he longed to think and feel as Shakespeare felt, or as the Germans Wieland and Bürger felt, whom he had read so many years before, as far back as 1800, when he was living in Germany, the first of all Americans to read them. But his instinct also had been blighted by the long winter of Puritanism. The time had not yet come for New England poets.

The time had not yet come, but the time was coming, and Adams, in his pertinacity, represented the chill before the dawn. During those years in Germany, he had translated Wieland's *Oberon*. The poet, to whom his tutor sent the version, compared it with the English Sotheby's version. Adams's was more accurate, he said, but Sotheby's was more poetical. Alas, the more Adams had written since, the more he realized that, with poetry, there was a certain point that one might reach, by means of the virtues that New England knew, beyond which no vigils or vows would take one. But he was under a spell. What was he to do? Riding, walking, musing, he poured the verses forth, odes to Lucinda, Narcissa, Belinda, whose charms he could not refuse to acknowledge, translations of Juvenal's Satires, elegiac stanzas, versifications of La Fontaine's Fables, versions of the Psalms in rhyme, even a long poem, *Dermot McMorrogh*, a satire in the eighteenth-century mode that filled his mind for weeks and left him, at the end, like a pleasant dream, to dull and distressing realities. What could

he do when the rhymes insisted on coming and he found he
could sometimes hold in his mind fifty lines at once? Throw his
poems behind the fire? Or suffer a few, at least, to appear in
print? Certainly one of the greatest statesmen living, he was
content to be known as one of the smallest poets of his country. Meanwhile, as a searcher of the skies, who knew that
there are many kinds of stars and who liked to promote astronomy, he scanned the horizon every day for other and better
poets than himself.

*   *   *

Cambridge, across the Charles, was a quiet village, so quiet
that one could hear in Harvard Square the booming of the
guns in the navy-yard in Boston. One even heard the murmur
of the waves breaking on the far-away sea-beaches. Cambridgeport was a huckleberry-pasture, with a few wharves and houses.
Thence the sloop "Harvard," moored to its dock, a Viking ship
in the eyes of the village boys, sailed once a year to the coast
of Maine to bring back wood for the college.

Through the port, as first through the village centre, passed
the white-topped wagons that brought to the Boston market
the wares and products of the inland regions. They filled the
yards of the inns, the Porter House, for one, beyond the village, and the shouts and oaths of the teamsters rang through
the tranquil air. Around the ungarnished Common, where the
dust and the snow blew unchecked, a few old houses stood
amid their ample gardens. One of them, a gambrel-roofed
dwelling, General Ward's headquarters in the Revolution, was
the house of the Reverend Abiel Holmes, the author of the
Annals of America, a work, sufficiently bald, that was yet the
first of its kind. The house next door was that of the Higginson
family. On Dana Hill stood the Dana mansion. The family of
Chief Justice Dana, the first American minister to Russia, had
owned their Cambridge farm for six generations. On Brattle
Street stood the Craigie house, one of a line of spacious
Georgian villas that were known as Tory Row. They had been
built before the Revolution by opulent loyalist families, who

owned slave-plantations in the West Indies. In the careless eighteenth-century days, the great halls and chambers of these houses had echoed with the sounds of music and dancing. Elmwood stood a mile or so beyond, the last house in the row, formerly the home of Elbridge Gerry. It had been occupied for several years by the Reverend Charles Lowell and his household. Wide-spread lawns encircled these dwellings, covered with wine-glass elms and willows, with orchards at the rear. The windows of the Craigie house overlooked the placid meadows to the river Charles.

From these Cambridge windows peered,—one saw them from the street,—the faces of aging women, now and then with turbans on their heads and massive silver spectacles, eyes that had witnessed and remembered the passing of guns and troops in the Revolution. Mrs. Craigie's head was often seen, as she sat at her parlour window. Her house had been Washington's headquarters, in the winter of '76, and there Mrs. Washington had come, with a coach and servants in scarlet livery, to celebrate her wedding-day. The late Mr. Craigie, the Boston merchant, had been famous for his entertainments; and among his guests, in this house, had been Talleyrand and Queen Victoria's father. But the days of Queen Victoria had not arrived, nor the days of a Cambridge poet who was to make the house more famous still. Mrs. Craigie, once a well-known beauty, a widow now, much reduced in fortune, even to the point of taking lodgers, spent her days reading her favourite authors, Voltaire and the British reviewers. Her house was well-stocked with books, like all the other liberal Cambridge houses. Hume, Addison, Gibbon, Swift stood on every shelf, along with Milton and *Evelina,* Richardson, perhaps a polyglot Bible, Casaubon's Polybius, two or three Elzevirs. The library of the Reverend Charles Lowell, who had a church in Boston, numbered nearly four thousand volumes. Mr. Lowell had exiled to the attic the old prints that had filled his grandfather's study, heads of the ancient wise men, Plato, Pythagoras, Socrates, Cicero, Seneca; for, without thinking less of the

ancients, he thought more of the moderns. He had studied his
theology in Scotland and had visited Southey and Wordsworth,
the new English poets, whose work he enjoyed discussing; and
facing his chair in the dining-room hung a portrait of Wilber-
force, the symbol of his humanitarian interests. The Reverend
Mr. Holmes, who also made the most of the art of living, had
yet maintained the ancient faith. Indeed, he was deposed for
doing so, although he was only mildly Orthodox, for the Cambridge people were Unitarians as they were Whigs. Here and
there one found a Calvinist, as here and there one found a
Democrat, like Mr. Timothy Fuller of Cambridgeport. But one
had to be a personage, a Member of Congress or a magistrate,
a man who could afford his coach and pair, to carry off these
odious opinions. The Cambridge people knew what they believed, and they did not propose to discuss it. But Mr. Holmes
had literary compensations. His house overflowed with books.
Amid the lumber in the attic, one found Erasmus's *Colloquies*
and queer old Latin works on alchemy. Sometimes, in the evening, Mr. and Mrs. Holmes and their sons and daughters
gathered about the London-made piano, and one of the daughters, who was the family minstrel, sang the *Irish Melodies* of
Thomas Moore.

All of these ampler houses, those of the ministerial and legal
families, and some of the merchant families, abounded in
family portraits. They were the work of so many journeyman
painters, at ten, twenty or forty dollars a head, that they represented only a decent regard for fathers and mothers who would
have thought themselves passing rich on a thousand dollars a
year. If one had a Copley or a Stuart, one had the right to lift
one's chin a little. On the shelves of the closets lay bundles of
mint and catnip, lavender, sweet-marjoram, pennyroyal. Apples
were stored there, and peaches spread their fragrance on the
darkness, as if waiting to inspire strains and strophes. For little
boys were growing up in Cambridge who were to be known as
"household poets," and often as something better. Their parents
even wished them to be poets. The Cambridge fathers and

mothers were not poetic, but they respected poetry. Their gardens were full of marigolds, hollyhocks, larkspurs, with the humbler vegetables of the working kind, carrots, parsnips, beets, —as if to remind the sons of the Revolution that classes were provisional in republics, that a deserving carrot was better than an undeserving lupin, that hollyhocks were only hollyhocks when they were plucky enough to withstand the wind, each on its own stalk (which made them pleasing vegetables indeed), and that the man who had the family portraits must always prove himself on other grounds. One of the "household poets" was to make this clear. The Cambridge flowers had a moral meaning, as good New England flowers ought to have; but they had a poetical meaning that was even more apparent. So did the sounds one heard on summer evenings, the bells of the cows ambling home at twilight, the lullaby of the crickets in early autumn, the hymns of the frogs, in spring, in some neighbouring swamp, not to speak of the creaking of the winter wood-sleds, dragging their loads of walnut over the complaining snow. Every sound and odour had its value. One heard the carpenter smoothing his knotty boards, and the whips of the four-horse coaches rattling by; one heard the ticks in the joints of the old bedsteads; one smelt the salt of the sea in the summer breeze. What a store of allusions and similes, drawn from the homely facts of his daily living, a Cambridge boy might pack into his poems! When it came to associations and recollections, such as all New England boys shared in common, buried under the leaves of many summers, the Cambridge boys who were to write their poems were to understand the meaning of Byron's line about "striking the electric chain."

In Cambridge, other facts pressed themselves upon one's attention. There was the village churchyard, where one puzzled over the Latin inscriptions on the gravestones of old theologians and presidents of the college, the diamond-shaped cavities in the stones from which the leaden escutcheons had been removed to be used for bullets in the Revolution, the graves of ancient scholars, with virtues ending in *issimus* and

errimus. One somehow acquired the sense that learning was a
very distinguished object, which made the scholar a natural
leader of men. The spot where Washington took command of
the army was near the spot where President Langdon of Harvard had offered prayers, before the assembled troops, and sped
them on their way to Bunker Hill. Learning might indeed be
quaint and queer, as, for instance, with those living tutors who
had so steeped themselves in Latin that their English was a
foreign babble, men who said "intramural aestivation" when
what they meant was town-life in summer, men who might
have written a poem beginning—

> *In candent ire the solar splendour flames;*
> *The foles, languescent, pend from arid rames.*

But all the New England statesmen were also scholars, and
many of them had come to nurse in Cambridge. There had
been set up, in the year the town received its name, the first
printing-press in the commonwealth, brought from England in
1638, the press that had produced for two-score years all the
printing in the colonies, including Eliot's Bible and the *Freeman's Oath.* Learning was immemorial in Cambridge. Learning
was omnipresent. In a population wholly derived from England,
one counted the foreigners on a single hand: two Scotch gardeners, a hair-cutter of nebulous antecedents, one Irishman,
the master of a spade. And the Irishman knew his Latin, like
everyone else: he had learned his Horace at a hedge-school
and was always ready to lean on his spade and test a boy's
knowledge of the *Quo me, Bacche.* The shopkeepers around
the square added tags of Latin to their signs. The janitor of
the newly established Law School was a notable spouter of
Virgil. The height of wit in all the Cambridge circles was a
thoroughly sound Latin-English pun.

The schoolmasters in Cambridge, as in Boston, were cut on
the ancient pattern. They drove the boys with switch and
ferule, and even drove the girls, all the more when the boys

and girls were children of the learned families; for everyone in Cambridge was precocious, and only a dunce could fail to be ready for college at fourteen or fifteen. The best-known school, soon to be opened, for Greek and Latin only, was that of William Wells, an Englishman. It was he who had published in Boston the Cicero in twenty volumes. He had also edited Tacitus. His school was a Gehenna of blood and tears. At Cambridgeport, there was another school where, in the process of flogging the Latin in, and pulling the boys about by the ears, the master almost pulled their ears off. One of the little Dana boys, the grandson of the old Chief Justice, never forgot how his ear had felt. He had his mind made up in regard to floggers, especially when he sailed before the mast and saw the sailors flogged; and in days to come he was to speak his mind. But the boys had pleasures, too. They pitched hay with the hired men, and even with their fathers, on occasion. They knew all the trees by their bark and leaves, and all the birds by their notes and manner of flying. They scoured the country in search of flowers and insects; they fished for pouts and waded for water-lilies; they searched for powder-mills and old redoubts, left from the Revolution. They lay and chattered on the grassy slopes and fought the battles over again. They haunted the Boston wharves, redolent of the ocean and swarming with ear-ringed seamen. Moreover, they had their parties with the Cambridge girls. Strangers who came from less heroic regions sometimes found these parties a little chilly. One of them said that, during the quadrille, his partner touched his hand as if she were feeling for cucumbers in the dark.

Harvard College was the heart of Cambridge. Seven generations before, every New England household had given the college twelvepence, or a peck of corn, or its value in unadulterated wampum peag. But those were the good old days when the Orthodox faith reigned in every mind. Established now on a Unitarian basis,—for the founding of the Divinity School, with Dr. Henry Ware as its chief professor, settled the character of the new regime,—the college was considered, in the

country districts, dangerously lax and liberal. West of Worcester, and up the Connecticut Valley, the clergy, Calvinist
almost to a man, united in condemning the Cambridge collegians, in the very words of Whitefield, as "close Pharisees,
resting on head knowledge,"—the same collegians who had
called Whitefield "low." But as for this "head knowledge," no
one denied that they possessed it. More than a few of the
Orthodox admitted that it was what collegians ought to possess.
Harvard still had an exalted prestige. The patrician families
of Boston and Cambridge regarded it as more than a family
affair. It was a family responsibility. They sent their sons to
the college, as a matter of course. But they considered it a
public duty, not only to endow and foster it, in the interests
of the meritorious poor, but to maintain its standards and over-
see it. They founded chairs that bore their names, the Boylston
chair, the Eliot chair, the Smith professorship. They watched
and brooded over its progress and welfare. Who would have
respected wealth in Boston if wealth had not, in turn, respected learning? And, if the professors' salaries were very
small, everyone knew they were partly paid in honour.

It was true that the standard of learning was not too lofty.
In this, as in certain other respects, the well-known "Harvard
indifference" resembled that of Oxford and Madrid. Intellectual things took second place. The object of study was to
form the mind, but this was to form the character; and Massachusetts knew what its character was and took a certain satisfaction in it. Everyone was aware of the best Boston and Cambridge type, the type that Josiah Quincy represented, or the
late Chief Justice Dana, formed on the classic models. A clear,
distinct mentality, a strong distaste for nonsense, steady composure, a calm and gentle demeanour, stability, good principles,
intelligence, a habit of understatement, a slow and cautious
way of reasoning, contempt for extravagance, vanity and af-
fectation, kindness of heart, purity, decorum, profound affections, filial and paternal. A noble type, severely limited, which
Boston celebrated in its marble busts. Comparing it, trait for

trait, with half of Plutarch's characters, one might have felt that Boston deserved its busts. Moreover, beneath its cold and tranquil surface, burned, though the fires were low, the passions and convictions of the Revolution, ready to flame forth on a fresh occasion. But would the occasion ever recur? That was what a stranger might have asked, face to face with the marble busts. The surface, at least, seemed somewhat tame, suited for the merchant and the lawyer, and the man of God after the Boston fashion.

This was the type, and almost the only type, the curriculum of Harvard contemplated. Whatever studies favoured its formation, whatever were the best ways to form it, these were the ways and the studies that Harvard knew. Whatever studies did not favour it, or favoured the formation of other types that Boston did not like or had never heard of, these were no concern of Harvard, or its concern only to oppose them. Josiah Quincy was not enthusiastic. Why should Harvard be? Mr. Dana was eminently decorous. He had caused the arrest, for contempt of court, of a butcher who, appearing at the bar, had left his coat behind him. Decorum was a Harvard characteristic. Neither Mr. Quincy nor Mr. Dana cared a button for the German language, which had been spoken by the Hessian troops, a half-barbarous tribe of Europeans who had been hired out to the British king. German, from the point of view of Harvard, always excepting John Quincy Adams, who, as everyone knew, was a little queer,—German was an outlandish dialect; and, while it was not improper to speak French, the language of Lafayette, which it was quite improper not to know, more than a few felt that Bonaparte had destroyed its respectability. Greek was esteemed as the tongue of a group of ancient republics that possessed some of the virtues of New England. Greece had produced a number of orators who were more eloquent even than Samuel Adams. Search as one might, however, in Massachusetts, one could not find a play of Euripides; besides, compared with Latin, which everyone drank in with his mother's milk, Greek was a little questionable. The

Roman word "convivium" meant "living together." "Symposium" had a similar sense in Greek, but what did "symposium" imply? "Drinking together." Was not this alone enough to prove that the Romans were more respectable than the Greeks? Cicero had made the point, and everyone knew that Cicero must be right.

These were the days of the genial President Kirkland, who, after conducting an examination, regaled the boys with a fine dish of pears. He was an easy-going man, a Unitarian minister, like most of the professors, sympathetic and of the gentlest temper, naturally frank and cordial, with all the delicate feeling for human behaviour that characterized the best New Englanders. It was said that he threw his sermons into a barrel, as the farmers threw their corn into the silo, and that on Sunday morning he fished out enough for a discourse and patched the leaves together. The story had a symbolic truth, at least. It signified the president's "Harvard indifference," which was accompanied by the best intentions and a notably warm heart. He never took the narrow view. Hearing that the flip at the Porter House had proved to be too attractive to the students, he dropped in to see the proprietor. "And so, Mr. Porter," he said, "the young gentlemen come to drink your flip, do they?"—"Yes, sir," said Mr. Porter, "sometimes."—"Well, I should think they would," the president said. "Good day, Mr. Porter." Any sort of illumination, physical or spiritual, might have taken place under his eye. He was kind to the rich young men whose fathers, at their graduation, gave them dinners in a great marquee, with five hundred guests and dancing in the Yard. He was kinder to the poor young men whose black coats were turning green. He was not a man to oppose any important change in the system of studies; and before the end of his long reign, in fact, certain changes were to occur that were eventually to transform the college. But he could not see why changes should occur. He thought the old ways were good enough, and he played into the hands of firmer men who thought that all other ways were bad. Four hours a day for study and recitation were quite enough for anyone. A library of twenty thousand books was certainly large enough. In fact, the Harvard library was a wonder. No other American library was larger, except perhaps one. A young man with literary tastes could find Hakluyt's *Voyages* there, Cotton's Montaigne and Dodsley's *Old Plays,* as well as the books that he ought to have at home; and the window-sills were broad enough to sit on, if he was too fidgety to keep his chair. What more, in reason, could one ask for? For the rest, the teaching consisted of recitations. No nonsense on the part of the professors, no lectures, no unnecessary comments, no flowery illustrations. One ground in one's Latin and mathematics, under a pair of candles, and the next day one ground them out again. Professors were not nurses, neither were they dancing-masters. One did not go to Harvard to stimulate a dubious fancy. One went to learn to deserve a marble bust.

A few imaginative persons had their doubts. The college was dying of antiquated notions,—so, at least, they thought. Twenty years before, one of the students, who was known later as a writer, had printed certain strictures on the college. He had called it "the death-bed of genius." How many immortals, he asked, had Harvard educated?—and how could it expect to produce immortals? The delicate muse of belles-lettres could never be induced to visit Harvard. "No, she would recoil at the sight of our walls." And very properly, the professors thought. The college was not for ladies, neither was it meant for men of genius, or any other sort of extravagant creature. For a thorough Boston lawyer, a merchant who desired a well-trained mind, a minister who did not indulge in raptures, Harvard had proved to be an adequate nest. It fostered polite, if not beautiful letters, it sent one back to Plutarch for one's models, it sharpened the reasoning faculties, it settled one's grounds for accepting a Christian faith that always knew where to draw the line.

In short, the college was a little realm as fixed and final as a checker-board. The squares of the various studies were plainly marked, with straight lines and indisputable corners. All one had to do was to play the game. Dr. Popkin, "Pop," was Professor of Greek. Over his cocked hat he carried a circular canopy that Cambridge learned to know as an umbrella. The doctor was a sound grammarian. He found his poetry in the Greek roots; he did not need to seek it in the flowers. A second umbrella appeared in the Cambridge streets, in the hands of Professor Hedge, who had written a famous *Logic*. He had spent seventeen years composing this work, with the aid of the other members of his household. No Logic could have been better, and he hoped his students would learn it word for word. For logic was important. Unless one knew logic, one could not read Locke; and who that had not read Locke could ever be certain that his Christian faith had a solid bottom? Logic was the Golden Calf of Cambridge, the muse of Theology, the muse of Law. For Hebrew, one went to Professor Willard; for Latin, to Brazer or Otis; for Natural Religion, to Professor Frisbie, whose taste for the ethically severe was modified by his love of graceful ease. He enjoyed Maria Edgeworth as well as the rigours of Tacitus. Dr. Ware presided over Divinity. Dr. Ware's favourite phrase was "on the one hand, on the other hand." He knew he possessed the truth, but he did not wish to slight its minor aspects. He was famous for the accuracy of his definitions. No one could distinguish better than he between "genuineness" and "authenticity"; and, although he had nineteen children, he never used the rod. He punished infractions of the household law by the hydropathic treatment.

Towering modestly over the other professors, Andrews Norton symbolized the *zeitgeist*, a word that he would have deprecated. It savoured of those antic tricks which the young men were beginning to play with language (or were so soon to begin to play),—German barbarisms, exclamations, inversions, coarse and violent metaphors, innovations which, to Mr. Norton, seemed both *outré* and *bizarre*, much as he would have disliked to use two foreign words in a single sentence. His own greatest days had not arrived, but Cambridge was prepared for his fortunate marriage. The heir of John Norton, who had proclaimed his line a "royal priesthood," not himself ordained, was yet a potent theologian, the Dexter Professor of Sacred Literature. He was more than a match for the daughter of a Boston merchant who kept a variety-store on Dock Square and who, after sending his son to Europe, to make the grand tour in his own carriage, wished his daughter to live in becoming style. Mr. Norton's father-in-law purchased Shady Hill for the promising couple, made a gentleman's house of it and bought the fifty acres of Norton's Woods, as the domain was henceforth to be called, an elegant park, unrivalled in homely Cambridge, where, in time, were to blossom, along with little Charles Eliot Norton, the handsome daughters whom the college knew as the "Evidences of Christianity," a reference to their father's famous book. Shady Hill was to have a notable history long after its first lord, the "Unitarian Pope," as Carlyle was to call him, who, for a generation, was to fight, on behalf of Harvard and common sense, against the Germanizing radicals, the Transcendentalists and their noxious crew, metaphysicians of the wilder sort,—long after the great Andrews Norton had laid his cold head in the colder tomb.

These days were still remote. Professor Norton was not married yet. He was not yet the "tyrant of the Cambridge Parnassus," nor was there an Emerson to call him so. He had not yet edited Mrs. Hemans, although he had written his own devotional poems. He had not visited his English readers; nor had he produced his commanding work, the *Evidences of the Genuineness of the Gospels,* which proved, to the satisfaction of honest men,—whatever the Germans might say, in their so-called higher criticism,—that Matthew, Mark, Luke and John had really written the books that bore their names, a demonstration as clear as Hedge's *Logic.* The four great volumes were still unborn, but Mr. Norton had won his spurs already. His head was long, his head was firm, his mind never wavered or misgave him. In Cambridge, chiaroscuro, a word unknown, would have been thought to savour of corruption; and the man who had put the

Calvinists to rout, by sheer force of reasoning, was not the man to be upset by any other appeal to the vulgar "feelings," that of the pantheist Schleiermacher, for instance, with his notion that the verities of religion rested, not on the letter of the Scriptures, but on "the soul's sense of things divine." Odious phrase, how German! Mr. Norton's lectures had spread his fame. There was not a lawyer in Boston or Cambridge who could find a crack in his chain of logic. No one could prove that he was mistaken; and, inasmuch as a lawyer-proof religion was exactly what Boston wished for, Mr. Norton's eminence was uncontested. Was he a little petulant and vain? That was beside the point. And if he was called a Pharisee by certain ill-bred persons, that was wholly a matter of definition. Mr. Norton, like Professor Ware, was a master of definition. He was benevolent, he was conscientious. Moreover, he was the only professor,— or he was soon to be,—who had his private carriage. One saw it every Sunday, drawn up beside the president's carriage at the entrance of the college chapel.

Such was Harvard College, as it might have appeared in the eyes of a travelling Persian. It resembled Paley's watch. One found the watch on the seashore and instantly inferred that some intelligent mind must have designed it. One found Harvard College in the village of Cambridge: the evidences of design were also there, the wheels and all the parts in perfect order. The mainspring was useful common sense, based on a thrifty view of Christian ethics; and, if it resembled the watch in other ways, if it was small, cold and mechanical, was it more mechanical than Oxford, where they also put the Apostles in the witness-box and drowsed over their bottles of port? Oxford was torpid also, droning along in its eighteenth-century grooves, waiting for its great awakening. Harvard was only a more provincial Oxford, as the travelling Persian would have seen at once. A sympathetic stranger, an aspiring student, especially one who had been born in Cambridge, would have seen it in a rosier light. The Cambridge boy would have known the "Cambridge elm," with its suggestions of the Revolution, the old houses with their charming customs, the gracious lawns, the birds, the luxuriant flowers, stuff for a dozen poets, especially when the naturalist Thomas Nuttall became curator of the Botanic Garden and wrote his books on botany and ornithology, drawn from observations of the local scene. The Cambridge folk were intelligent and kind; and, if it was one of their foibles to put other people in their places, this was an indication, after all, that other people's places were not Cambridge. They were serious, devout, cultivated, stable. They were not given to excesses, even on the side of righteousness. The "ministers' sons" who became proverbial were the sons of the brimstone God of the inland regions. The ministers' sons of Cambridge never knew repression and therefore had no wild oats to sow. Neither in its action nor in its reaction was the Cambridge mind marked by a waste of force. Its only danger was a certain smugness. Its only excess was an excess of caution.

Harvard, moreover, was on the brink of change. Woe to the student, woe to the youthful tutor who counted overmuch on the signs of the times, who interlarded his speech with foreign phrases, sported embroidered waistcoats or even thought that modern languages ought to be included in the course of studies. Harvard was intellectually sound, and the sound intellect makes its changes slowly. But the changes were plainly imminent. President Kirkland might have been indifferent, but he was also liberal in temper. The ethics that Professor Frisbie taught might have been cold and dry, but the warmth with which he taught them,—he was a poet himself, in a modest way,—gave his pupils an impulse to study ethics instead of accepting them on authority. The Harvard philosophy was not exciting,—Locke, Paley, Reid,—but one became excited over it. One acquired a taste for philosophy. One acquired a sceptical attitude that opened the way for other points of view. Even Andrews Norton promoted this sceptical attitude. He had no sympathy with the new ideas that were dawning in people's minds, but he had demolished the old ideas. One could not, after hearing Mr. Norton, revert to the Calvinist view; and if one had disposed of Nortonism, to one's own satisfaction, at least, one was obliged to go forward to something else. And Mr. Norton's positive tone aroused the desire for combat in his pupils. They learned to fight, in the world of the mind. Their intellectual life was filled with zest.

In a word, the students learned to think. Moreover, they learned to write. Whatever might have been said of the Harvard professors, their taste could not have been impugned. Their taste was as refined as their ethical instincts. Their standards were severe. Their students might have certain limitations, but certain others they could hardly have. Their style was almost sure to be marked by grace and, as often as not, by force. Their scholarship was sure to be exacting, especially when Edward Tyrrel Channing, the younger brother of Dr. Channing, became professor of Rhetoric,—two years after the birth of a Concord boy, Henry Thoreau by name, who was to acknowledge, in later years, that he had learned to write as Channing's pupil. In fact, the whole New England "renaissance" was to spring so largely from Channing's pupils, Emerson, Holmes, Dana, Motley, Parkman, to name only a few, that the question might have been asked, Did Channing cause it?—

> *Channing, with his bland, superior look,*
> *Cold as a moonbeam on a frozen brook,*
> *While the pale student, shivering in his shoes,*
> *Sees from his theme the turgid rhetoric ooze.*

That the rhetoric oozed from his pupils' themes, under his bland eye,—that is to say, the "turgid" rhetoric,—was one of the secrets of his influence; for turgid rhetoric was the bane of letters in the days of the Boston orators, the orators whom every boy adored. He had a remorseless eye for the high-falutin, the swelling period, the emphatic word, morbid tissue to this ruthless surgeon whose Puritan instincts had been clarified by a sensible classical culture. None of his pupils grew the sort of feathers that required the ministrations of Artemus Ward.

One of these pupils kept his college themes, and a list of some of the subjects that Channing set might go as far as any other fact to explain why his pupils were to go so far. Bearing in mind the careers of his pupils, poets, historians, essayists or whatever, one asks oneself what must have been the effect, on adolescent minds, prepared and eager, of questions like the following,—on which they were obliged to write, and to write with perspicuity, whether they shivered in their shoes or not: on keeping a private journal, the anxieties and delights of a discoverer, the cultivation of the imagination, the pleasures and privileges of a literary man, the duty and dangers of conformity, the superior and the common man. These were the subjects that Channing discussed and urged his little classes to discuss, these and the topics of his brilliant *Lectures,* a writer's preparation, a writer's habits, permanent literary fame. The literary life, as he described it, seemed very important and very exciting. Moreover, he spoke of its problems in a way that brought it home to the rising generation. He referred to the confident freedom of thought and style that comes from a writer's pride in his own people and gives him a fine "bravery and indifference to foreign doubts and censure." He showed how the world in general values most the writers who bear the unmistakable stamp, the pungency and native sincerity, of their own time and place. The early Roman writers,—like the American writers of the past,—depended on foreign examples and supplies. In Rome, at least, this question had found an answer in the praise the Romans bestowed upon their writers for turning home at last for their themes and their style.

Judging by the fruits of his instruction, one might almost say that Channing sowed more of the seeds that make a man of letters,—when the seeds fall on a fortunate soil,—than all the other teachers of composition and all the writers of ingenious text-books that have ever taught a much-taught country. A Harvard student of his generation had certain advantages of an inward kind that were not likely to be soon repeated. One of them was that, reading Plutarch, in this sympathetic atmosphere, he might have understood Cicero's youth,—how, consulting the Delphic oracle, he listened to the pythoness who advised him not to regard the opinion of other people, but to make his own genius the guide of his life.

III. THE COAST AND THE HINTERLAND

In every corner of this New England country, where the ways of the eighteenth century lingered on, a fresh and more vigorous spirit was plainly astir. On the granite ledges of New Hampshire, along the Merrimac river, in Essex and Middlesex counties, where the spindles whirred, or westward, on the lovely Housatonic, life was filled with a kind of electric excitement. The air resounded with the saw and hammer, the blows of the forge, the bells in the factory-towers. In all directions the people were building turnpikes, hundreds of miles of straight lines that cut athwart the old winding roads. The Green Mountain boys had erected their State-house. Dwellings were going up in clearings and meadows, or, being up, were carted bodily off to better sites. Churches grew like snowdrops in early March. Villages, towns sprang from the fields. A current of ambition had galvanized New England. The "era of good feeling" was on its way.

As yet there were no signs of a similar movement in the intellectual life of this humming region. No poets, no historians had arisen, none or few, feeble as they were few, to celebrate and record men's thoughts and feelings. The mind of the country, torn, since the Revolution, with other anxieties and preoccupations, was tired and too busy with the present. It had no use for its own imagination. The ways of the folk, the deeds of the past, of the notable sires and grandsires of New England, if surely not unhonoured, were unsung. The seaports, like the inland villages, bristled with their legendary lore, tales of the wars, tales of Indian fights, of painted Indian faces at the farmhouse window, of the war-dance, the pow-wow and the forest, of great snows in which men had lost their lives, of haunted bridges, buccaneers and redcoats, of Yankee maidens and their tory lovers, of shipwrecks and battles,—themes for a New England Scott or Byron. One heard of the "screeching woman" of Marblehead. One heard of "witches' hollows," groves of beech and hemlock, where the Indians had held their demon-worship and burning crosses appeared in a greenish light. There were popular ballads and folk-songs,—"Skipper Ireson's Ride," for one,—sailors' chanties along the coast, ballads of village murders, rockaby songs, sugar-makers' songs, sung by weavers and carpenters, by farm-wives and wandering fiddlers, by hunters, trappers, guides and lumbermen, snatches and refrains and longer pieces, brought from the old world or natural outgrowths of the American soil. But the rhymesters, for there were plenty of these,—the rural colleges and academies were turning them out in hundreds,—the rhymesters, unmindful of Burns, whom they imitated, ignored these rude materials of their art, as they were unaware of the greater themes which the history of their country offered them.

They felt, these rhymesters, one and all, as later writers felt, —as Hawthorne was to feel, in his earlier days,—that the American scene was too prosaic. How could one write poems and romances about a world that seemed so spick-and-span?—a country that had no shadow, no picturesqueness, no mystery, no pageantry of the past, none of those romantic associations that gathered like moss about every roof and tree, about every hill and valley of the older countries? A land where everything sprawled on the same dull level, in the broad, simple, garish light of day? It required a vision that no one as yet possessed to detect the stores of poetic interest that lay beneath this commonplace appearance. Among these living poetasters, whose style and tone were so flat and thin, whose only thought was to follow the current fashion, or who were busy translating Horace's Odes, or giving new twists to the Psalms, there was not one who had the diviner's eye. But for two hundred years the New England people had been actively working their minds. They had been striving to educate themselves, thinking, brooding, keeping their journals, reading their Bibles, their classics, their books of sermons; and all this life was preparing to bear its fruit. In the country schools, no doubt, in the grammar schools, even in Boston, Cambridge and New Haven, the masters droned along in their ancient ruts. No business of theirs to produce Virgils and Livys! They made the scholars spell aloud in chorus. One learned, at the rod's end, the longest words in the language, learned them to the last sad syllable, a method which, if it failed to rouse one's mind, taught one that every error meant a rap. One saw the schoolmarm, with her willow switch, pinning the boys and girls to her terrible apron, when they were restless and unruly. One found, in many a village, the methods of some old "Ma'am Betty," who kept school in her bedroom and chewed tobacco and drank from the nose of her tea-kettle. But other, more promising methods were rapidly growing, in the Latin schools about the capital, as well as in the towns along the seaboard.

At Newport, Salem, Portsmouth, where the great square mansions faced the sea or lined the stately streets, with their beautiful gardens, cultivated by Scotch and Irish gardeners, there were notable scholars in charge of the young, Harvard men or Englishmen, French tutors, Italian dancing-masters, the dim dawn of a cosmopolitan culture. There were public reading-rooms in Newport and Portsmouth. Salem, like Boston, had its Athenæum and a Philosophical Library, one of the prizes of the late war, second to that of Philadelphia. In Portland, in the cultivated circles, where many spoke French and a few Italian, they were beginning to criticize Dr. Johnson, whom no one had ever criticized before and who had been so unjust to the poet Gray. Music, so long the symbol of the ne'er-do-well, began to be heard on summer nights. The strains of the harp and the flute had ceased to suggest the danger of a drunkard's grave. Here and there some carver of figureheads, or of pumpheads and wooden urns for gate-posts, some young whittler, fired by a book on Rome, which he had found in the reading-room, dreamed of a sculptor's life. If he could carve these eagles for McIntire doorways, these heads of Galen for the apothecaries, why should he not create a marble group that would fill the portico of the county court-house?

In all these bustling ports, or ports that had recently bustled, where the forests of masts rose at the wharves and Portuguese sailors sauntered through the streets, the wide world was omnipresent. Everyone talked about voyages "up the Straits," or to Hong Kong and Calcutta, towns that seemed closer to Salem or Portsmouth than Hartford or New York had ever seemed. The lofty chambers of the great dwellings, hung with French or English tapestry, adorned with arches and columns and carved Italian mantel-pieces, were papered with bold designs, brilliantly coloured birds and tropical flowers and scenes from the Mediterranean lands. The massive bedsteads in the upper rooms were draped with curious curtains of India linen, covered with quaint pagodas and figures in turbans. Canton shawls and Smyrna silks were as common as linsey-woolsey. There were parrots and pet monkeys in half the houses. The children played with coconuts and coral and spent their pennies for tamarinds and ginger, or spent their Russian kopeks and their British coppers, which circulated as freely as American coins. The men wore Chinese gowns at the Salem assemblies, and the horn-pipe was taught in the dancing-schools. At the great merchants' houses there were formal parties, where the heads of the Federal government came to dine, with ambassadors from the European countries. One of the Salem magnates of the previous decade was the largest shipowner in the world.

All these towns abounded in interesting persons, sometimes eccentric or droll, often witty, almost always learned. At Salem, the most imposing of the seaports, dwelt a circle of distinguished men who were to leave their mark in American history. One of them was Joseph Story, already Mr. Justice Story, who wrote for the *Monthly Anthology* in Boston. Judge William Prescott was another, the son of the old hero of Bunker Hill, who lived on his farm at Pepperell. Both these worthies were men of renown and both the fathers of sons who were famous

later. Another was John Pickering, the son of Timothy Pickering, who had learned Arabic in his youth, while travelling with
his father, and had mastered twenty other tongues. He had
refused, as a busy lawyer, the chairs of Greek and Hebrew at
Harvard and was at work on a philological project, for the
spelling of the American Indian tongues, that was to lead to a
world-wide movement for the study of all the primitive languages. Presently, Rufus Choate joined the circle, the great
Boston orator of the future, a weirdly exotic creature in appearance who might have come over in one of the ships from Java.
All the members of this Salem group,—like Daniel Webster
of Portsmouth, Choate's more famous fellow-orator, who had
already made his mark in Congress,—were soon to move to
Boston, as the fortunes of Salem waned and the capital spread
its tentacles through New England.

So was the most illustrious of the Salem worthies, the great
mathematician, Nathaniel Bowditch, the author of *The Practical Navigator,* a little, nimble man with burning eyes, with
silky hair prematurely white, who darted about, rubbing his
hands with excitement. This second Benjamin Franklin, the
son of a poor cooper and mechanic, who had learned his Latin
as a boy in order to read Newton's *Principia,*—in which he
found an error,—had found eight thousand errors in the best
English book on navigation. The book he had written himself,
the *Navigator,* had saved countless lives and made the American ships the swiftest that had ever sailed. Everyone knew that,
as a supercargo, bound for Sumatra and Manila, Bowditch had
mastered astronomy so well,—between the stars that he watched
from the deck and the books he carried with him in his berth,—
that he was able to revise Laplace. Everyone knew how, on a
Christmas night, in the midst of a blinding snow-storm, when
he was captain of his own ship and there was not a landmark
to be seen, Bowditch had sailed straight to his Salem wharf,
as if it had been a sunny day in June. He had taught all his
sailors navigation, and every one of them became a captain.
And what a work was this *Practical Navigator,* a work that was

still to be in active use a century after his death. The literary circles in Boston and Cambridge blushed over the taunts of the British reviewers, the clever men in London who were always asking, "Who reads an American book?" They felt so helplessly mortified. But here was an American book that every British seaman had to read if he hoped to get ahead of the Yankee skippers. It was a classic in its realm, as stoutly built as one of the clipper-ships for which Dr. Bowditch had prepared the way. If the Yankee mind could produce a work like this, what could not the Yankee mind produce when it turned its faculties in other directions? Even here in Salem, where the Prescotts lived, where a little boy, also called Nathaniel, the son of another skipper, was reading his *Pilgrim's Progress*.

In all these centres of the seaboard life, there had arisen a buffer generation that lay between the hard old Puritan ways and the minds of the younger people. Alive itself to literature and thought, prosperous, interested in a larger world, creative, though only, or mainly, in practical spheres, it was a kind of *cordon sanitaire* against the repressive habits of the past. The lawyers, merchants, ministers and scholars who formed the society of these towns preserved the faith in discipline and standards that had marked the older culture, and yet they encouraged in their sons and daughters a free mind, a knowledge of mundane things, the study of languages, music, drawing, dancing, an education of the eye and ear which, from the point of view of the inland regions, savoured of the frankest paganism. The Unitarian cause had won the day all along the sea-line. The leading families professed the "Boston religion." Their intercourse with other lands and peoples had mollified their mental habits; indeed, almost as much as their wide-flung commerce, a little good Madeira softened the old rigidities. They smiled at the faith of their forbears, when they were not shocked by its consequences. For which of them had not seen, in some neighbouring farmhouse, or even in one of the mansions or beside the wharves, some poor crazy woman, chained to a bed, or held by a staple in the floor, driven mad by some hysterical sermon about some unpardonable sin? Wherever one turned, in these prosperous ports, far more in the towns of the hinterland, one seemed to encounter simpletons, and worse, idiots and harmless lunatics, freely walking about, as if the supply of chains were insufficient; and the young people drew their own conclusions. They respected the old ways and the old religion. But they felt there was something unwholesome in this life from which their own minds had been liberated.

For among the younger folk of all these towns, on the sunny side of this buffer generation, these lawyers and merchants and scholars and experienced skippers, there were boys, growing up in dozens, who were to thrive on these new influences. Newport was already reaping its harvest, for there the Channing family lived. William Ellery Channing, the Boston preacher, had spent half the hours of his childhood wandering about the beach and the towering rocks, listening to the music of the waves, with the wide ocean before him, filled with a sense of awe and rapture; and there he spent all his vacations now, in the house surrounded by the charming garden, which had been laid out by the son of Gilpin, the famous writer on the picturesque. At Newport, on winter days, the air was soft and springlike, tempered by the Gulf Stream. There the northern blizzard seldom came, and the English ivy grew on the old stone walls and covered the well-known Mill. Legends throve in the languid atmosphere, and the British arms still hung in Trinity Church, near Bishop Berkeley's organ. And there, in a setting half rustic, half cosmopolitan, the Southern planters brought their families and mingled with the New York and Boston merchants. One could almost see in imagination the Brighton or Baden-Baden of the future. On the promenade, as in Italy or France, the men took off their hats to one another; and the ships set sail from the strange little wharves for Mozambique, Fayal or Zanzibar. The sailors talked of the East and the West Cape and a voyage to the Indian Ocean, perhaps in some fishing-smack of fifty tons.

Newport, the "American Eden," so like the Isle of Wight,

had fostered in Channing a feeling for Wordsworth and Byron, those two romantic poets who had shared his moods. There, as a boy, after some sulphurous sermon, dealing with infant damnation, he had heard his father whistle. That was the end of the old faith for Channing. If his father did not believe in it, life was not so dismal, after all. Mingling with the Southern families, he had come to dislike what he called the avarice of the North, the selfish prudence of his fellow-Yankees. He loved the spontaneous ways of the Southern folk, who took no thought for the morrow, ways that should have fostered poetry and art. He had spent a year as a tutor in Virginia, and it was the Jeffersonians there who had weaned him away from his Federalist prepossessions, strong enough, at first, in a Newport boy whose father had entertained, as he well remembered, Washington, Jay and the other Federalist leaders. In the South, he had read the French philosophers, Godwin's books and Mary Wollstonecraft, and first conceived those dreams of social justice that were to find a voice in his later years. His health had never been strong since those early days when, with a stoic desire for self-improvement, he had slept on the bare floor, subjected himself to a rigid system of diet and prolonged his studies till two or three in the morning. But the slender, pallid, nervous little man, grave, reflective, fond of lonely rambles, teemed with the new ideas that were slowly coming to birth along the seacoast. All thanks to Newport!—where the South and Europe seemed so close at hand. And if Newport had also sheltered the great grim author of the *System of Doctrines*, Dr. Samuel Hopkins's views had gradually melted away from people's minds. They were no longer "willing to be damned." All that the Newport people wished to recall was the doctor's prediction that the millennium was bound to occur within two hundred years.

In this little corner of New England, Roger Williams too had lived and toiled for the cause of religious liberty. Channing's brother, Edward Tyrrel Channing, had also spent his childhood there. So had the cousin of the Channing brothers,

Richard Henry Dana, the poet and critic, the son of the old
Chief Justice. So had Washington Allston, the painter and
poet, the child of one of the South Carolina families who
flocked to Newport for the summer season. His father and
mother, distressed by his early talent, and fearing that he
would disgrace a planter's household, had sent him North to
cure him of his folly; and at Newport he had fallen in with
Malbone, the unrivalled painter of miniatures. Allston, whose
first wife was Channing's sister and who was later to marry the
sister of Dana, had played as a boy with both of his brothers-
in-law, both his friends at Harvard and both the inseparable
friends of his Boston years. At Newport, Gilbert Stuart had
lived, and there the great Berkeley had dwelt for a while. In
his house Whitehall, near the sea, he had planned his new-
world university. He had written his *Minute Philosopher*
among the rocks where the Channings, Allston and Dana had
dreamed and wandered. One might have imagined that Berkeley's benign spirit still lingered in the gracious Newport air.

Other writers and poets were to draw from Newport the
themes of poems and stories. There were themes enough,—
the writers had only to pluck them,—in the burying-ground of
the Portuguese Jews who had settled there after the Lisbon
earthquake, in the Mill, which, as people supposed, the Norse-
men had built, in the old black houses and rough-stone mansions, in the anomalous figures, vaguely savouring of the great
world, whom one saw on the promenade or behind the curtained windows, one the reputed sister of an English queen,
one the heroine of a strange romance, an impoverished lady of
title who paid her washerwoman with costly lace. There were
themes near by on the Providence Plantations, where lingered,
and were to linger for many years, the great feudal dwellings
of the rural magnates, households of seventy, eighty, ninety
persons, where the master of his twelve thousand acres, his
fox-hounds and his four thousand sheep kept twelve dairy-
maids at work, each with another girl to wait upon her, and
two dozen cheeses, as big as cart-wheels, vanished into the void

every day. There were stories enough to the north and west, in the valleys and plains of Connecticut, on the green hill-slopes of Vermont, where the Scottish ballads, on the lips of immigrant weavers and shepherds, bloomed again as in their native air, and the farmers and hunters were building a commonwealth. Themes enough for the novels and the poems, waiting for the novelists and the poets.

But still, or more than ever, in these inland regions, not poetry, or history, or romance, but a more sombre form of exercise possessed the people's minds. They did not care for stories. They thought that fiction was a fraud, and worse. Religion was their only poetry. The cultivated few, the "mansion people," those who had seen something of the world, or knew at least Boston or New York, the families of the rural magistrates, the squires, the village notables who had connections in the capitals, made an exception of Scott, whose Waverley novels were in every house. They read Scott for his moral tone, just as they read Richardson's *Clarissa* and the tales of Maria Edgeworth, which all the leading families enjoyed and discussed,—often with the families of the Boston merchants, who, in their travelling-carriages, constantly made tours across New England, to Stafford Springs, through the Berkshire hills, to Round Hill, Mount Holyoke or Graylock, perhaps on their way to Niagara or Trenton Falls, for a little holiday outing, stopping to see their cousins on the way. These novels, so moderate and so elevating, served them as patterns of manners. Scott, who adorned and beautified all that was growing old and passing away, appealed to their conservative feelings, and Richardson's Grandison was their beau ideal. Many a girl said she would never marry until she found his like. Novels like these were hardly "fiction." One read them without loss of self-respect, as one read the works of Hannah More, or Mrs. Chapone on the bringing-up of girls.

This was only in the mansion-houses. The mansion people formed an invisible chain, stretching across the country, through which the currents of the great world passed. Outside, the village life continued in its primal innocence. Even the rural aristocracy, touched as it was by foreign influences, retained its strong indigenous character. America was the only land it knew, or that its forbears had known for seven generations. In towns near the seaboard, one found a loyalist family here and there. A few old ladies lingered on who spoke of themselves as "eating the King's bread," because their father had fought on the tory side and they still received a British pension. Miss Debby Barker of Hingham, a town that was much like "Cranford,"—as everyone saw at once when the book came out,—went into mourning, donned a purple dress, at the death of George the Fourth. There were many Miss Debby Barkers in Boston and Newport, but most of the country aristocracy had always opposed the crown. The village folk in general, mainly of the purest English stock, carried on their ancient village ways, not in a spirit of Anglophobia, but rather as if England had never existed. They formed a self-sufficing Yankee world, separated by a pathless ocean from the ways of the mother-country. They were farmers almost to a man, aside from a few mechanics. Most of the ministers tilled their own soil. Each village had its Indian population, a cluster of huts on the outskirts, a few Negroes who had once been slaves, sometimes two or three Irishmen and one or two beggars and paupers. The larger towns had public reading-rooms, possibly a Franklin Institute, where a few odd volumes of Shakespeare, Hume and Milton, Young's *Night Thoughts,* Thomson's *Seasons,* Rollin's *Ancient History,* filled the shelves with old books of sermons, Owen on Sin or *An Arrow Against Profane and Promiscuous Dancing.*

Every village had its squire and parson, a Deacon Hart, living on the turnpike, where he raised the golden squashes, the full-orbed pumpkins, the rustling Indian corn and the crimson currants that straggled by the painted picket fence. Further on, dwelt some Abihu Peters. An Ebenezer Camp contrived the shoes. A Patience Mosely made the village bonnets, hard by Comfort Scran's general store. There were always two or three hired men, a handy-andy, usually a fiddler, who had made his violin from the bole of a maple and strung his bow from the tail of the family horse. Now and then one found a village drunkard, who might have been a poet, perhaps some scalawag of a Stephen Burroughs, the worst boy in the town, who was often kept in chains in the county jail. There were a few Yankees of the swindling kind who found their proper sphere in the peddling business. Sometimes they were caught as counterfeiters. The Yankee mind was quick and sharp, but mainly it was singularly honest. Everyone who travelled through the country marvelled that the New England farmers' doors were seldom locked or barred, even at night; and, while the land flowed with rum, and even overflowed, the great popular drink was homely cider. The cider-barrel was never empty at weddings and ordinations, on training-days, at huskings, at Thanksgiving, when the sounds of chopping and pounding and baking and brewing rose from the smoke-browned walls of the farmhouse kitchen. Those who grew up in these inland regions, looking back on the old village life, saw it in the light of Goldsmith's Auburn, abounding in mild virtues, faithful swains, rural virgins, peace and innocence. The goodman's daughters made his shirts and stockings; his garments were provided by his flocks and herds. So were those of the women-folk, who, as they spun and knitted, discussed the weekly sermon.

For religion filled the horizon of the village people, all that was left by politics and law. On Sunday morning, in the church, one heard the Psalms repeated, in Sternhold and Hopkins's version, which some of the old women believed were the very strains King David had sung to his harp,—"The Lord will come, and he will not," and, after a pause, another line, which most of the children thought was another idea, "Keep silence, but speak out." The old-fashioned polemical sermon followed, fortified with texts and garnished with quotations in Greek and Hebrew, for most of the clergy were still learned men. Perhaps only the week before, the minister had driven in his one-horse chaise twenty or thirty miles across the country to meet some reverend brother and settle some nice point in theology on which he was writing a treatise: he could not agree with Dr. Stern that God had created sin deliberately, and he wished to lay his case before his flock. Many of the village ministers, whose cocked hats and gold-headed canes were symbols of their unquestioned authority, as shepherds and judges of the people, devoted their lives to writing these treatises. The farmers discussed them over their ploughs, and the farm-wives over their spinning-wheels. For religion was their romance. They named their children after the biblical heroes, and the Bible places, Chimmin and the Isles, Dan and Bathsheba, Kedar and Tarshish were stations on the map of their El Dorado. The congregations followed the web of the sermons with a keen and anxious watchfulness, eager to learn the terms of their damnation. And they talked about fate and freedom and how evil came, and what death is, and the life to come, as familiarly as they talked of their crops and the weather.

All New England seethed with these discussions. One heard about "potential presence" and "representative presence" and "representative identity," and Dr. Bancroft's sermon on the fourth commandment. Blacksmiths and farriers, youths and maidens argued about free will and predestination, about "natural ability" and "moral ability" and "God's efficiency" and "man's agency." Sometimes it was a morbid interest, when the children sat on "anxious seats" and wept over their wicked little hearts. The conscience of New England was precocious. Even Cotton Mather had observed that "splenetic maladies" throve among the people, maladies that were scarcely allayed by some of the more emotional preachers. One heard of "sweating" sermons and "fainting" sermons, followed by "convulsion-fit" sermons, in the best tradition of Whitefield. Sometimes, in the frontier settlements, on the borders of the wilderness, in the forests of New Hampshire and Vermont, where men almost forgot that they had voices, and only the axe and the hammer broke the silence, where, on the frozen slopes, the snow fell for days together, strange and terrible thoughts rose in the mind. A Green Mountain boy with an axe in his hand might sing his happy songs in the busy summer, rejoicing in the Alpine air, scented with fir and hemlock, for the Green Mountain boys had their mountain freedom. But when the snow began to fall, and he sat brooding beside the stove, over his calfskin Bible, in the close, foul air of the farmhouse kitchen, digesting food that was never meant for man, then, as he conned the mystical Revelations and the savage mythology of the ancient Jews, visions of blood-atonement swept his brain. Among the native ballads of the Vermonters, bloodshed was an omnipresent theme. They felt the presence of the God of Vengeance. They heard voices that were not benign. From them, was to spring, a few years hence, the cult of Joseph Smith and Brigham Young, where flourished now, as foretastes of the Mormons, the quiet murder and the loud revival.

Sometimes, on the other hand, these wrestlings over sublime abstractions rose, in some lonely soul, to the loftiest heights, where the mind was lost in mystical raptures over the universe and its great Architect, and men conversed with angels. Here and there, in the woods of Maine or among the hills of western Massachusetts, some spinster or some godly man, like Benedict in his solitary cell, seated on the mount of transfiguration, kept his days of appointment with the Eternal. What hopes, what rhapsodies possessed his soul, what meditations on a time and space in which all transient ills were engulfed or muted! He saw the whirling of the puppet-world with the eye of the mounting eagle that faces the sun. What mattered this changing planet with its petty cares, lost in the unfading light of moons and stars? There was a fire in the New England heart, in the intellectual depths of Calvinism, which the cold minds of Unitarian Cambridge possessed no knowledge of, a hunger for righteousness and a thirst for truth, a passionate dream of perfection. Concord knew this dream, and Concord was to express it. Not for nothing had this vigorous race invested in its flaming ancient faith all the treasures of its thought and feel-

ing. Deep in its mental caverns lingered still the spiritual passions of the Middle Ages. Deep in its mental caverns lingered
the passions of the Roundheads, who had suffered and fought
for freedom and human rights. Let the trumpet sound again,
let the God of Hosts unfurl his banners! New England was
prepared, when the time was ripe, for another holy war.

At the moment, the state of mind of these inland regions,—
even Connecticut, which faced the sea,—seemed hardly aus-
picious for the man of letters. It was not quickened by the
mental currents that brought new light to the towns of the
Eastern seaboard. It was wrapped in an atmosphere of gloom;
and its doctrines of total depravity and the utter vanity of
human effort paralysed the literary sense. Whatever mobility
this mind possessed was all but confined to the theological
sphere.

One could only say that in this sphere its mobility was surprising. The great New England schism had broken out, thirty
years later than in Boston. The theocratic Church was giving
way. Many of the farmers were moving westward; others were
in revolt against the blue laws. The Church had been forced
to yield in its main positions, as the democratic movement grew
apace, for the democratic movement, with its faith in equality,
could and would no longer tolerate the aristocratic doctrine of
"election"; and, breaking at the centre, it had begun to branch
at the outer edges into forms that were often fantastic. Many
of the congregations were held together by the prestige of some
ancient minister, who still ruled the village as of old. But as
these ministers vanished, one by one, the congregations fell
apart in factions, and hundreds of conventicles arose,—poor
little ugly scraps of wooden Gothic,—in the shadows of the village churches. The mansion people, up and down the country,
had begun to be touched by the Unitarian movement. Some of
them, as in Boston, were Episcopalians. All of them had lost
their taste for the Orthodox phraseology; and to please them,
or to express their own views, which were also rapidly changing, numbers of the Orthodox clergy let down the bars of the

old religion. Their sermons wandered from the ancestral standard. The humbler folk, meanwhile, who were breaking away,
the farmers, mechanics, factory-hands, were offered a wide
choice of isms, some of them brand-new, an assortment as ap-
petizing and variegated as that of any Connecticut pedlar's
pack. The more emotional sects, the Methodists, throve on the
sudden reaction against the logical sermons of the past. The
Universalists promised salvation to all. For the Adventists,
Christ was coming at once; they did not have to wait for a far-
away judgment. Perfectionism captured some; Restorationism
captured others. According to the Come-outers of Cape Cod,
the word was written in the human heart, a doctrine that
pleased the unlettered who had heard too many texts in Greek
and Hebrew. As for the question of punishment after death,
one could choose between No Punishment, Eternal Punishment, good for most of one's neighbours, or a strictly limited
punishment that stopped after the first million years.

All this represented a movement of mind that was to find
expression in other spheres, the practical sphere, the scientific
sphere,—for it promoted enquiry and the feeling for action,—
but whether in the sphere of literature was rather open to
question. At present, the intellect of the rural regions was
largely confined to two of these factions: the mansion people,
with their broader leanings, and the still potent Orthodox
party. The sects, appealing to the simpler-minded, contributed
to the abolition movement, which was to make its appearance
presently; but they had little to give to thought or letters. The
Unitarians were still few and scattered. There remained the
Orthodox leaders who, to regain their power, as the dissolution
of the Church advanced, redoubled their ancient threats of
hell-fire. To stop the Unitarian movement, the "icy system,"
as Lyman Beecher called it, they founded the Andover Seminary and built the Park Street Church in the centre of Boston,
fortresses of the old faith, in the heart of the enemy's country,
from which to pelt the enemy with their sermons,—"each one
fresh, like bullets from a mould." They denounced the "vandal

spirit of innovation," as Robert Treat Paine had denounced the "vandal spirit of puritanism." They reaffirmed the glory of the Pilgrim Fathers. As far back as New England history went, the "Connecticut school" had had its own tone, distinct from that of the "Massachusetts school"; and now more than ever, with Lyman Beecher,—as erstwhile with "old Pope Dwight," Timothy Dwight, the president of Yale, who died in 1817,— the Connecticut school was conscious of its strength. Its efforts were futile to capture the stronghold of Boston, but on its own ground it stood firm. The ancient Puritan faith had been re-vived in a new and powerful cult.

This energy seemed to promise an abundant life in various other realms. At Yale, for instance, the great centre of learning, the second capital of the New England mind, a notable school of science had arisen, with Benjamin Silliman as its presiding spirit. Harvard, with all its literary prospects, had nothing to show as yet, or for years to come, beside this genius of the laboratory, who formed for Yale its collection of minerals and its physical and chemical apparatus, along with the *American Journal of Science.* Silliman's pioneer work in science might have been expected to offset the obscurantist theology of the college, for Yale, like the other and lesser centres of learning, Williams, Amherst, Bowdoin, Brown and Dartmouth, those minor Paley's watches, continued to be stoutly Orthodox. Through Silliman's *Journal,* the science of the world passed into the mind of the nation; and Yale was in other respects nationally-minded, with broader political sympathies than Harvard and a much more all-American student-body. But it was isolated from the great-world interests, outside the field of science, that were so soon to stir Boston and Cambridge; and this, in addition to its religious thinking and the relative pov-erty of the institution, portended little good for literature. Cer-tainly there was little enough at present. Timothy Dwight, the "last of the Puritans,"—as people had called him once, before they became aware of Lyman Beecher,—Timothy Dwight, Jonathan Edwards's grandson, a mighty man, a prodigy of learning, even a poet himself in earlier times, had frowned on "song" and the "arts of the pencil and chisel." He had made every effort to restore the Puritan modes and methods. Of the New Haven poets of the hour, James A. Hillhouse was symptomatic. The son of a well-known senator, a college-mate of the novelist Cooper, he wrote long poems, correct but decidedly dismal, on biblical themes.

At Hartford, the political capital, the second New England seat of the Federalists, which had grown in about the same proportion as Boston, the literary scene was scarcely brighter. A few of the "Hartford Wits" lingered on. Humphreys, Barlow and Lemuel Hopkins were gone, but Theodore Dwight remained, the "old Pope's" brother. One saw him strolling about the Hartford streets, filled to the brim with anecdote and learning, Dwight who had once pursued the Jacobins with the vigilance of a beagle in the brush. John Trumbull still lived in Hartford, the once-famous author of *MacFingal*, old, small, emaciated, bent, tottering on his cane, his fine little face alive with Erasmian humour. One could not forget that the Hartford Wits, whatever their faults and limitations were, had laughed away the popular taste for bombast, at least for a generation. They had had a vigorous interest in poetry which the Boston of their day could only match in the bilious rhymes of Robert Treat Paine. But their day was already remote. Hartford had lost its tincture of intellectual life, and Mrs. Sigourney and her little *salon* still belonged to the future. A youthful poet who, at this moment, oscillated between Hartford and New Haven, cried to the empty air for someone with whom he could talk. A mere author had no place here. The only society that he could find was a handful of indolent and dyspeptic tutors, one or two lawyers without ambition and the illiterate mistress of a boarding-house.

The Connecticut mind, as travellers often noted, was keen, strong and witty, but usually narrow, educated rather than cultivated. It abounded in prejudices that were often small, like most of the "Yankee notions." It lacked, as a rule, the power of generalizing, which had been marked in New York, in Virginia and in Boston. It was a village mind, in short, that had never breathed a larger atmosphere. It bore few of the fruits that spring from an intercourse and collision with other minds from other mental regions. The only important Connecticut man of letters, a man of great importance, a symbol of his world in many ways, was the famous lexicographer, Noah Webster, who was more concerned with "education" than he was ever concerned with "cultivation," but who was doing more with his education than all the American pedagogues put together. A tall, lean, black-coated man, with black small-clothes and black silk stockings, with the oddest, quaintest, old-fashioned air,—if you had met him in China, you would have known that he hailed from Connecticut,—always a farmer's son in his heart of hearts, a busy-body, self-important, vain, but upright and honest, aggressive, enterprising, pertinacious, a schoolmaster, lawyer, journalist, who had written on banking, medicine and statistics, and yet, for all these multifarious interests, possessed a vast and accurate fund of learning, he was at work, at New Haven, writing his Dictionary, for which his Spelling-book had prepared the way,—a new Declaration of Independence. His object was to establish a national language as a bond of "national union," for Webster, with his democratic tastes, was an old-school Federalist in politics. Already an elderly man, he had lived through the Revolution; and, filled as he was with patriotic fervour, he had not failed to note that, while the Americans boasted of their freedom, nevertheless their arts, their dress, their customs still aped the ways of the mother-country. Why should they receive, in this supine way, everything that came from a foreign press? A spirit of the blindest imitation stifled all American enquiry, benumbed the intellectual faculties. During the years of war, when the intercourse with England was interrupted and American schoolbooks had to be improvised, he had supplanted Dilworth's Spelling-book with his own popular speller. He saw no reason why American children should learn that the letters

"Ast. P. G. C." meant "Astronomy Professor of Gresham College," on the other side of the ocean. He had worked up his own vernacular word-book, based on the common usage of New England. The store-keepers, up and down the country, laid in supplies of Webster's Speller, along with their hogsheads of rum and their kegs of molasses. The pedlars carried it from door to door until, as the decades passed, fifty million copies had been sold. It had given the population a uniform spelling.

The irrepressible Cobbett, in his will, bequeathed five pounds to Noah Webster to pay for a new engraving of his portrait, so that the children who used his speller might no longer be frightened out of their wits by the grim Websterian visage. But the visage had its work to do. Webster was a fighter. He had fought for an author's copyright law, travelling through the South and the Middle States, working on the minds of the legislatures. He spoke in terms that farmers understood. The copyright, he said, was the "author's soil." Only the products belonged to the purchaser; the soil should be vested in the owner. He fought for his mother-tongue in a similar fashion. He toiled along the road from village to village, visiting every country printing-house, handing the compositor a printed slip, saying, as he did so, "My lad, when you use these words, oblige me by spelling them as here,"—*theater, center, honor,* etc. He had such a passion for detail, for the fruits and even the process of enumeration, that he often counted the houses in the village, counting up one side of a street and down the other side. For the rest, he saw no reason why the language should not be spelled as the average man pronounced it, even,—he had his little crotchets,—dropping the final *e* in *fugitive*; for he had no use for the formal grammarians. As a patriotic gesture of a wholesome kind, he used, as illustrations in his work, quotations from the American fathers, Hancock, Barlow, Livingston, along with Burke and Johnson. It happened that all his own affiliations, in spite of his prodigious store of learning, had been with the plain people:

a fact which, accounting for his success, also indicated his limitations. For he had little literary feeling; he had no sense, or only a primitive sense, of the flavour and the history of words, well as he knew his etymology. He had a somewhat arid emotional nature, and the relatively thin, pale speech that had come to prevail among the Yankee farmers, who had lost, in the dry American air, much of their ancestral heartiness, sounded as rich and full in Webster's ears as the deep chest-notes of the men of old, whose tones were maintained in cultivated usage. His temper, as befitted a man of Yale, was rather scientific than humanistic; and his influence, as a result of this, was very far from happy. When it came to the niceties of language, whether in spelling or pronunciation, Webster's work was always to be challenged. But he did his task so well, within his limits, adding his thousands of words, adding his tens of thousands of definitions, which no previous book had ever contained, that "Webster," with its countless modifications, was destined to remain a standard work for the English-speaking peoples of the world.

In short, the great Connecticut Dictionary stood, as a monument of New England learning, beside Bowditch's *Practical Navigator*. Only by courtesy works of literature, these two solid books rose like a pair of imposing gate-posts at the opening of an epoch. Indeed, the lonely scholar, Noah Webster, who, for a generation, prowled round and round his study-table, shaped in a hollow circle and piled with dictionaries of Greek and Latin, Hebrew, Arabic, twenty other tongues, was a highly symbolic figure; for learning, at this moment in New England, was in a very active state. The new sects paid less attention to it, but there were many ministers still like the old poet Edward Taylor of Westfield, who took such delight in Origen's works that, not being able to purchase them, he copied them out in four quarto volumes. One heard of ministers who, rebuked for heresy by a group of others, defended themselves in Latin, Greek and Hebrew, and, when they were cornered in all these tongues, retreated into Arabic, where they were safe from pursuit. Here and there, some secular scholar, dressed in his decent black coat,—old but not untidy, neatly bound at the cuffs,— conned his Christian fathers and his Cave and Stanley while he composed his work on the universe. The children of the ministerial households, whose mother, as often as not, read Virgil aloud in the afternoon, talked about Homer and the ancient myths while they were milking or learning to bake, or, in New Hampshire and Vermont, sugaring-off in the spring. Serving-women were not unknown who read their Latin with the boys and girls and heard them recite, after washing the dishes. Young girls, who rose at five and asked themselves, "What hard good work have I to do today?" began with two or three books of *Paradise Lost,* to give them the proper tone. They talked about Dugald Stewart and Alison on Taste, or perhaps about the *Life of Sir William Jones,* which was spreading an interest in Oriental studies. Older sisters advised their younger sisters, who were filled with the *furor scribendi,* to discipline their minds by studying Butler's *Analogy.* One little girl of seven, who had read a book on the ancient gods, telling how much they had been loved and honoured, they whom no one worshipped any more, felt her heart fill with pity. Entering the woods near by, she built a little altar of stones, decked it with flowers and shells and laid her favourite toys on the summit. Then she apostrophized the god of gods: "Poor old Jupiter, I love you! Nobody else worships you, but I will, dear old god. You shall have my doll, and I will bring you flowers every day."

All over New England, not only in the "Literary Emporium," as Boston was called far and wide, there was a passionate interest in self-culture. Countless households followed Miss Edgeworth's theories, or some other theory of education, and practised on their friends and youthful cousins. All the sons and daughters of the well-to-do were sent to the "literary institutions," the colleges and academies. Children of the poorer families, who could not afford to buy paper and ink, made their own, or used chalk or charcoal, and learned to write on the kitchen floor; and here and there some group of boys and girls, who had read Washington Irving's *Salmagundi,* edited a family magazine. This interest in reading and study, in books and authors, laid trains of feeling in the general mind that were about to burst into expression. Throughout the region, as throughout the nation, there was a widely spread presentiment that a great native American literature was about to make its appearance. Everyone read English books, histories, poems, essays, in which people found the moulds of their minds and manners; but they already felt that these English authors described a world that had ceased to be their own. They read about beggars, in the British novels, just as they read about kings, but few had seen a beggar, no one had seen a king. They read about skylarks and nightingales, but a skylark was as rare as a "pampered menial." Who had seen a pampered menial? Most of the distinctions and conventions which they found in the European writers were foreign to their own experience. They were ready to welcome tales and poems without the kings, the menials and the beggars,—with bobolinks instead of larks, with the blue-bird and the wood-thrush where the nightingale had been, and fresh American flowers instead of the far-away verdure of the British poets,—whenever the authors appeared who were able to write them. They were ready for historians and poets who might prove to be as independent as their statesmen had already been.

Of this frame of mind it was symptomatic that a New England author of the future, describing the generation that preceded his own, wrote a story about a valley in which the people cared so much for greatness that they were watching for the man to come, the child born in the valley, who was to be the greatest of his time. The story of *The Great Stone Face* had its prophetic element. It also had a foundation in fact, which it could not have had a century later; for it was true that the New England air was filled with a sense of expectation.

THE SOUTH: 1800–1870

1. 1800

THE SOUTH in 1800 was a land of contrasts, of opulence and squalor, ignorance and learning, of exquisite gardens bordering on Amazonian swamps, fine mansions, beggarly taverns and roads that were rivers. One often met some great lady on a progress through the woods, drawn through the mud by four horses, seated in a splendid coach, made perhaps in London, and followed by a train of magnificently liveried servants. In the Virginia tidewater counties and in the lowlands of South Carolina, this was an everyday occurrence, while the "valley of humiliation between the two mountain peaks of pride,"— the pioneer state of North Carolina,—was a wilderness of log-huts, black hogs and wolves. Georgia was equally primitive, as were the Western regions, although at any time, in a clearing in the forest, one might happen upon some great plantation-house with all the amenities and elegances of Williamsburg and Charleston. The Southland suggested feudal Europe before the rise of cities and the bourgeoisie.

Because, in the South, the towns were few and of less importance than in the North,—the region of manufacturing and commerce,—the roads were even worse than elsewhere; and American roads in general were mediæval. In the best parts of Virginia, one struggled hub-high through the mud, fording creeks and runs and mired in marshes, and crossing Albemarle Sound, for instance, one sometimes had to wait two days for a ferryman who would brave the snarling water. The taverns were like ale-houses in the remoter parts of Russia, where travellers slept three in a bed and six in a room, with bare bleak dirty walls and a few old broken chairs and benches, desolate, noisy, cold and alive with vermin. One recognized these taverns by the hogs at the door and the sign of an earthen jug suspended from a pole, and a corner of the public-room was

128

railed off for a bar, with a rum-keg and a row of dingy tumblers. This bar was often thronged with Major Billies and Colonel Dicks, like so many former nobles of the Polish republic; and if one happened to close one's eyes one was certain to be awakened soon by drinking songs inspired by the flowing grog. Among these favourite songs were "Tony Philpot" and "Boony Bet," and gaming, cock-fighting and wrestling were pleasures of the taverns, which were no ruder, for the rest, than the country inns of Spain, as Washington Irving found them a few years later. In Spain a traveller had to supply his own provisions and his own bed, whereas in the South one could count upon hoe-cake and pork, whiskey and a bed stuffed with shavings. Besides, one was seldom obliged to resort to a tavern because the plantation-houses were "free hotels." To have taken this for granted would have been to treat with scant respect the famous hospitality of the Southern gentry; but the taverns were so ill-equipped because there was no real incentive, on the part of the tavern-keepers, to make them better. Strangers were besieged with invitations the moment they appeared, and many a free-living planter kept Negroes on the lookout to announce the coming of a possible guest on the road. When a carriage or a horseman appeared on the horizon, the Negro donned his livery and accosted the stranger, and sometimes boys were stationed at the door of the inn with a tray of fruit and cider as an invitation. Occasionally, a planter himself was known to meet the coach and vaguely bow into the window, hoping for a guest. Sometimes the humblest Yankee pedlar, crossing the lawn of a mansion, with his basket over an arm and a bundle on his shoulder, found himself welcomed for a night and even for a week. He was certain to cause a stir in the house, with his trinkets for the girls and his jack-knives, brushes, razors, combs and ribbons; and if he brought news from the outside world or possessed an amusing gift of the gab he was treated as often as not like a visiting cousin.

Most of the great Virginia houses were spread along the tide-water rivers, the James, the York and the Rappahannock, and more thinly to the valley of the Shenandoah; and one usually reached the plantation by one of the long winding roads that branched and forked from the highways in every direction. Each plantation had its name, Hordumonde, Bizarre, Roslin, Westover, Olive Hill or what not, and the vast Virginia cousin-hood linked them all together, for most of the established families were in some way related. Among these were the Carters, the Lees and the Bollings, the Pages, the Paynes and the Blands, the Pendletons, the Randolphs and the Cabells. Tobacco-planters mostly, with scores and usually hundreds of slaves, the heads of these houses were nominally Episcopalians, and the plantations were self-contained villages, where the slaves were taught all the trades, and the planter's wife often conducted a school of her own. She directed the chambermaids with their knitting, taught the Negro girls to sew and supervised the work of the reel and the churn, while she kept an eye on the out-kitchen, the smoke-house and the dyeing-room, the fowl-yard, the hot-house and the garden. Sometimes this garden was laid out with terraces, arbours, box-hedges and parterres. In his turn, the planter superintended the sheep-shearing, the sowing of the crops, the orchard, the hoe-house and the grain-house, the cutting of timber for new cabins and the pressing of the tobacco and cotton, which was usually shipped in bales from his own wharf. He visited the servants' quarters and often doctored the slaves himself,—Caesar, Pompey, Scipio, Agamemnon, Cato, with Sappho, Venus and Chloe among the women, for the slaves, more often than not, bore classical names; and he made the rounds of his lands on a pony, with an umbrella over his head, to direct their work and consult with the overseers. There was much coming and going of company, neighbours, kinsfolk, visiting lawyers; the parson was a frequenter of all the big houses; and the table groaned with ducks and turkeys, geese, beef and mutton, while there was usually a pitcher of iced toddy in the hall. At Monticello, Jefferson's daughter sometimes had to find beds and provide meals for fifty people. Whole families, as many as three or four at a time, would arrive with their carriages and servants. There were stalls at Monticello for thirty-six horses, only about ten of which belonged to the master. The guests often remained for weeks, sleeping on sofas all over the house and amusing themselves with billiards, piquet and loo, riding about the grounds in the morning, shooting larks and partridges, breaking colts with the sons of the house and discussing dogs, horses, guns and duels. Horse-racing and horse-breeding were constant themes of conversation, the merits of Lamplighter, Psyche and the Shark Mare; while the serious talk of the older men dealt with law and agriculture, the virtues of different kinds of ploughs and the raising of Indian corn. Especially they discussed politics, the leading theme of every mind, the affairs of the county, the state and latterly the nation.

Such, more or less, was the daily life of all the plantation-houses and people from Maryland to Savannah and the Western regions, for even in Kentucky there were plantations already, following in a ruder style the tidewater model. Florida was still in possession of the Spaniards, and the Louisiana territory belonged to the French: the Spaniards ceded it to them in 1800, and it did not enter the Union until 1803. Maryland was noted for an extra measure of sociability, the cavalier *joie de vivre*, good humour and mirth; and the plantations of South Carolina, along the Ashley and Cooper rivers, devoted to rice and cotton, were famous for their gardens. The Middleton place brimmed over with Roman laurels and camellias that were planted by the elder Michaux, and Joel R. Poinsett later was a Charleston man who brought the poinsettia from Mexico and gave it a name. Another was Dr. Alexander Garden, after whom the gardenia was named by the great Linnæus. Of all the states South Carolina remained the most aristocratic. With a constitution drawn up by John Locke and Shaftesbury, it had even had for a while a peerage of its own, three orders, Carolinian barons, cassiques and landgraves; and more than other Southern towns,—Annapolis, Baltimore, Williamsburg, Norfolk,—Charleston was luxurious, brilliant and gay. Nowhere else, for instance, did one see so many splendid coaches, so round, of so bright a yellow, so besprinkled with gold, or footmen with such sumptuous liveries, or households with so many servants, or so many peacocks' plumes for the ladies to be fanned with; and where else did one hear epigrams so wittily bandied about by raconteurs who set the table on a roar? Charleston, moreover, had a club of duellists in which the members took precedence according to the number of times they had been "out." For the winter social season and race-week in the spring, the planters abandoned Drayton Hall, Magnolia, Archdale, Fairlawn and Clifton; and then the picturesque little city, with its balconies, walls, oleanders and jasmine, and its figs and pomegranates and jonquils and hyacinths from Holland, gave itself over to music, the theatre and the races. Charleston had the oldest theatre in the country, in which Otway's *The Orphan* was performed in 1736, and it also had a French theatre, for the town itself was half French, overflowing with Huguenot families and refugees from Santo Domingo. Meanwhile, the St. Cecilia Society offered concerts of Mozart and Haydn, and the best singers, musicians and actors were engaged for long seasons in Charleston, among them Mrs. Siddons's sister,—Mrs. Whitlock, born a Kemble,—and the family of Thomas Sully, who grew up in the town. There, in 1737, John Wesley, who lived for a while in Georgia, had published his first collection of psalms and hymns, written in Savannah where, as an apostle to the Indians, he had founded the first of all the Sunday schools. In Charleston at present lived David Ramsay, the historian of the Revolution, and the miniature-painter Charles Fraser, who left in his water-colours a charming record of the town, its greens, churches, taverns and plantation-houses. A visitor there in 1800 was Edward Malbone of Rhode Island, Fraser's master and rival, and Sully was already studying in Charleston. The portrait-painter that was to be saw fine examples of his art, a dozen Copleys, three or four Romneys and several by Sir Joshua Reynolds.

Like many of the South Carolinians, the Virginia and Maryland planters, secluded as they were on their forest estates, were conversant with the great world of London and Paris. Some had been educated in Europe, at Eton or Harrow and Oxford or Cambridge, as various New Yorkers and Bostonians had also been, and others had gone further afield,—for instance, Charles Carroll, the signer, of Maryland, who had studied at Rheims, Bourges and Paris before he went to the Temple in London. This descendant of Lord Baltimore, the only Catholic "founding father," a young man of fashion whom Reynolds had painted, had signed the Declaration with his full name "Charles Carroll of Carrollton," as if he wished to imperil his great estate. The younger men, since the Revolution, more generally went to American colleges, William and Mary, Harvard and oftener Princeton, but numbers who made the grand tour and kept up their correspondence were in touch with the literary news and the gossip of England. Their houses were full of furniture, pictures and musical instruments brought from Europe,—pianofortes, harpsichords, guitars and flutes, and engravings from Hogarth and Claude,—and in their libraries, large or small, one found old folios and quartos, occasionally a few Elzevirs and Shakespeare, Montaigne and Jeremy Taylor. Bacon, Boyle, Locke and Hooper were often included, the *Letters of Junius,* Dr. Johnson, Burke, Hume and the Roman historians, with *Tristram Shandy, Roderick Random, Don Quixote* and Madame de Sévigné's *Letters,* and especially the beloved authors of the days of Queen Anne. The queen herself had a special place in the hearts of Virginians, who had bestowed her name on a system of rivers, the North and the South Anna, the Rivanna, the Fluvianna and the Rapidann. Pope, Prior, the cheerful Addison, Defoe and Swift were favourites in the South, as in the North; and the young ladies studied their polished diction and used them as models for their letters. The libraries were sometimes magnificent and contained books in many tongues. Among the books of Thomas Jefferson were a first edition of *Paradise Lost,* a black-letter Chaucer and other treasures; and William Byrd had had at

Westover the largest library in the country, with the exception perhaps of Cotton Mather's. Byrd himself had read Greek and Latin, French, Italian and Dutch and had often begun the day with a chapter of Hebrew.

This Byrd of an earlier generation, the founder of Richmond and Petersburg, who had named valleys, streams and mountains, had been thrown, as a young man in England, with Congreve, Swift and Pope, and had made heroic efforts at home to maintain his early standard of culture. A member of the Royal Society as well as of the world of fashion, he had lived in Virginia three or four lives at once, as a planter on a large scale, a soldier, statesman, scholar and author, a lover of horse-flesh and horse-play also and a great fellow at country dancing. Between romping with his wife and "playing the wag" with Indian girls, he pondered Dr. Tillotson's sermons and read the Latin poems of Milton. It was he who drew the boundary-line between Virginia and North Carolina, on the expedition described in one of his books. Another great planter, Colonel Carter of Westmoreland county, was a composer of minuets and other more serious music. Many of these magnates took great pains with the education of their children, catechising the tutors, who were usually Yankees or Englishmen, and selecting French governesses with the utmost care. Often the tutor had a schoolhouse of his own, perhaps by the joiner's cabin or the poultry-yard, where he slept in the best corner for keeping out the rain and instructed the planter's children by the door or the window. Girls of eleven were expected to repeat by heart Pope's *Ode to Solitude* and Collins's *Ode to the Passions*. Thomas Jefferson's daughter Martha, who had been placed as a child in Paris under the care of Madame de Genlis, was busy at home from eight in the morning till five o'clock and supper-time with music, letter-writing, drawing, dancing and French. In the evening she read the English authors, and, when her father was away, he required her to write to him in detail about the first whippoorwill's whistle and the coming of the swallows. Were the strawberries ripe? Had the peas blossomed? Was there any sign yet of the martins? Had she read her *Don Quixote* every day? How went her grammer in English and Spanish? John Randolph, the rising Virginia statesman, a brilliant writer of letters himself, who had studied at Princeton, Columbia and William and Mary, supervised the education of his nephew Theodorick Dudley, whom he all but adopted as a son. Wifeless and childless, condemned, as he said, to a solitude like Robinson Crusoe's, he directed the young man's reading, studies and manners, his penmanship, his Greek grammar, his associations with other young men, his exploits on the hunting-field and the training of his dogs. Dash, Clio, Echo and the pointer Dido must also learn their manners. He sent his nephew money, preferring not to know how it was spent, and urged him to learn to write in French, so that he could think in the language of the arts and arms. He was never to give promises and never to betray a secret, and he must be invariably courteous, truthful and brave.

In this plantation world of leisure, there was time for sports and horsemanship, for talk, hospitality, reading, study and friends; and the plantations were happy hunting-grounds for travellers, impecunious cousins and portrait-painters. It was a life of out-of-door activity, easy-going, generous, hearty and free, where nothing seemed remoter than the kind of introspection that flourished in the Northern regions, especially New England. Ideas played little part in it, outside the realm of politics, and the Southern mind was seldom detached and never analytical; and, while many of the planters, parsons and lawyers amused themselves with "capping verses," and writing satirical odes and epigrams for albums, the conception of the literary life was unknown among them. Writing was an accomplishment merely, as it largely was in the North as well; and the genius of the Southland and the careless, active life there were long to prevent its becoming anything else. There was no more Southern literature, and little more promise of such a thing, than there would have been in similar circles in England if there had been no London; and the few men who "burned," like John Randolph, "with literary ambition" seldom did anything about it. They were rather despised, they were apt to be snubbed if their writing suggested anything more than "hours of relaxation" and entertainment. It was in this spirit that William Wirt "threw together" the *Letters of the British Spy*, a case in point, a bland Addisonian series of papers that contained a pleasant account of Virginia, supposedly found in a seaport inn where an Englishman had left them. William Wirt, a Maryland lawyer who practised in Virginia, was later attorney-general under Monroe, and by far the most illuminating papers in the book were those that dealt with oratory and "forensic encounters." There, in the region of statesmanship, the Southern mind declared itself, and its real and vital interests appeared in Wirt's descriptions of Patrick Henry's "Gothic magnificence" and the "Herculean club" of Marshall. It was an observation of the "British spy" that every Virginian of talent was bred as a lawyer, and in the pages of William Wirt one felt that one was overhearing an actual conversation of these men of law, perhaps on a progress from court to court when a group of them, booted and spurred, looked less like learned clerks than like merry huntsmen. With what animation the British spy compared the traits of the various orators and the "great boast" of all, the famous Henry, whose bold and overwhelming speeches had never appeared in print and were only preserved in fragments in the memories of his hearers. In manners and appearance a plain back-country farmer, hesitant, with an air of depression, unassuming, lowly, with what splendour he blazed when slowly his fancy took flight!—and William Pinkney and John Marshall and half a dozen others were characterized with equal precision and zest. This one excelled in Grecian elegance, another in force and purity, a third in tender pictures of distress; one was ornate, one was severe, one was like a martial trumpet, while some were preëminent in melody and others in pathos.

William Wirt and every Southerner took oratory seriously, and one and all were serious about agriculture, soils, crops, farm-animals, fruit-trees, breeding and feeding. This was true in the North as well, where many of the public men of the time were concerned with these questions as deeply as the men of the South. John Jay discussed with his correspondents experiments in agriculture, a novel use of plaster as a kind of manure, a new variety of rye which he introduced on his Bedford farm and a new breed of mules of which he had heard. Gouverneur Morris recorded his rapture over the well-tilled fields of France, though he found no soil there as good as the soil at home. He observed minutely the variations of soils and grasses, while Joel Barlow sent home from France a root of the sugar-beet, which was hitherto unknown in the United States. Chancellor Livingston of New York was the author of an *Essay on Sheep* that was read with delight by William Cobbett; and Fisher Ames constantly corresponded with Christopher Gore and Timothy Pickering on cattle-breeding, milch-cows, fruit-trees and orchard-grasses. He exchanged the "pig wisdom" that he had acquired on his farm at Dedham for Pickering's "potato knowledge," gathered in Salem. But the Northern men were interested also in commerce and manufacturing, while agriculture in the South was all in all; and John Taylor of Caroline, for instance, was a philosopher in this field and might have been called a veritable poet of farming. As for Thomas Jefferson, his great estate, Monticello, on the summit of the Charlottesville "mountain" near which he was born, was a vast out-door laboratory for experiments in agriculture, unique in the United States and the Western world. There Jefferson, hearing of any device that might be of service to farmers, examined, improved it, if possible, and spread it abroad, importing the best new threshing-machine, which he further developed in certain ways, and inventing a plough that was later in general use. He introduced into Virginia the nectarine and the pomegranate, promoted the culture of mulberries, peaches and figs, cultivated grapes for wine and brought to Monticello a group of Italian viniculturists. He experimented with orange-trees, Italian cherries, apricots and four varieties of almonds, while he also tried to raise olives; and, hoping that the Southern states might soon produce their own oil, he sent two shiploads of olive-plants to Charleston. As for South Carolina and Georgia, the wet rice they raised there caused a fearful loss of life in summer, so he imported from Africa some heavy upland rice that proved to be successful in the Georgia hills. He had sent from France some Egyptian rice, and to study the Piedmontese rice he went on a week's excursion beyond the Alps and smuggled over the border a few pocketfuls of this, which he also sent to South Carolina. He examined almost every tree and plant in Western Europe, and he kept his farm journal as carefully in France as at home. Meanwhile, John Taylor, the "Virginia Arator," philosophized and experimented on his three plantations. A graduate of William and Mary, a master of five languages, he wrote four books on government besides the *Arator* that was read all over the country by statesmen and farmers; and the agricultural library of this learned lawyer-planter was larger than George Washington's at Mount Vernon. John Taylor's great farms in Caroline county, Hazelwood, Hayfield and Mill Hill, were bounded by interminable cedar hedges, with avenues of towering holly-trees, and they too were famous for their practical devices, their admirable soil, their verdure and the abundance of their crops. In his essays Taylor discussed the problems that occupied most of his neighbours, the travels and observations of Arthur Young and Sir Humphry Davy's analyses of fertilizers, for the state of Virginian agriculture was always on his mind and he felt that his friends were ignoring much-needed improvements. The conclusion of his *Arator* was a glorification of agriculture that warmed the heart of every honest planter, for he exalted as all but divine the virtues of this art, which fed the hungry, clothed the naked and filled the soul with health and vigour. What other art compared with it for building a life that was truly complete, so close to nature, so pleasurable, so joyous, so moral?

Such were the questions the planters discussed when they

met, for instance, at church on Sundays, strolling about before service and after the sermon, exchanging business letters, comparing notes on crop-prices and inviting one another, with their families, to dinner. For whatever their private faith was,—and many of them were deists,—they were mostly Episcopalians, at least in name, although the Episcopal Church had grown more and more perfunctory and was generally in a state of decay both without and within. There had been no colonial bishops to supervise the clergy, who were often wasters, idlers and hangers-on, and there were many who felt that the Church had gone too far to be revived, although most of the planters supported it as a matter of form. Numbers of the old churches had long been in ruins. Their roofs had fallen in, and they were lost in the fields or the forest, with chancel-floors and stone aisles buried out of sight, and sometimes a huge sycamore overspread the ruins, rising out of the spot where the altar had been. Such was the great church on the Rappahannock that stood between Rosegill and Brandon. The ploughshare had passed over many, and one sometimes found an old communion-table that was used as a chopping-block, while fonts served as punch-bowls in taverns. The churchyards overflowed with weeds and brambles, and, scattered in neglected meadows, lay tombstones adorned with heraldic emblems and panegyrics that related the virtues of some long-dead lady in the grand eulogistic rhetoric of the past. Occasionally on loaves of bread one saw the prints of tombstones that housewives had employed for kneading their dough, and one often discovered in farmhouses rich altar-cloths and communion-plate and bits of superb old carving that had strayed from the churches. One church was used as a nursery for silk-worms.

This was all part of the general ruin that had even preceded the Revolution when the planters, investing nothing and saving nothing, had recklessly lived on their capital, fleeced by the traders, building ever finer houses with stabling for a hundred horses, buying more and more splendid coaches, more silver and more Madeira. They had maintained their lordly style of the days when the price of tobacco was high, when the price of slaves was low and the soil was virgin, and they did not know what had happened to them when tobacco sold for less, when slaves cost more and more and the soil was exhausted. Now the plantation-system was on the rise again,—indeed, its most prosperous days lay in the future; and, after an age of infidelity, the South was to experience soon a notable revival of religion. Even the free-thinking Anglicans were to think less "freely," although the Episcopal Church remained small in the South; and meanwhile the Methodists and Baptists, despised by the planters, were making multitudes of converts. These evangelical sects appealed to the less cultivated classes, and they throve especially in the frontier regions, North Carolina, Georgia and the turbulent West; but in 1800 Francis Asbury was active in Virginia, and Lorenzo Dow, the free-lance Methodist, was known all over the roads of the South. Peter Cartwright, the backwoods preacher, a Virginian by birth, was a boy in 1800, living in Kentucky; and this "dark and bloody ground" and the neighbouring Tennessee were peculiarly favourable settings for the "sons of thunder." There an educated clergy was regarded as undemocratic, although some of the early Methodists were as learned as any New England minister. Asbury, the first Methodist bishop, who was scarcely ever out of the saddle, pursued on horseback his study of Hebrew and Greek, while he sang hymns and shouted hosannahs, riding from hamlet to hamlet, sometimes in a concourse of preachers, till the forest rang with his jubilation. Arriving in the colonies in 1771, he travelled three hundred thousand miles, visiting every state in the Union and almost every town and wearing out half a dozen horses. He lived on the corn and wild fruits that he picked up as he rode along, sleeping on the floors of cabins on verminous bear-skins, longing now and then for a "nice clean plank," and his favourite ritual was a lively song and a fervent prayer, followed by an earth-shaking sermon and an earnest hymn. The tall, spare, severe old man, in his Quakerish broad-brimmed hat, had less success in the North and least in New Haven, that "seat of science and of sin"; but the somewhat more emotional South was prepared for his methods and doctrines and he was welcomed even by some of the planters.

Most of these, however, preferred the decorous Church of their fathers, though the clergy were worldly and dissolute and their faith was dim, while infidelity was triumphant and bishops resigned in despair, until deism itself went down in popular disapproval. One of the Methodist preachers even found a living Virginian who had never heard of Jesus Christ. On the other hand, some of the planters were seriously religious, and the deism of Jefferson, for instance, was profound and devout. He shared this with Madison, Monroe and scores of others. Patrick Henry, before his death, had returned to the ancestral Church and had even composed a reply to *The Age of Reason*. Every Sunday evening his household joined in sacred music, which the old orator accompanied on his violin. John Randolph, who had been a deist and was even drawn to Mohammedanism, despising the Cross, as he said, and preferring the Crescent,—a result of his early reading of Voltaire and Gibbon,—erased from his *Decline and Fall* the notes he had scribbled on the margins approving of the historian's deistical views. Disavowing all these tokens of his unhappy youth, Randolph also returned to the Church of England, for he would not accept its new name,—he detested the phrase "the Episcopal Church" and insisted that he was a diocesan of the Bishop of London. Meanwhile, Jefferson, who had established religious freedom in Virginia by enforcing the separation of Church and State, was a deist in bone and grain of a noble type who wished to restore the original ethics of the Christians. While never admitting a right of enquiry into other people's religious opinions, he was clear and sure about his own, and he felt that Athanasius and Calvin were usurpers of the Christian name whose doctrines were crazy perversions of the teachings of Christ. They were impious dogmatists, he thought, who had made a Babel of a faith that was friendly to liberty, science and the expansion of the mind. Divested of the rags in which they had enveloped it, Christianity was the most moral and sublime religion that had ever been preached to man; and, if the doctrines of Jesus had been preached as pure as they came from his lips, the whole civilized world would now have been Christian. So thought Jefferson, and a few years later he compiled a little book of his own called *The Life and Morals of Jesus of Nazareth*. In this he selected, as far as possible,—with the Greek, Latin and French texts in parallel columns beside the English,—the actual words of Jesus, and these alone.

The great class of the Southern planters, small in numbers but large in mind, had been singularly prolific of eminent statesmen; and the nation was full of the labours of the famous Virginia men of affairs, while in this respect South Carolina vied with Massachusetts. The Southerners were congenital politicians; for the plantation was a school of statesmanship, and the management of a great estate trained one to manage a larger world. Many of the planters were not only lawyers but also church-wardens, legislators and commissioners of roads. Moreover, the plantation life developed the paternal sense,—no doubt, the germ of patriotic feeling; and the planters, who were responsible for hundreds and sometimes thousands of souls, came naturally to feel responsible for the state as well. Bred on the Greek and Roman classics, they were republicans by example, and the monarchy had wounded their self-esteem, so that, while most of them had no sympathy with democracy whatever, they were largely of one mind in the Revolution. Having lived in dependency upon Europe, they had watched the politics of Europe, about which they were surpassingly well-informed; and the problems involved in converting their colonies into an independent nation had made them past-masters of statecraft and its issues and perils. In their young country, they had to think everything out anew, and government in all its aspects was their chief occupation, from the settling of boundary disputes to the care of their slaves; and they knew the ancient historians and orators as well as the modern political thinkers. Even a generation later the women of the South were famous all over the country for their political knowledge. They spent parts of their winters at Richmond or Washington, visiting the Springs in the summer, constantly thrown with statesmen and political talk; and on their plantations they were busy all day long with questions that were political in essence.

While New England and its town-meetings contributed much to American statecraft, the experience of Virginia was riper in political matters; and the country between the James and the York was the scene of the earliest legislature, the first *habeas corpus* case and the first American trial by jury. There had been heard the first American protest against tyranny, and the Bill of Rights, the heart of the Constitution, was a document of the state of Virginia first. More than by anyone else indeed the political creed of Americanism was first conceived by Virginians of a certain type, planters such as Jefferson who, whatever else they were, had roots in the hinterland, which they called "the forest." Patrick Henry was born a woodsman of the pioneer stock of the "Qu'hoes," the men in buckskin breeches from the upper counties, so called in distinction from the "Tuckahoes," the aristocrats of the tidewater region; and it was these up-country men who supported him in '75, when many of the Tuckahoes were lukewarm about independence. As for Jefferson, while his mother was one of the Randolphs, he had grown up on a frontier farm, the son of a pioneer, and, although from early youth he was thrown among the gentlefolk, his sympathies largely remained with the humbler people. He never forgot his backwoods neighbours, the small tobacco-growers of the upper rivers and the hunters and trappers of the hills; and they were in his mind when he introduced his great reforms, abolishing entails and primogeniture, establishing religious freedom and drawing up his famous bill for the general diffusion of knowledge. These early Virginia reforms had won him the hatred of the landed aristocracy and the clergy, although John Taylor of Caroline was a Jeffersonian democrat; but how could there have been a permanent landed aristocracy when land all over America was so abundant and cheap? Jefferson profoundly believed in the intelligence of the people, while he was determined that the rich should not prey on the poor; and it was this measure of trust in the goodness of ordinary men, as well as in their ability to set things right, that established the American principle in political thinking. No doubt the work of the Federalists was necessary to establish the country, to render a nation possible and sustain its existence. But they cared for the body of the state alone, while the Jeffersonians endowed this body with a soul, concerned as they were not merely with the existence of the nation but with the making of the nation unique and great. The Federalists perpetuated European forms; the Republicans devised and developed forms that sprang from the habits and history of the American people. They represented new men in a new world.

So this Virginia school of democracy was the great school of American statecraft, and Jefferson, who looked to the West, was trusted by the West in turn. The first Western statesman, Henry Clay, was his disciple, and so was John C. Calhoun in South Carolina; and the first statesman of the Southwest, Sam Houston, was a Virginian born, like the first governor of Louisiana, William C. C. Claiborne. Even Abraham Lincoln had roots in the state,—his Virginia grandfather crossed the mountains and settled in Kentucky. The statesmanship that characterized American civilization was an outgrowth of Jefferson's ideas; yet these ideas came to little, for special but obvious reasons, in the very region where they grew. There were few towns where they could spread and few urban folk to spread them,—and the spreading of ideas is usually a function of towns,—while the Southern middle class was small and scattered; and meanwhile the plantation-system was aristocratic by definition and pushed the lower orders to the wall. Slavery, moreover, denied the beliefs upon which the

ideas of democracy rested and was bound to prevent the realization of them. Nobody defended slavery, everyone abhorred it,
Jefferson as much as Paine or the Quaker John Woolman, or
Asbury, or George Wythe, or Richard Henry Lee, while John
Randolph freed his slaves, and Henry Clay and John C. Calhoun were both opposed to slavery in their earlier years. Clay
was an ardent abolitionist in Kentucky in 1799, and his anti-
slavery impulses were always breaking through the apologies
he made for it later. In those after days Calhoun was the chief
defender of slavery, but he had agreed in 1800 with the best
young men in South Carolina. They all felt that somehow slavery must be wiped out or it would lead to civil war; but, like
John Taylor of Caroline, they could only see the awful problems that would be sure to follow emancipation. They remembered that the Negroes of Santo Domingo had massacred the
whites when they were freed.

The economic life of the South was founded upon slavery,
and the question seemed too difficult to solve; and meanwhile
the lower orders of whites were all but beyond the reach of
democracy. It would have been impossible to raise their status
without a reorganization of the Southern system, and, humane
as the planters often were towards both their tenants and their
slaves, they were all involved alike in this feudal regime. The
small farmers and tenant-farmers were half-starved and miser-
ably lodged and frequently idle, besotted and fever-stricken,
even along the Potomac; and they lived on bits of salt pork
three times a day, with whiskey "to keep the cold out" and still
more whiskey to ward off ague. There were plenty of generous planters who insured the crops of their poorer neighbours,
but thousands of these grew up necessitous and friendless,
barred from any hope of escape or advance. They had no
market for their crops, and they usually had the poorest soil,
for they were pushed back to the sand-lands, the pine-barrens
and the swamps. The more the forests were cleared away, the
less they were able to hunt any longer; and, reduced to a diet
of cornpone and razor-back hogs, they grew more and more

dispirited, sapless and shiftless. They had little or no education, for only the planters could pay for tutors, although Jefferson made heroic efforts to educate the people at large; and,
while there were numbers of schools in Virginia,—indeed, in all
the states,—there were towns of three thousand people without
a single schoolmaster. Teaching was generally regarded as a
low-caste job.

Thus evolved the "poor whites," whom even the Negroes
regarded with scorn, among them the "sharpers of the South,"
the Georgia crackers, the lean, white-headed, yellow-skinned
folk who lived in mean cabins in the waste-lands, the only
Southern men against whom the Yankees were said to have
had no chance. The energetic could always go west, where
the forests were still full of game and there was good soil
for all comers, the land of the valiant borderers who built their
log-huts in the woods and throve on wild turkeys, partridges,
venison and bear's meat. It was they who were to build in
time,—indeed, they were building already, side by side with
emigrants from the Northern regions,—the Western states
where democracy came into being.

II. 1825

From his Virginian mountain-top, the sage of Monticello
surveyed the Blue Ridge twenty miles away, while, glancing
through his telescope, year after year, in the other direction, he
watched the rising of the walls at Charlottesville. Eighty-two
years old in 1825, when his university was opened, he had ridden over the rough road on horseback almost every day to over-
see the carpenters and masons. Architect, founder and father
of this "darling" of his old age, where he himself gave lessons
in Anglo-Saxon, Jefferson was the father too of the higher education of the future South, for the university set a standard
that was followed down to the Civil War. It was the model
for most of the new Southern colleges. Meanwhile, all of the
eight professors dined every week at Monticello, the beautiful

half-domed Italianate house that shed its influence far and wide. For Jefferson gladly threw off plans for others, so that country-houses all over the newer South reminded one more or less of Monticello. Just so, in matters of education, he counselled all and sundry, and he had been the author of one of the most mature educational plans that had ever been proposed in the world. He hoped to find by education the natural aristocracy that was fit to occupy places of trust and power, seeking out virtue and talents from every condition of life to defeat the competition of mere birth and wealth.

Fifty years had gone by, in 1826, since the signing of the Declaration of Independence. On the Fourth of July, the actual anniversary, John Adams died on his farm at Quincy. He said as he was dying, "Thomas Jefferson survives," not knowing that Jefferson had gone earlier in the day. The two old statesmen had broken off relations, out of conceit with each other, years before, but Benjamin Rush had persuaded Adams to resume a correspondence that he knew would give them both a world of pleasure. For Adams, the irascible, and the calm and wise Virginian admired, revered and even loved each other. "Labouring always at the same oar, with some wave ever ahead, threatening to overwhelm us," Jefferson wrote, they had ridden "through the storm with heart and hand and made a happy port"; and he agreed when Adams remarked, "You and I ought not to die before we have explained ourselves to each other."

Thus had begun the correspondence, so touching to later American readers, between these ancient worthies of the Revolution, one the spokesman of Massachusetts, the other of Virginia, the states that represented best the culture of the North and the culture of the South. This famous correspondence was so regular and long,—for it began in 1812,—that all the postmasters along the route soon became aware of it, and the postriders watched for the letters. Adams, sitting down to write, felt like the woodcutter on Mount Ida,—he could not see the wood for the trees. He could not write a hundredth part of what he wished to say, and so many subjects crowded upon him that he knew not with which to begin, while Jefferson, knowing that they could never have changed their fixed opinions, avoided any suggestion of controversy. But they had few thoughts now of old unhappy far-off things and battles of politicians long ago, though they liked to review the labours and perils through which they had broken away from what Jefferson called the "dull monotony" of "colonial subservience." Both agreed that the world on the whole was good. Even for Adams no individual was "totally depraved," and Jefferson, the ever-sanguine, steered his bark with hope, preferring the dreams of the future to the history of the past. Both had developed what Jefferson described as a "canine appetite for reading," though he had little time to read himself. From sunrise till one or two, and often from dinner to dark as well, he drudged away at his writing-table, civilly answering every letter, while Adams either ignored his or gave "gruff, short, unintelligible" answers,—"mysterious, enigmatic or pedantical," —to discourage intruders. So Adams was able to spend his days with Chateaubriand, Grimm, La Harpe and Sismondi and the twelve volumes of Dupuis on the Origin of Cults. These were his "marbles and nine-pins of old age." They were "romances all," and especially Grimm,—"the most entertaining book I ever read"; and Jefferson, remembering this old French gossip whom he had known so well in Paris, the ancient friend of Jean-Jacques and Catherine the Great, longed for a similar work by an American hand. Fifteen volumes of anecdotes, within the compass of his own time, written by a man of equal genius and taste, would have turned back the scale for him in favour of life; but he would not read the "fan-colouring biographers" who painted small men as very great. Both had gone through Plato again, Adams with two Latin translations, together with an English and a French, comparing them with the Greek, and they discussed this and also the uses of grief, about which Adams had found a fine passage in Molière. He was for taking no notice of malice,—"Were such things to be answered, our lives would be wasted in the filth of fendings and provings";

and he felt with Jefferson that, for all the distress and pain of his life, he had really had ten times more ease and pleasure.

With the passing of these spacious minds, the classical age of the Revolution seemed suddenly dim to Americans and far away; and the new statesmen who had emerged, Webster, Calhoun and Henry Clay, were by no means men of such wide horizons. Relatively, indeed, they were provincials. They had neither the time nor the taste to read Livy once a year, delighting in *Tristram Shandy,* like Patrick Henry, and, while Calhoun and Webster were scholarly enough, their sympathies were severely circumscribed. Their regions or, at most, the nation alone concerned them. They had none of the planetary interests of the men of old, whose principles were of universal meaning. As for Jefferson, his thoughts had been as bold and large as he was benevolent, sincere, cheerful and candid; and his mind had ranged through so many fields,—even more than Franklin's,—that he recalled the men of the Renaissance. A lover of music and the poems of Ossian, he had corresponded with Dr. Burney, and with Madame de Staël and Humboldt and Dupont de Nemours, philosophers, artists, writers and men of affairs, and his literary feeling was as marked as the "friendly warmth" that Adams said was natural and habitual to him. His conception of America enchanted the young men who flocked about the oracle of Monticello: "It is part of the American character to consider nothing as desperate . . . Let those flatter who fear: it is not an American art."

The contrast between the old and the new was especially striking below the Potomac, for the South, which had given birth to the largest number of world-minds, had withdrawn more than any other region from the movement of the world. It was committed to a patriarchal mode of life and a primitive system of industry and labour-system when progress was the watchword everywhere else, while its economic mainstay, slavery, an obsolete institution, was opposed to the conscience and professions of the American people. St. George Tucker had expressed the view of the older Virginians that slavery was at

variance with the Bill of Rights and that it ought to be eradi-
cated, while the new generation defended it as an institution
blessed by God and a positive good to be guarded at any cost.
The wild revolt of Nat Turner in 1831 was one of the turning-
points in this change of opinion, for it sent a shock of fear
through all the Southern states and intensified the will of the
masters to repress the slaves. Then the Northern anti-slavery
movement produced a reaction in the South in favour of "our
domestic institution," while the rise of "cotton capitalism" in
what came to be known as the Deep South destroyed the liberal
ideas of Jefferson's time. The Virginian aristocracy sank in importance as its wasteful system of production exhausted the
soil, and many of the Virginia planters moved to Mississippi
and Alabama, where more primitive modes of thinking were
the order of the day. Yet slavery was altogether opposed to the
current of economic thought and indeed of all the genuine
thought of the time, and in consequence the Southern mind,
which was driven to defend it, cut itself off from the mind of
the rest of the world. It fell out of step with modern civilization, and the defence of slavery involved a sort of censorship
that precluded either freedom of the press or freedom of
thought. Meanwhile, the Southerners ceased to send their sons
abroad for education and more and more ceased to send them
to college in the North,—they even ceased to have Yankee
tutors at home; and, in short, the South closed door after door
through which the thought of mankind had passed and became
by its own desire a forbidden region. Even the European immi-
grants, who might have brought in fresh ideas but who could
not compete with slave-labour, avoided the South.

This shrinking of the Southern mental horizon was especially
marked and singular because of the breadth and freedom of the
Southern mind in the recent past, and it accounted largely for
the relative sterility of the new mind of the South in literary
matters. There were other reasons for this, to be sure, the
absence of towns, for example, and the lonely and sporadic
nature of the plantation life. The people of education were

widely scattered and had few chances indeed to exchange ideas, and the universal Southern system of an out-of-doors existence was in any case unpropitious to the growth of ideas. It was apt to dissipate the mind, it was too pleasant for concentration, and there was little to encourage mental variation in the simple unchanging routine of the planter's life; while, much as the gentry might like to read, they seldom heard of new books and continued to live with the authors and thoughts of the past. They encountered few of the outside forces that modified a Northern taste for the writers of Greece and Rome and the days of Queen Anne; and the South, with its fine social culture, tended to be static and to live, at the expense of the present, in a world of tradition. Its intellectual habits, like all its other views and ways, were generally handed down from father to son with an ever-diminishing fund of original feeling. Then even Virginia, as compared with the North, was scarcely a reading community, as its own cultivated spokesmen were the first to complain; and the South had few publishing facilities and small respect for men of letters, who were offered the least of incentives to pursue their vocation. Besides, all Southern thought was guided much more by the spoken word, in the law-courts, at political conventions, at camp-meetings and barbecues, than it was ever influenced by the written page.

The wonder was that in these conditions the South produced any writers at all; yet Simms, Maury, the Cookes and others, not to mention Poe, were proofs of the tenacity of its literary instinct. At the moment, John Randolph symbolized in various ways the life of the Southern man of letters, for Randolph, although he published nothing and seldom wrote indeed, was distinctly of the literary order. His speeches were improvisations, but what invariably distinguished them was his literary feeling, his reading and his gift of the phrase, and, as he poured out his beautiful sentences, lolling in the House,— booted and spurred, leaning against a pillar,—one realized that Randolph was an artist. Confident, proud and imposing, in his blue coat and buckskin breeches, with the skeleton figure that was mounted as if on stilts, he fascinated high and low, the groundlings and the learned, and whether in Congress or at hustings or the dinner-table. His voice, occasionally shrill, was silvery often,—it was as sweet as a flute, Lord Melbourne said,— and the flow of his imagination and memory was endless; and, arch-individual that he was and otherwise typical of nothing, he was yet an exemplar of the literary caste in the South. He impersonated its loneliness and its dilettantism. For Randolph would not condescend to cultivate his gifts, in this resembling many Southern writers, and as the "wild man of the woods," as he liked to call himself, he was only a little more isolated than most of these writers. For the rest, his statesmanship, which was all in the mood of the time, might alone have explained the shrinking of the Southern horizon; for his passionate love of Virginia and the moonstruck logic that governed his mind had led him to defy the republic that Virginia mothered. Virginia was a sufficient world for Randolph and his followers, and moreover he opposed the admission of any new states. His hand was against every other statesman, for, having fought the Federalists who wished to extinguish the rights of states, he fought the equalitarian Jefferson also, and he left directions to have his body buried facing west, so that he might "keep an eye on Henry Clay." Detesting equality as much as he loved liberty, he sneered at "Saint Thomas of Cantingbury,"—Jefferson, his cousin; and he had virtually preached from the first the right of secession by force and prepared the way for Calhoun and Jefferson Davis.

Insolent, wilful, quixotic, John Randolph dwelt in a world of his own that had come to seem more and more like the House of Usher as, touched with dementia, living on opium, he waved his wand-like fingers and forbade the star of the nation to advance in its course. A voluntary exile at Roanoke, he had broken with his family, exchanging his great house with its formal gardens for a pair of rude log-cabins in the desolate forest, and there he kept his hundreds of slaves and his ample stud of blooded horses and his English coach and plate and clothes and books. A centaur, always on his horse, trotting to Charleston for the races or galloping about the plantation when he could not sleep, at midnight, in a cloak, with a brace of pistols, he was silent for days and weeks together or excitable, restless, abusive and harsh; and he nursed the melancholy that had so much of Byron in it, while it also suggested Leopardi. Arrogantly proud of his race, he was impotent, he could have no children, and this most romantic of men was deprived of romance,—the bitter secret that wrapped him round with mystery and darkness as, more and more, his mind fell into decay. He sometimes carried a bell in his hand, ringing it slowly as he advanced, muttering half aloud, "It is all over," for he thought that Virginia was degenerating along with himself; and he called himself the "stricken deer" in a letter to Francis Scott Key, his cherished correspondent and only crony. In what he described as his long "privation of human intercourse," he counted on Key, who wrote to him and tried to cheer him, and he often visited Key at his house in Georgetown, where the orchard sloped down to the Potomac. He said that Key was "as near perfection as our poor human nature can go," and he confided his literary ambitions to this friend. Randolph had fought a duel over a matter of pronunciation, and questions of language and literature interested him deeply. He thought he would like to edit a magazine.

The present was less intellectually exciting in the South than in the North,—if only because there was less variation there,— while the South was proportionately prouder of its own past. The relatively simple, easy-going out-of-doors existence there tended to develop types rather than persons,—that is, from a psychological point of view; while, at the same time, the Southern mind was not given to analysis or detachment. The novel properly so called had scarcely appeared in America, aside from Brockden Brown and one or two others, but already Cooper and presently Hawthorne exhibited traits and attitudes that were seldom found in the regions below the Potomac. The North was more open to new ideas and methods, and besides, the existence of slavery and the mental habits that sprang from it disabled and even paralysed the critical sense. The sort of social criticism that vivified some of Cooper's romances was all but inconceivable in the South, and a Hawthorne would hardly have been possible there because the Southern mind was indifferent to psychological observation. This was the burden of the advice that St. George Tucker gave William Wirt when the latter was planning to write a Virginian Plutarch,—inasmuch as the Virginians had never observed their notable men, Wirt would be unable to collect the material with which to compose these lives of eminent Virginians. Wirt had begun with Patrick Henry, whom he had never seen, the beau ideal of all that was grand as a patriot and orator, and this biography, which became a full-length book, was in fact the only one he wrote. He could find few written records even of Henry; he could scarcely find anything tangible indeed about him. The fame of his hero rested on a vague, gigantic, shadowy memory in the marvel-loving minds of the people, and in consequence the book was not really a biography but rather a "discourse on rhetoric, patriotism and morals." It was disconcerting to a man who wished to write about Patrick Henry as English authors wrote about Fox and Burke, and Tucker had tried to dissuade him from doing it, saying that in any case no one would be interested in the book. Nor would anyone care for lives of Pendleton or Wythe. All these great men had been forgotten the moment the earth was thrown on their coffins, for no one had been sufficiently interested in them to keep any kind of record of their talk or their lives. Writing to Wirt, Tucker asked who knew anything of Peyton Randolph, the most popular man in Virginia in his time. Or of George Mason, or Dabney Carr, or the majestic Colonel Innes. No trace of the flight of the latter remained behind, save only an abridgement of one of his speeches, and this might be compared to the sparks that issue from a furnace which is invisible itself.*

On the subject of Virginia all the Tuckers spoke with authority, and what was true of Virginia in matters of this kind was undoubtedly still more true of the rest of the South. Biography, as Tucker observed, was a "hopeless undertaking" there, and so, for much the same reason, was novel-writing, for, generally speaking, the Southern mind was an extroverted mind and it had small native interest in the study and observation of character. It found its natural outlet in action and the kind of thinking that fostered action, as befitted a world of lawyers and planters who were soldiers by instinct as well. Thus the Southern mind excelled in political and juristic thinking, while the writings of Matthew Fontaine Maury also belonged in the sphere of action. What science, indeed, had ever produced more striking results in application than the science which, as Humboldt said, Maury created? This was the physical geography of the sea, its nature and the influence of its currents on climate and commerce. It was Maury who discovered the level plateau on the sea-bottom that made it possible to lay the transatlantic cable, and his wind and current charts shortened voyages all over the world and brought the markets of the world closer together. Maury also lessened the dangers of navigation, and, moreover, the weather-bureau resulted from his studies. He had first conceived his charts as master of a sloop-of-war, in 1831, on a voyage to Rio. Thinking of this sort sprang naturally from the Southern mind, which, for the rest, produced few novels. It produced few novels dealing with the

* "They have all glided down the current of life so smoothly (except as public men) that nobody ever thought of noticing how they lived or what they did . . .

"The truth is that Socrates himself would pass unnoticed and forgotten in Virginia, if he were not a public character, and some of his speeches preserved in a newspaper; the latter might keep his memory alive for a year or two, but not much longer."—Letter of St. George Tucker to William Wirt, 1813.

present, while its chief imaginative resource was the historical romance.

For to the martial Southern mind the present was inglorious as compared with the age of the Revolution and the golden colonial time. Those were the days of noble exploits, both military and patriotic; and who was not proud of the past of a state that had mothered four presidents whose faces smiled down from the walls of every log-cabin? Southerners everywhere were full of local and sectional feeling, and South Carolina was producing the greatest of Southern romancers in the prolific and admirable William Gilmore Simms; while the passion for Sir Walter Scott was foreordained throughout the South, for his note was loyalty to the soil, to the family, to the clan. Scott pictured brave men of heroic deeds and women devoted and pure, and he spoke for an unquestioning fidelity to the feudal past and all the primary virtues of an unchanging order. Jefferson had detested Scott precisely because of his feudal sympathies, while John Randolph preferred Fielding, who held the mirror up to nature. The older Virginians were realistic and had small use for the "mere romances" that pictured men as they should be, not as they were. But the realistic mind had vanished for a while in the South. The new generation preferred to cherish illusions, and one of these illusions was that the age of chivalry was *not* gone and that they could perpetuate feudalism in the teeth of the world. The pride of the Virginians was proverbial, meanwhile, and they carried Virginia with them wherever they went, to the Delta of the Mississippi that suggested the "low grounds" of the James and the prairies of Texas that recalled the meadows of the Valley. Every Virginian county had its great men, and a hue of romance invested the past of them all, and the Virginians loved to think of the early days of the Old Dominion, the courage of Captain John Smith, the gallantry of Sir Walter Raleigh. They dwelt with delight on the story of Virginia Dare, the first white child who was born on American soil, Pocahontas and John Rolfe and the old courtier George Sandys, who translated the poems of Ovid in the primeval forest. They liked to remember that their Hampton was named for a friend of Virginia, the Earl of Southampton who was Shakespeare's friend, and they tried to solve the riddle of the colony that disappeared mysteriously from Roanoke Island. They visited the ruins of Jamestown, romantic in the moonlight, with its old brick enclosure and crumbling arches, where ancient sycamores and mulberries rose among the scattered tombs by the broken and moss-covered tower that was mantled with ivy. Scarcely less appealing was the wide street at Williamsburg that stretched along the ridge from the capitol to the college and the beautiful building designed by Sir Christopher Wren; and many an eccentric old country gentleman cherished recollections of the days when the salaries of the clergy were paid in tobacco. They told tales of a heartier time when oxen were roasted whole at feasts and the head of the pirate Black Beard, defeated in battle, was brought up the James as the figurehead of a ship. And who could forget that once upon a time the British monarchy existed in Virginia only? When Charles the Second was a fugitive, decrees were issued in his name in this most loyal of all the colonies, and Colonel Richard Lee was dispatched to Holland to invite him to set up his throne there. Later, the king wore at his coronation a robe that was woven of pure Virginia silk. Nor was it forgotten that the first Eppes of Virginia was a gentleman of the bed-chamber of Charles the First. The cavalier tradition was as firmly based in Virginian history as the stories of the Tubal Cain of the Old Dominion, the illustrious Governor Spotswood who opened a passage over the range and started iron-mining in the mountains. He had set out with a company of gentlemen, dressed in green velvet himself with a plume in his hat, and he had taken possession of the Shenandoah Valley in the name of the first King George. In order to encourage his companions to venture back and explore the West, he instituted the order of the Golden Horseshoe, presenting them all with horseshoes of gold that were made for him

in London and covered in a number of cases with precious
stones.

The Southern romancers lingered over all these themes,
while they described the Valley, Jamestown and the Blue Ridge
and the shores of the Rivanna and the Rappahannock. Their
characters followed standard patterns, while the tone of their
writing was oratorical and their action was often melodramatic.
These remained for many years the general traits of Southern
writers. They reflected the drift of the Southern mind towards
a certain unreality that all but invited the shock of the Civil
War.

III. 1850

Philadelphia was the port whence the great stream of Scotch-
Irish settlers had spread through Pennsylvania to the West and
the South, flowing down the Valley of Virginia and covering
the clefts and mountain slopes with red-brick dwellings, ham-
lets, spires and manses. Most of the new Southern leaders
were of Scotch-Irish descent, Calhoun, Toombs, Alexander
Stephens, Jefferson Davis, and theirs was the stock of "Stonewall" Jackson, who was living and teaching at Lexington,
where the blue limestone streets looked hard and grim. So, at
least, thought John S. Wise when he rode over from Richmond
to call on the Presbyterian girls who lived there. He never
forgot their vault-like parlours, the horsehair sofas, the drawn
curtains, the engravings of Oliver Cromwell and the Rock of
Ages. It was all as chilly as a dog's nose, formal, dark and stiff
and very unlike the Virginia in which he was at home.

There was much else, to be sure, in the Valley, where the
novelist John Esten Cooke was born,—he still returned to spend
his summers there,—much that was warm and expansive too,
Virginians of the convivial sort, sportsmen, lovers of scenery,
lovers of horses. This was the region that Spotswood had explored, and Cooke had gathered in his boyhood there from the
country people and village folk many of the stories that appeared in his romances. The Valley, with its green floor, teemed

with historical memories, as thick as the blossoming locusts and the blue-grass verdure, the oaks and the climbing red roses in the quiet gardens, but the suggestion of coldness and grimness that John Wise found in Lexington was also a part of the atmosphere, especially at the moment. While, generally, the Southern way of living was genial, elastic and hearty still, an icy wind blew over the mind of the South, which had grown singularly narrow and bleak in many a notable case as compared with its warmth and breadth in earlier times. It had lost its universality and the spaciousness of feeling that characterized so many of the older statesmen, the sympathetic amplitude that went with Jeffersonianism, which the new Southern thinkers derided or ignored. The day had long since passed when Stephen Girard of Philadelphia named his ships after Voltaire and other free-thinkers, and especially in the Southern states people spoke of deists now as they spoke of thieves and murderers. For the evangelical sects were in power,* and political heresy-hunters were active in a land where people were constrained in their opinions. The liberal old Virginians had yielded to the "cotton snobs," the new-rich cotton planters who reigned over the region and who were determined to spread their empire through Cuba, Mexico and Central America, controlling the government at Washington by acting as a group. With none of the scruples of the older gentry, they bred slaves for the market and presently reopened the long-abandoned slave trade, directing the policy of editors and colleges and churches that had formerly opposed the system, like Calhoun himself. The ministers supported slavery, citing Scripture for it, professors acclaimed and extolled it, citing the classics, and more and more boldly the leaders of thought in the South defended the principle of caste and the law of force.† They vindi-

* The South became, so to speak, officially Calvinistic just at the moment when New England ceased to be so.

† E.g., Thomas R. Dew, William Harper and George Fitzhugh, whose writings suggested at many points the later apologetics of Nazism and Fascism in Europe.

cated the order of nature in which animals preyed on one another and the natural propensity of men to grovel or to rule, and this new Carlylean point of view,—for the vogue of Carlyle was widespread in the South,*—was peremptorily enforced by law or controlled opinion.

It was true that the older type of mind, spacious and humane, survived and even flourished here and there, in the most intolerant regions, moreover, or those where the new thought most prevailed, Calhoun's South Carolina and Mississippi. There was no living American who was more truly a citizen of the world, in the old Jeffersonian way, than Joel R. Poinsett, the Charleston friend of Petigru and William J. Grayson, the poet, who were also opposed to the sectionalism of the adored Calhoun. This first American minister to Mexico retained the universal mind, together with the courtier's manner and the versatile charm, of the days before cotton filled the horizon of the South. In years of travel in his youth he had visited Madame de Staël, studied at Edinburgh, lived for a while in Russia, and in 1811 President Madison had sent him to Chile and Argentina to cultivate friendly relations with these embryo republics. As one of the Americans, like Madison and Clay, for whom their country was ordained to establish an order superior to that of the old world, he encouraged the liberals in these insurgent colonies of Spain on this first of the inter-American "good will" missions. Then Poinsett, as Secretary of War, furthered the exploration of the West, enabling the Charlestonian Frémont to show what he was made of, while he appointed Charles Wilkes to command the South Sea expedition and tried to secure George Catlin's pictures for the nation. A naturalist and an antiquarian, always a patron of learning and art, he had helped Prescott in his work on the Mexican conquest, preserved examples of the Indian crafts, rescued Peruvian manuscripts and made a collection of ancient Mexican sculp-

* The Carlyle admired by these Southern thinkers was the author of *Cromwell* and *Frederick the Great*. It was mainly the author of *Sartor Resartus* who was admired in New England.

ture. Still later, on the Pedee river, he had experimented with grapes and rice, assembling countless specimens of trees and shrubs from all over the world in the park that surrounded his plantation-house. Benjamin L. C. Wailes of Natchez, the Mississippi planter, showed some of his Jeffersonian breadth of mind, although Wailes's interests were those of a naturalist mainly whose father had been one of Audubon's hosts and friends. He studied the aboriginal mounds, collected fish for Agassiz and reptiles, eggs and shells for the Smithsonian Institution, assisted Joseph Leidy in his work on prehistoric life and arranged and conducted an important museum of his own.

No doubt there were many Southerners still of this old and delightful classic type like Wailes of Mississippi and Poinsett of South Carolina, the states that were leading the others in the movement for secession, but certainly the new public men had none of their universality and even Calhoun seemed bigoted and insular beside them. The leaders of the "cotton kingdom" knew little of the world outside and they looked towards Europe chiefly for aid, towards the West merely to extend their power, towards Latin America only as a field of conquest. Too self-absorbed for curiosity, narrow, legalistic, with scarcely a trace of the older disinterested mind, they studied antiquity in the main for the purpose of bolstering their own regime and looked to the future for an endless repetition of the present. They took John Randolph as their model, the enemy of Jefferson, who resented the democratic changes that his kinsman had wrought and who wished to revive primogeniture and entail, while he clung to the past, contemned the West and reverted to an outworn colonialism in matters of culture.

Survivors of the old school were apt to look down on the new politicians, regarding them as partisans rather than statesmen, yet they represented the mind of the region, as the cotton-power had formed it, better perhaps than the novelists and men of letters. Where the mails were closed to dissentient books and agents were punished for selling them, the writers were "tongue-tied by authority," at least in a measure,* and they very seldom rose above the conventional grooves of thought and feeling, while the statesmen, who shared none of their doubts, were bold and frank. The writers, moreover, were not highly esteemed; in fact, they were scarcely respected at all; they were commonly treated with "contumely and a thinly veiled contempt," as Paul Hamilton Hayne observed in a letter. This attitude had never changed since the days when Ralph Izard of South Carolina had been sent as minister to Tuscany in the seventeen-nineties. Finding himself in Paris one evening at Benjamin Franklin's house, in the company of Buffon, Turgot, Condorcet and D'Alembert, he asked, "Why couldn't we have some of the *gentlemen* of France?" Three quarters of a century later, Mrs. Chesnut in her *Diary from Dixie* referred to writers generally as "literary fellows," and the scorn and neglect they had to endure, their discouragements, their embarrassments, were a constant burden of comment in their essays and their letters. They were driven to complain of their isolation, the uncongeniality of the atmosphere, the limited audience at best which the South afforded, conditions that obliged them to publish their work in the North or abroad if they wished it to receive the least attention. The thinkers of the "cotton kingdom" contemplated a great society where art, philosophy and literature were to rise and thrive, while actually the system they sustained still further blighted a literary mind that had scarcely as yet begun to develop in the South. They did not correct the disesteem in which writers had always been held in a region where Hugh Legaré lamented that the literary fame of his earlier days had hampered his pro-

---

* "The Southern Thackeray of the future will doubtless be surprised to learn that if he had put in an appearance half a century sooner he would probably have been escorted beyond the limits and boundaries of our Southern clime astraddle of a rail. Thackeray satirized the society in which he moved and held up to ridicule the hollow hypocrisy of his neighbours. He took liberties with the people of his own blood and time that would have led him hurriedly in the direction of bodily discomfort if he had lived in the South."—Joel Chandler Harris, editorial in the Atlanta *Constitution*, 1879.

fessional advancement and local recognition. It mortified Henry Timrod, the poet, to compare the standing of the Northern writers with the stolid indifference of the Southerners towards their own, while Hayne expressed to Lowell the sadness that he felt when he thought of the literary society of his friends in Boston.

Few and depressed as the writers were,—at least, as they were apt to be whenever they cherished serious aspirations,—they shared John Randolph's tendencies in retiring from national to sectional concerns, in clinging to the past, in reclaiming the heritage of England. At the moment when literature in the North was making its independence good in the name of an autonomous America with a genius of its own, the Southern writers, disconnected from this larger movement of the national mind, resumed their ancestral feeling for the mother-country. They remembered that Shakespeare was inspired to write *The Tempest* by a romantic event in the history of the Dominion, and it pleased the "first families" to give their places English names like "Stonehenge" and to think of the English pimpernel growing in their soil. More than ever the writers dwelt on the cavaliers of colonial times, who appeared in John Esten Cooke's novels, in the train of Caruthers, and they delighted in recalling that the Old Dominion was the oldest community of Englishmen outside England. In their dream of "Southern books written by Southern gentlemen," they repudiated the potent influence of the New England writers, seizing on Poe's remarks discrediting them, although Simms broke only at the last his lifelong friendship with Bryant's circle and Hayne was devoted to Emerson, Whittier and Lowell. The Northern writers were too often tainted with a dangerous anti-slavery feeling. Just so Southerners more and more withdrew from the Northern colleges and schools, to the vast numerical advantage of the colleges of the South, and they travelled at home rather than abroad, rambling through western Virginia, summering in the mountains, visiting the caverns and the springs. They felt a sort of obligation to show the world outside the graces and beauties of the Southland and its picturesqueness, a motive that General Strother shared in his charming *Virginia Illustrated,* the book for which he assumed the name Porte Crayon. He related in this the engaging story of the belle of Cacapon valley, the true Virginia girl Sally Jones, who refused to follow her father west when he sold his fertile ancestral farm and set out for the Rockies, the Pacific, the Columbia river. She offered herself to any young man who had the spunk to ask her to stay, and Porte Crayon did not fail to remark that if all the girls were like Sally Jones the prosperity of the Old Dominion would be permanent and solid. Meanwhile, the new plantation literature, as it was called in later days, became a political instrument of the cotton regime, an apology for it that was also a glorification, and the critical attitude itself was felt to be disloyal after *Uncle Tom's Cabin* appeared in 1852.* Many writers rose at once to give the lie to Mrs. Stowe and to prove that the Southern system was both lovable and just, and scores of "domestic romances" appeared, creating a picture of the South that lingered on for decades and became a legend. They were tales of palatial plantation-houses where all the men were cavaliers and the women exquisite heroines, tender and true, where the slaves were invariably devoted and happy and visiting Yankees were abashed and amazed by a culture that had never been heard of in benighted New England.

This rapturous vision of the Southern romancers was destined to survive the Civil War,—in which flags were commonly described as oriflammes,—and it sprang partly from the need of defending the South in the face of a world that was hostile to Southern institutions. It was true too that the new-rich

---

* The editor of the *Southern Literary Messenger* wrote as follows to the reviewer of this book: "I would have the review as hot as hellfire, blasting and searing the reputation of the vile wretch in petticoats who could write such a volume."

The obsession of slavery completely dominated the critical mind. For another instance, Webster's Dictionary was ostracized in Tennessee because of its definition of a slave as "a person subject to the will of another, a drudge."—See F. G. Davenport, *Cultural Life in Nashville, 1825–1860.*

planters wished the writers to create a noble Southern past that enhanced their prestige. Yet this was only half the story,— there were other elements behind the vision,—it conventionalized much that was actual, authentic, true. The convention was largely shaped by Scott, whom Southerners especially idolized, and other historians and romancers of the feudal world,— Froissart, for one, a favourite of the Southern writers,—and it gained its power not merely because it expressed an ideal of the South but because it corresponded in a fashion with the realities of life there. Ancient ways survived there, vestigial remains of earlier times, and in many respects the region was still genuinely feudal, while, as Thackeray observed when he visited Richmond in 1856, the Virginians were more like the English than Americans elsewhere. They had remained more like the English because their life had changed less and because their American nationality had never been very real to them as compared with their allegiance and devotion to the region, to the state. The Revolution, for the South, had been much more political than social and had left the old order largely as it was before, while the industrial revolution that severed the link with the feudal past had touched the South even less, far less, than England. The gentry in the older states had carried on without a break immemorial customs that had long since vanished elsewhere, and tournaments were held as annual events in Maryland, Virginia and South Carolina in spite of the disapprobation of the killjoy preachers. Young men tilted on decorated steeds and the Queen of Love and Beauty, surrounded by her maids of honour, crowned the victor, a relic of the antique fairs that vanished as the rising puritanism more and more steadily blighted the gaieties of old. Fox-hunting remained a pastime not of the fashionable few alone but of many a simple old country doctor also, who was passionately fond of the chase and kept his own hounds, while men of spirit followed the *code duello*, in perfect good faith, well into the seventies and beyond. Certain of these customs were revived artificially in later days and much of the mediævalism was factitious in the fifties, worked up to lend an air to the new regime, as the so-called domestic romances showed only the amenities of Southern life, dissembling or glossing whatever was unjust or unpleasant. But the feudal note in these romances existed here and there in fact, and Scott was really closer to this old plantation world than writers who spoke for the nineteenth century elsewhere. When the Southern ruling class called itself "the chivalry," it challenged the wit of others who were less self-immersed, though Southerners were generally cavaliers in the most primitive sense, at least,—they spent much of their lives on horseback, always armed. And as for their dream of chivalrous times, one saw how genuine it could be when Sidney Lanier set out for the Civil War, a Georgian who had been brought up on Scott and Froissart in his father's house and thought of himself as a knight who was also a minstrel. He saw in himself, in all sincerity, a troubadour wandering about the world, with a lute and the ribbon of his lady-love slung on his back. The fact that the lute was a flute did not alter the vision.

These actual Southern states of mind and these customs and modes of behaviour, together with the singular characters who expressed and upheld them, appeared occasionally in the books of the time, enough to excite one's regret that literature so failed to do justice to life in the South. Would not readers in later days have given much for a genius of the fifties, a Virginia Turgenev, a Gogol of South Carolina, who could have amplified the glimpses that actual writers conveyed of the picturesque, noble or fantastic people of the South? What made many of these characters so striking was that they lived in a timeless world, a society that was little touched by modern conditions, so that they embodied traits of the eighteenth, seventeenth, sixteenth centuries, either wholly unaltered or so altered as to be still more striking. There was William Walker, for one example, the filibuster from Tennessee, a well-trained surgeon who had studied medicine in Paris, in whom all the accretions of the modern man merely threw into bolder relief a character that properly belonged in Elizabethan times. Half-consciously an agent of the cotton kingdom that aspired to be an empire, this latter-day Cortes had much of the original in him, and Sam Houston had still more of the ancient swash-buckler in a composition that savoured, like so many others, of the militant South. Knight-errantry and quixotism throve on every hand there, ideals of the moment were mingled with ideals of the past, and men could be taken for practical leaders who ignored in their dream of romance the most essential elements in the situation. Robert Barnwell Rhett, for instance, was wholly oblivious of economics when he strove to make South Carolina an independent nation: he proposed to liberate it as Perseus freed Andromeda, and he thought of this purely in terms of knightly prowess. The romantic type of the soldier of fortune existed in the North, of course, in stirring figures like Samuel Gridley Howe, the champion of the Greek revolution and later of the Poles, but it seemed more congruous with the South when James J. Pettigrew, the Charleston lawyer, fought for the "sacred liberty" of the Italians. For the Southerners were generally less given to counting costs. It was part of their code to think of life as something to be "put in risk," as Shaler said, "in the pursuit of manly ideals," and this explained the violence of the South, and some of its courtliness too, survivals of the seventeenth century or the Middle Ages. By no means defending this violence, the Kentuckian Shaler pointed out how much that was obviously admirable lay behind it, how much could be said for a view of life as something to be recklessly cast away for honour, for a generous impulse or the merest whim. This careless irresponsible indifference to life had characterized the greatest ages, which had given more nobility and ability to history than others, and one might have said that the burden of proof lay rather on the modern concern for continued mundane existence at any price. Sometimes blackguardly, often rowdy, especially along the frontier, where it merged with the border ruffianism of the unsettled regions, this headiness and touchiness was a genuine survival of the chivalrous life that appeared in a variety of types all over the South. Many different points of view had chivalrous defenders there, and the deadliest of all the foes of slavery was also a Southerner born and bred, the first candidate of the new Republican party. Frémont in 1856 brought to the abolitionist cause the ardour with which others championed the Southern system. He fought for the freedom of the Negroes as he would have fought for Jerusalem if he had lived in the days of the Crusaders.

Bizarre or noble, these provocative types seldom appeared on the printed page, not merely because there was no one with the genius to describe them. It did not interest Southerners to read about themselves or people they knew and encountered in their ordinary living, and this alone was enough to discourage the writers. There were many readers like Mrs. Lightfoot in Ellen Glasgow's *The Battle-ground* who detested Dickens's common chimney-sweeps, while, weeping as they did over *Thaddeus of Warsaw,* they would scarcely have preferred realistic pictures of people they admired and respected. They were not given to analysis or the discussion of motives, and nothing could have bored them more than to read about the life they were living with such cheerful insouciance every day. In books they looked for something else, for something far away from home that left the placid flow of their minds unruffled, something that savoured of the past, of England, of a stable unchanging social scene that was undisturbed by new ideas or "progress."

It was related that John M. Daniel, the best-known Richmond editor, had a "sovereign contempt for the so-called 'literature of the day,'" and in this he reflected the general feeling of a world in which letters to the press were still universally signed "Vox Populi" and "Scrutator." The Charleston Library, piled to the ceiling with venerable works in morocco and calf, contained, as the librarian said, "but few new books," and the pleasant little "neighbourhood libraries" in the country, established for the families of the planters, were seldom invaded by nineteenth-century authors. Only a few old French books were mingled with the dust that covered the fine editions of the English classics; and this was true also in private houses where men who still wore ruffles and wigs read Addison aloud in the evenings while the ladies embroidered. They discussed the question whether Fanny Burney, undoubtedly the greatest, was not also the last female novelist who would probably appear,—for who was there since her day worthy to hold a descriptive pen and what had been written since that was worth one's reading? Old gentlemen recited Swift with the zest of a schoolboy, or perhaps two hundred lines from *The Rape of the Lock*, quoting Spence's anecdotes, the maxims of La Rochefoucauld and the letters of Madame de Sévigné and the witty Walpole. They questioned their nephews and grandsons, who had returned from the grand tour, about Westminster Abbey, St. Paul's and the London streets. Had they remembered to look up the haunts of Steele and Goldsmith? Was Dr. Johnson's coffee-house still open for guests? Anything more modern than *Bracebridge Hall* or *Swallow Barn* was likely to have too much "nature" in it, which had nothing to do with literature that one called polite, and men who were faithful to the classic muse continued to model their own lucubrations on the writings of Matthew Prior, Shenstone or Johnson. When the Charleston poet Grayson was asked to mend a lady's quill, he returned it as a matter of course with a copy of verses, and *The Bee* was in Mr. Turner's mind when he established *The Countryman* as late as 1860 on his Georgia plantation. This was the weekly on which Joel Chandler Harris, who was twelve years old that year, learned to set type. In the most enlightened Southern circles Wordsworth was a bone of contention still when that question had been settled in New England for thirty years, and Grayson attacked the "hypocrites" who dared to disparage the poet Pope in the book that he wrote on Petigru in 1863. Timrod was one of these hypocrites, the brightest of the younger Charleston minds, who constantly lamented the "backwardness" of the literary South.

Despite these many handicaps, more books than ever were appearing in the South, for the abolition movement roused its literary consciousness and put the Southern authors on their mettle. Of these books many were merely defensive; others teased the imagination,—unhappily, they could not satisfy it,— with flashes that illumined the scene and the people at moments. In Miss Wormeley's novel *Our Cousin Veronica* one caught delightful glimpses of certain of the "visiting Virginians" and their drawing-rooms and houses, Clairmont and the seat of Governor Tyrell, the courtly old survivor, in his feelings, tastes and habits, of Jefferson's times. Who could forget the dinner-party, with the governor himself as the Lord of Misrule, that so surprised the decorous English cousin, at which there were twenty-eight chairs for thirty-five guests, for the host was "too genuine a Virginian" to count them in advance? What most amused the alien observer was the total change from foreign ways, the absence of city airs and modern conventions, the jokes, the merriment unconfined, the guests that foraged for themselves while a crowd of Negroes scrambled round the table. Everything was at sixes and sevens, with the small darkies dodging about, while over all the gaiety and humour that recalled a mediæval feast the distinguished old governor presided with stately grace. The drawing-room at Clairmont was littered with oboes and flageolets, flutes, fiddles and guitars that all the cousins played, too busy and happy with picnics and cards, horses, dogs, hunting and talk to bother their heads with books or the writing of letters. There was always a place at the breakfast-table for the kindly old tailor Mr. Felix, who passed from house to house in summer and winter cutting out clothes for the Negroes and who was admitted without apology to any circle at any time in this world where so few existed between the nobles and the serfs.

What would Aksakov not have done with these patriarchal scenes that were so much the same in Russia as they were in the South, true survivals of a feudal world that appeared in *The Two Country Houses,* Philip Pendleton Cooke's skeleton of a novel? This tale of the Hunters of Winisfalen and the Cars of Cotsworth owed something,—the banshee perhaps,—to the author's reading, but the wild young heir, the stable-boys, the generous old magnifico were authentic reflections of the place, the people and the time. So was the splendid hospitality and the mean little family attorney who might have stepped straight out of Hogarth or Sterne. But Cooke, who wrote on scraps of paper that he carried on his hunting trips, stowed in his hat, for gun-wadding, was too casual and careless, too much the spendthrift Southerner to develop the sketch, and most of the books remained unwritten that might have given after times an adequate and veritable picture of the ways of the South. Most memorable of all perhaps, *Memorials of a Southern Planter,* the life of Colonel Dabney of Mississippi, a Virginian who had moved southwestward in 1835, published after the Civil War, remained the classic story of the model country gentleman of the old regime. The narrative was interspersed with letters relating the daily life at Burleigh, the great plantation near Vicksburg where the children grew up with governesses and music-teachers, Belgian and German, and with Negro "aunts" and "uncles" who were cherished as if they were nearest of kin, while the colonel with fatherly care watched over all. The archetypal "good master," stricter with his children than he was with his servants, a passionate lover of music, affectionate and kind, he was always ready to sign notes for friends who were sometimes untrustworthy or present a sick pedlar with a horse to help him on his way. This was the nobly courteous Dabney, ruined by the war, all too confiding as he was and as generous as proud, who after he was seventy performed the household laundry-work, for he could not permit his five daughters to do manual labour.

IV. 1870

A number of writers from the South, unknown or famous, old and young, appeared in New York after the Civil War, finding that there was no place at home for men of their complexion in the general devastation of the Southern plantations and towns. Among them was John R. Thompson, the poet, who had edited *The Index* in London,—the journal of Confederate propaganda,—during the war, and who had returned to Richmond from England in 1866 in the vain hope of finding employment there. Within two or three years he was literary editor of Bryant's *Evening Post*, and he and the poet of *Thanatopsis* toured Cuba together. George Cary Eggleston soon arrived, Edward Eggleston's Virginian brother who also became a literary editor in New York, with Dr. George Bagby, who observed, "Baronial Virginia is dead. Ilium, nor Carthage, nor Thebes is more so." John Esten Cooke appeared as well, and the young poet Sidney Lanier came up from Alabama, where he was teaching, with the manuscript of a novel called *Tiger Lilies,* while at about the same time the veteran William Gilmore Simms was trying to reëstablish his career in New York. The metropolis was tolerant as it was large: two laudatory lives of Stonewall Jackson had been published in New York during the war, with several others books by Southern writers, and there had been no protests from the government about it. Then, as Whitman said, while New York was a bad place for literary farming, it was a good market for the harvest.

Other Southerners flocked to Baltimore, "that almost sole harbour of refuge," as a later writer called it,—the town was half Southern,—where "Little Aleck" Stephens was to live for a while, the Confederate vice-president whose career was so far from finished. Richard Malcolm Johnston, who had lost the whole of his large estate, settled there as a schoolmaster in 1867, and Sidney Lanier and Basil L. Gildersleeve joined him there a few years later when both were teaching at the new university, Johns Hopkins. The novelist and poet Maurice Thompson moved from Georgia to Indiana, and the geologist Joseph Le Conte, after teaching in Georgia and South Carolina, joined the hegira to California in 1869. There this old student of Agassiz opened his well-known career as a teacher in Berkeley. The great diaspora had begun in the desperate South. Thousands of ex-Confederate soldiers thronged to the Pacific coast, drawn by the appeal of cheap land and the spirit of adventure that were bred by the war and the ruin of the farms of the South, while others, in the disorganization of institutions and property alike, emigrated to various foreign countries. There were those who went to Paris or to London, where the former Confederate Secretary of State, Judah P. Benjamin, established himself as a lawyer and Robert Toombs also lived for a while as an exile. Five ex-Confederates became officers in the Egyptian army. Many left for Mexico, Brazil and Venezuela, which had offered them land and the hope of prosperity with it. A colony of Southerners settled in the coffee region of Brazil and another from Alabama went to Honduras, where some were so shocked by the intimate relations of the Negroes and the whites that they were happy to return to the United States. The great oceanographer Matthew F. Maury, who had gone to Mexico, made plans for the establishment of a new Virginia there. As imperial commissioner for Maximilian, he pictured the good fortune of prominent ex-Confederates who had already joined him.

But with all these movements hither and thither the vast majority remained at home, for all the misery and havoc and waste of a time that was worse in many ways than the years of the war, following the example of the great-hearted Lee, who discouraged Maury's plan and who never knew "one moment of bitterness or resentment." His only answer when English noblemen offered him houses and large estates was that he could never leave Virginia in her time of trial, and, urging "silence and patience on the part of the South," he looked for some quiet little dwelling with a farm in the woods. Then, mounted on "Traveller," he rode off to the Valley of Virginia where he had accepted the presidency of a half-ruined old college. He was only too happy to play his part in educating the future South, while he advised his sons on the problems of farming, admiring and honouring his fellow-officers, affluent once, who were cheerful now as porters perhaps or as farmers who did their own ploughing. One of them was grateful that, having lost one of his arms, he had a chance to use the arm that was left. There were many other sons of planters who drove pie-wagons and warehouse-drays, peddled wood for fires and moulded bricks, while their plantations went back to forest or were reduced to two-mule farms and the broomsedge and the scrub-oak grew over the fields and the ruins.

From Harper's Ferry to New Market the country was a desert, virtually eighty miles without a fence or a horse, with roofless dwellings, burned barns and chimneys without houses, while vast regions of other states were scorched, dilapidated, trodden by war, and the old mansions had vanished or were tenantless wrecks. One saw them in South Carolina and Georgia, battered, with windows fallen in, rifts in the bricks and plaster lying on the steps, perhaps with a wing that was occupied by a swarm of gaunt poor whites who greeted the passer-by with a vacant stare. As for the destitute "quality folk" who had never thought of money in their lives, they were unable to think of it even now, though they did not know how in the world to get on without it, and, powerless as they were to improve things, they could only endure. They had been quite content to leave the shipyards and the foundries and the coalmines to the North, proud that the South had few arsenals, factories, machine-shops, proud that Southerners had never stooped to trade, mechanics or engineering and had never been anything but soldiers, planters and statesmen. They could no longer be soldiers now, and simple farming was all that was left to the lords of the soil who had ruled the Southern world,—who had all but ruled the nation, at Washington, for decades,—and politics were closed to them by laws that gave votes to their former slaves and disfranchised all ex-Confederates, whether soldiers or civilians. The "bottom rail" was "on top" and the struggle to restore the top rail to its former position was to form the "Solid South" in these years of unrest, when the spoilsmen of the North and the carpet-baggers, with the lib-

erated Negroes, repressed the political life of the old master-
class. The Southern whites were helpless in the presence of
this alien horde, together with their own bushwhackers, de-
serters and outlaws, and the Ku Klux Klan inevitably rose to
provide them indirectly with political work and reëstablish, if
possible, the supremacy of the whites. With its emblem of the
fiery cross, its uniform of sheets and pillow-cases, its masks and
infantile mummery that frightened the Negroes, it undertook
to "regulate" a region it could not control by law and retrieve
for the disfranchised overlords the power they had lost. The
force of the revolt was proportional to the strength of a
thwarted political sense that was almost a primary instinct with
the people of the South.

In a future that was not too remote the South of broken fortunes was to bring forth writers far better than those of the
past,—with the exception of Poe and two or three others,—
proving again that, as Ernest Renan observed about this time,
"Discomfort is the principle of movement." The old South of
the articulate class had been too happy, too satisfied merely to
exist, to bestir its mind. On the other hand, these violent years
of chaos, ruin and destitution, these years that preceded recon-
struction, were too much for the writers. Many had been
Confederate soldiers,—Timrod, Hayne, George Eggleston, Lanier, George W. Cable, Gildersleeve, Maurice Thompson,—
and many were adrift after suffering the miseries of war. Some
were even homeless, and all were obliged to construct again a
basis on which to exist before they could hope for any calm of
mind. Simms's plantation-house The Woodlands had been destroyed by fire, though in this case the Northern general had
given orders for the place to be spared, saying, "Simms and
his fame belong to the Union." The house and the great library
had been burned by the Negroes after the Federal troops had
left the region, but gone it was, like Paul Hamilton Hayne's
fine house in Charleston, which had been burned to the
ground in the bombardment of the town. Maurice Thompson's
house was in ashes, Richard Malcolm Johnston was poor and

Henry Timrod was walking the streets in 1866, "weak for the want of a good meal," as he wrote to a friend. He had tried to open a school in Charleston, but no one could pay his tuition-fees, and he had asked Hayne what were the prospects in New York,—was there any chance of his finding employment there? His family was reduced to "beggary, starvation, death," and he was willing to be a grocer's clerk or a hack-writer on a third-rate paper. Timrod was "swallowed up in distresses," Simms wrote to Hayne, lonely as he also was and dying of consumption,—the manuscript of his translation of Catullus had been lost,—while Hayne was scarcely better off, camping out as he said he was in the "shanty" he had built in the woods not far from Augusta. He could not send his son to school, a Christmas turkey was a dream of the past and the children saw plum-puddings only in visions, but at least he was able to work on serenely while his wife papered the little house and made chairs, tables, bookcases, benches and lampstands. He cherished the autographs on the walls of Simms and Timrod, who came to see him, enraptured by the sight of new books in this literary dwelling,—so few had been seen in the South during the war-years. For Hayne was in touch with the publishers and continued to write: some of his best verse was written on this windy hill. In much of this, he followed Tennyson, the poet whose idylls of the feudal world appealed as deeply to the Southern mind as Scott, exhaling as he did the feeling of caste, revelling in traditions of knights and chivalry and the splendour that fell on ivied castle walls. It was there Hayne collected the poems of Timrod in 1873 when he was himself the oracle of the younger writers. He inspired Lanier with a faith in his own vocation.

But the veterans Hayne and Simms were exceptional cases. As Lanier wrote to Bayard Taylor, "With us of the younger generation of the South . . . pretty much the whole of life has been merely not dying," and most of them were a long time getting under way. The magazines of the South were dead, readers were fewer than ever and writers were driven to work for quick returns, and they were therefore apt to turn to rapid, shallow story-telling and the hasty historical writing that was required at the moment. For they were asked and they naturally wished to justify the Southern cause and uphold the ideals of the Confederacy for the world of the future. This was the motive of John Esten Cooke in his lives of Lee and Stonewall Jackson and the novels *Mohun* and *Surry of Eagle's-Nest* in which he continued his earlier work as a romancer.

With a present that one could scarcely face and without any visible future, only the past was tolerable to the Southern mind, and this came to seem all the more wonderful in contrast to the sordid facts that were virtually identical with reality in these years of trial. The so-called "plantation tradition" had been clearly established before the war, partly by way of defence of the cotton regime, and it bloomed afresh with the younger writers and with Southern novelists for decades to come who were under the spell of the cause that was lost with the war. It was scarcely checked by the critical mind that carried weight with the Northern writers who developed the methods of realism during these years, for, unlike Howells and Henry James, the Southerners were not open to the thinking of Europe or Matthew Arnold's ideas of the "provincial" and the "centre." In its dearth of new books the South missed Matthew Arnold, whose essays were appearing in the war-years and immediately after,* and it remained quite unaware of its own provinciality and the fertilizing doctrine of seeing things "as they are." The Southerners, moreover, had not been given to travelling as much as the Northerners travelled; they seldom saw their country in the light of others, while, as for their own past, the cynosure of the Southern mind, they knew this mainly through personal memories alone, through household stories that were

---

* "The current literature of those three or four years was a blank to most Confederates. Few books got across the line."—Basil L. Gildersleeve, *The Creed of the Old South*. Arnold's *Essays in Criticism* was published in 1865, and many of his other important prose writings appeared in the years following the war when the impoverished Southerners bought few books.

handed down by fable-loving aunts in place of the impersonal records, for example, of New England. St. George Tucker had pointed out that the lives of the old Virginian worthies had never been observed by their contemporaries, by diarists and thinkers: their talk had never been recorded, no "chiel" among them had taken notes or even collected their speeches in time to preserve them. Hayne made the same remark in Charleston, speaking of the times of Hugh Legaré, when he wrote his sketch of this worthy in 1869, referring to the "fast-waning traditions" of the days of the fame and prosperity of the town through whose streets he "shrank," as he said, "like a stranger and alien." Culture, refinement, hospitality, wit, genius and social virtue had seemed to have taken up their lasting abode there; and he saw that Legaré had prophesied truly when he said, "We are, I am quite sure, the last of the race of South Carolina." But what Hayne regretted most, now that the orators and statesmen were gone, was that their names and fame were perishing too, for their words had scarcely been recorded and their lives were unwritten. Calhoun lived in his writings still, but Legaré was the only other exception,—his works alone had ever been gathered together. A generation later, Boston men were also to lament the passing of the prestige of their city, but at least the Bostonians had amply attested their progress and were always to know whereof they spoke. In the South much of the reality of the past was utterly forgotten or swallowed up and blurred and confused by legend. Because it was not really known, it was idealized the more and lent itself to a singularly deceptive treatment.

Thus for years the Southern writers were marked by a curious unreality that led to a kind of revenge on the part of their successors. What Mark Twain called the "Sir Walter disease," which had, he said, so large a hand in making the Southern character before the war,—so that "in great measure" Scott was "responsible for the war,"—this disease raged still in the unreconstructed South in manners, names and customs as well as in books. Mark Twain, a Southerner himself, in full revolt against the South and its "maudlin middle-age romanticisms," as he described them, poked fun at its "absurd chivalry business" although to the end of his life he retained the peculiar sensibility that characterized it. For was not his feeling for Joan of Arc precisely the chivalrous feeling and quite in the vein of a man of Joan's own time? He said the South needed another Cervantes and attempted the role several times, when he pictured in *The American Claimant,* for instance, the Rowena-Ivanhoe College where Sally Sellers was known as Gwendolen. The South was full of these castellated buildings with towers, turrets and an imitation moat and with everything redolent of royalty and names out of Scott. As for Colonel Sellers, who thought of himself as the Earl of Rossmore, he was a Southern mediævalist on the Western frontier. Mark Twain liked to contrast this "chivalry" with the facts of life as he saw them in the South,—in the newspaper-clippings he took such pleasure in assembling,—the duels with butcher-knives fought in Virginia, the braining of a man with a club, the murder of a general and his son on the street in Tennessee. Later in *A Connecticut Yankee in King Arthur's Court* he attacked these mediævalist notions directly. Meanwhile, in *The Galaxy,* he described in 1870 a tournament that was held in Virginia during that year in which knights of the Shenandoah and the Blue Ridge with tinsel decorations and broomstick lances exhibited, he said, an "absurdity gone crazy." What could he think of modern men who accepted the mailed and plumed knight of romance while rejecting the unpolished verdict whereby history exposed him as an ignoramus, a ruffian and a braggart?

Perhaps only a Southerner could have been so angry with all these illusions of the Southern mind. But in satirizing daydreams that replaced realities at a time when so much that was real was far too distasteful for many to look in the face, Mark Twain anticipated the feeling of a later generation. Even the Confederacy had been a kind of day-dream,—except in so far as it spoke for the interests of cotton,—for the states, Virginia, South Carolina, Louisiana and all the rest, were the real ob-

jects of the passionate devotion it aroused. Its vision of the
future had scarcely more substance than Sidney Lanier's vision
of Macon as a great art-centre whose streets were to be lined
with statues. Lanier was one of a host of Southerners who
lived in a world of make-believe and his peculiar fantasies
typified the South, from the days when he organized the
Macon Archers and drilled them as Froissart said he should, to
the days when he shared in a tournament in 1879. When, two
years before his death, he addressed the "knights" in the Shenandoah valley, charging them "to do after the good and leave
the evil, and ever to live nobly in the service of their fair
ladies," was he not still living in the fantasy-world in which
he had drilled the Macon boys who thought of themselves as
English bowmen of Crécy? * When Burke felt, during the
French Revolution, that the age of chivalry was gone, his feeling was closely connected with historical fact, but with what
did the feeling of Lanier connect when he repeated this remark
at another historical juncture seventy years later? In convincing
himself that he was descended from a family of Laniers who
were court musicians and artists of the Stuart kings, was he
less willingly duped than Colonel Sellers, who held his supposititious earldom by as good a right? The biographers of
J. E. B. Stuart, the "Flower of Cavaliers," who asserted that
he was a lineal descendant of Prince Rupert revealed a type of
the will-to-believe that flourished like broomsedge in the South,
where the aspect of things "as they are" was so generally
ignored. Was it not ignored because the Southerners had lived
apart and remote from the world, unvisited, unvisiting, rapt in

---

* Another Southern poet, Maurice Thompson, and his brother were
the principal agents in the revival of the modern sport of archery.
Thompson, who wrote *Alice of Old Vincennes,* was the author of several
books about it, *The Witchery of Archery* among them, which led people to welcome archery as a real sport at a time when croquet was the
only outdoor game.

Maurice Thompson's poems, like Lanier's, were full of images drawn
in all probability from his reading of Froissart, cross-bows, old yew
bows, "the flaunting flag and the crashing lance," tournaments and
troubadours, Crécy and Agincourt.

their impracticable dream?—at the core of which lay an ugly fact, which sensitive people could not face, and had never faced, "as it was," with its ramifications. When by chance in Alabama Mrs. Chesnut of the *Diary from Dixie* saw a Negress sold on the auction-block, the spectacle made her, as she said, "faint" and "seasick." She had to sit down to discipline her "wild thoughts." How far had she realized what slavery meant when one glimpse of the naked reality could have shaken a mind as clear and firm as hers?

Thus the "plantation tradition" had thriven in the days that made the old South an "unfinished fairy-story," as a later writer called it, and it continued to thrive in days when the fairy-story was finished indeed but no new theme had arisen to possess the mind. Southern society in many respects still suggested the masquerade that W. C. Falkner described in *The White Rose of Memphis,* a vastly popular mystery-story about a voyage down the Mississippi from Memphis to New Orleans a few years after the war. The steamboat-company had organized it to amuse the passengers, who wore masks and fancy costumes, concealing their names, picnicking on the banks at landings while the cotton was loaded on the boat, strolling in the beech-groves and dancing on the greensward. The queen held her court on board and young ladies who knew *Lalla Rookh* by heart acted scenes from *Mazeppa* with the young men, while they were all disguised as Ingomar, Ivanhoe, Sir Walter Raleigh and other knights and ladies of chivalrous times. Behind the masks a real drama went on that involved a murderer and a desperado who were disguised with the others in the general rout, and here too the masquerade suggested the reality of Southern society that one saw when William Faulkner stripped away the masks. One could not say that this great-grandson of the author of *The White Rose of Memphis* saw only the murderer and the desperado,* but he saw more than one might have seen of old men who nail themselves up in

---

* In *Absalom, Absalom,* for instance, a novel of a period and setting closely corresponding with those of *The White Rose of Memphis.*

attics and aunts who slide down rain-pipes and run off with horse-traders; and this would never have been the case perhaps if the South had been more realistic in earlier days. In those times Southern gentlewomen were almost invariably pictured in fiction with exquisite hands always folded in their laps, when they were often as busy in fact as Eliza Pinckney of South Carolina who at sixteen transacted the business of three plantations. This was the lady two of whose sons were generals in the Revolution and who changed the whole face of the province when she discovered that indigo could be grown there with profit, when, versed in the difficult art of raising it, she distributed seeds to the other planters whose houses she visited on the rivers in her long canoe. Six Negroes swung the paddles, singing in cadence. Eliza Pinckney experimented with ginger, observed the habits of the mocking-birds and showed a fine taste in music and in poetry too, happy to find that, writing for Italy, Virgil had many times over written in a way that suited Carolina as well. For, entertained by his charming pen and what she called his pleasing diction, she studied agriculture also in this Roman poet. He would have delighted in turn in such a reader.

There were never many Eliza Pinckneys, but there were countless women in the South who were far more stirring than the phantoms that appeared in the romances, in which the men were so often Byronic like the gloomy and world-weary Mordaunt, with his taste for Arabic, in *Surry of Eagle's-Nest*. Mysterious and grand, with his dark proud eyes, Mordaunt was another St. Elmo Murray, the hero of the romance that bore his name. The author of this was Augusta J. Evans of Mobile, where Henry Timrod met her when he was a war-correspondent with General Beauregard's army in Alabama. St. Elmo, fierce, cynical, morose, had a basilisk's eye, and his midnight orgies and habitual excesses had stamped his Mephistophelean face, while his evil charm was as powerful as his unhallowed mind. The costly *bizarrerie* of his house in Georgia suggested Lucanian Sybaris, opulent and vast as it was, with

its Egyptian museum, its vaulted passages, high Gothic windows, Moresque frescoes, rotunda and park that was filled with
rare animals from Lapland, India and Peru. His favourite horse,
called Tamerlane, had been brought by him from the Kirghese
steppes on one of the long journeys that led him to the back
of beyond, and the whisperings of his conscience were as faint
and unexpected as the dim reverberating echoes from Morella's
tomb. But there was a core of nobility in him, as one might
have guessed, which Edna, the precious little prig, brought out
in the end. Edna, a prodigy of learning too, with her Greek,
Hebrew and Chaldee, was a mistress of Norse myths, runes,
scalds and sagas as well as the writings of Machiavelli,—so like
St. Elmo in his way,—and of archæology, ethnology, philology
and what not. She became a great and famous novelist whom
amorous baronets pursued at intervals when infatuated editors
left her alone.

Of all the Southern romances of the time *St. Elmo* was the
hugest success,—towns, hotels, steamboats and plantations were
named for the book,—the Cinderella story of the little barefoot
Tennessee girl who won "all this and heaven too." For Edna
was a prodigy of virtue as well as of learning, and the fantasy,
which recalled *Jane Eyre,* was obviously Southern: there was
something of John Randolph as of Rochester in the character
of the hero. In his Gothic madness he even suggested Poe's
Roderick Usher. Moreover, the picture of the Georgian village
with its coterie of "blues" was a Southerner's reply to the claims
of triumphant New England,* to which,—or New York,—her
countrypeople had been taunted with having to resort for their
French and German books, for the opera and for pictures. St.
Elmo himself preferred to read the London papers, having no
use whatever for *"soi-disant* republics." The story had been
shaped in every way to please the Southern public in the year
that followed the defeat of 1865, when few would have wel-

* As St. Elmo scornfully remarked, "Not even egoistic, infallible
'Brain Town,'—that self-complacent and pretentious 'Hub,'—can show a
more ambitious covey of literary fledglings."

comed the pictures of life that sprang from the realities of the local scene which certain writers were to produce in time. These writers were to take a savage joy in cutting the wires of the puppet-show that others had created so fondly in their heyday of illusions.

Characters

CHARACTERS

POE

Edgar Allan Poe had spent five years of his childhood in England. Then he had grown up in Richmond as a ward of John Allan, the merchant, whose wife was the daughter of one of the Virginia planters. Edgar, petted and rather spoiled, with his air of a Little Lord Fauntleroy, graceful, exceptionally handsome, winning in manner, had become an imperious older boy, a capital horseman, fencer and shot and a leader of the other boys at his school in Richmond. He swam in the river James one day six miles against the tide. Devoted to music, he played a flute, he wrote good Latin verses, he even had more than a little talent for drawing. He made a charming sketch of one of the young girls in Richmond, and his friends later remembered the skill with which he drew fanciful pictures in charcoal on the ceiling and walls of his room at Charlottesville. These drawings were suggested by a number of illustrations for Byron, the favourite poet of all the Virginia young men. Thomas Sully, a friend of the Allans, painted a portrait of Poe in a cloak in one of the romantic postures associated with Byron.

By 1826, when Poe was sent to the university, he was erect, pale, slender and seventeen, with large, grey, luminous, liquid eyes, a brow of the sort that was often called noble and the manners of a well brought-up young man. One might have taken him for the type of the *jeunesse dorée* of Virginia, surrounded with tutors, servants, horses and dogs, with clothes of the best that the tailors of Richmond afforded, and he was regarded in fact as the heir of one of the richest men in the state, for Allan, who had no legitimate children, had recently inherited a fortune of something round three quarters of a million dollars. The large, new, luxurious house of the Allans, with its empire furniture and busts by Canova and the spacious octagonal parlour on the second floor, left traces in some of the writings of Poe, who thought of it as home long after he had lost the right to live there. Along with the Medici Venus and the Etruscan vases, there was a niche on the stairs with an agate lamp, and a telescope stood on the balcony through which Poe gazed at the constellations whose beautiful names were scattered through his poems. Later he studied astronomy, as one might have guessed from reading his tales, but he knew the Pleiades as a boy in Richmond, "Astarte's bediamonded crescent" and the mountains of the moon. For the rest, he had always been thrown with the sons of the cultivated lawyers and planters who rode about the streets on their blooded horses. Most of the larger Richmond houses, with porticoes and pillars, reflected the classical feeling that prevailed in the town, where the clerk of the House of Delegates was translating the Iliad during these years and lawyers often carried in their pockets a Cicero or a Horace. On Sundays, at the Episcopal church, Poe sat behind Chief Justice Marshall, and he must have seen Madison too on a visit to town, while John Randolph sold some of his tobacco through Mr. Allan's agency and all but certainly appeared occasionally at the warehouse. One evening, as a little boy, Poe romped with General Winfield Scott at a party in the house of the Allans. Taken twice to the Virginia springs, he visited his foster-mother's plantation as well as the Allan plantation at Lower Byrd's, where he heard weird tales in the slave-quarters, whither his mammy took him, about graveyards, apparitions, corpses and spooks. His childhood was bathed indeed in the grotesquerie of the Negroes, which also certainly left traces in some of his tales, while he heard other stories of exploits at sea and adventures in the West, related by merchants and mariners who dined with the Allans. For the firm supplied some of the Western settlements with blankets, rum and powder and imported a variety of goods from England and Europe,—the docks were crowded with barques and square-riggers, and Poe knew ships and the ways of sailors, as one soon saw in his *Narrative of A. Gordon Pym.* This was the tale that might have been written, in part at least, by Fenimore Cooper and that placed Poe also in the age of *Moby-Dick.* He had crossed the ocean twice, besides sailing from Scotland to London, and he soon took several voyages on army transports. If, throughout his later life, Poe thought of Richmond as his home, it was because of the happiness he had known there as a child.

For, on the whole, he appeared to be a normal, healthy, lively boy, orderly in his way of living, punctilious in dress, and the professors at Charlottesville, as long as he was permitted to stay there, regarded him as well-behaved and a model student. The university had been opened only the previous year, the rotunda, the serpentine walls and the terraces were new, and, as Jefferson was still alive, Poe must have seen him often,—indeed, he probably dined at Monticello. For all the students were invited in rotation on Sundays. He certainly heard the bell toll for the death of the "American Confucius," whose wisdom, for the rest, meant nothing to Poe; for this brilliant young man, who cared little for politics, shared none of Jefferson's beliefs and even considered democracy a delusion and an evil. His writings were to bristle with allusions to the "rabble" and the "canaille," to democracy as an "admirable form of government—for dogs," to voting as "meddling" with public affairs and republican government as "rascally," while they also expressed the contempt of the writer for "reform cranks" and "progress mongers." Poe had no faith, as he often said, in human perfectibility or the general notions of equality, progress and improvement that characterized the Jeffersonian vision, and, if he had been politically minded, one might have thought of him as a type of the anti-Jeffersonian Southern reaction of the moment. Temperamentally, indeed, Poe was a type of this reaction. He had something in common with Beverley Tucker, who was deeply interested in him and remembered his mother as a charming young actress in Richmond.

Meanwhile, he acquired at Charlottesville a good part of the store of learning that marked his tales and his criticism in after years. In those days, and later, Poe was accused of all manner of dodges in the way of pretending to a learning he did not possess, and critics took pleasure in pointing out the absurd mistakes that he had made and that proved him "two-fifths sheer fudge," an impostor and what not. It was true that he made these mistakes, and he sometimes seemed to lug in his learning, like his own Signora Psyche Zenobia in *How to Write a Blackwood Article*. The editor himself instructed this aspiring young lady to cultivate an air of erudition, to sprinkle her pages with piquant expressions from Schiller, Cervantes and Lucan and never miss a chance to use a botanical phrase or a little Greek. Poe often made learned allusions for the sake of their effect, but were they not occasionally admirable for just this reason? Much of the wondrous atmosphere of tales like *The Fall of the House of Usher* was a result of these allusions to strange and exotic books and authors. Moreover, Poe was a well-read man, especially in English, French and Latin, and he was prodigious in the breadth of his general knowledge. He knew the language, as his writing revealed, of astronomy, chemistry and physics, of conchology, botany, medicine and mathematics, and no one could have written *Hans Pfaall* and *Maelzel's Chess-Player* without a considerable knowledge of mechanics as well. As for the other modern tongues, he read a little Italian and German, though he probably picked up his knowledge of Novalis, Tieck and Hoffmann from the papers of Carlyle and others in the British reviews. He was always a constant reader of the current magazines, and he had formed the habit of reading the foreign periodicals as a boy in the book-loft of Allan's warehouse. Inevitably Poe was steeped in Coleridge, Shelley, Moore and Byron, but how, in his hurried, anxious life, could he have stowed away such a mass of erudition and information? Obviously, this was because

as a boy he "felt with the energy of a man," as he remarked
of the hero of *William Wilson*, while he had, in a rudimentary
form, a universal mind, together with astonishing powers of
concentration. Poe, in the range of his curiosity, resembled
Jefferson, after all, and for him a single manual of ancient
history or natural science went further than hundreds of volumes in the minds of others. But this meant assiduity, too,—
he was always immensely industrious,—and a few months at
West Point were all the additional time that Poe was ever to
have for his education. He was complimented at Charlottesville
for a translation from Tasso, and he wrote *Tamerlane* there
and other poems.

While outwardly the attractive Poe was a clever young man
of the ruling class, with all the advantages and prospects of a
Cabell or a Lee, his life was built on quicksand really, as he
had always known perhaps, and certainly knew when he was
withdrawn from college. John Allan had never adopted him
and may have turned against him because Poe happened to
know too much about his private life, but, long before this,
when the two fell out, Allan had called him a charity boy and
threatened more than once to turn him adrift. Like some of
the other boys at school, he had sneered at Poe as the child of
actors, and he refused to pay Poe's expenses at college, as after-
wards, at West Point, he would not pay even for the necessary
textbooks and Poe did not have money enough for soap and
writing-paper. Of course, he played cards for money, not for
fun but to pay his way,—another humiliation, and he usually
lost,—so that he was followed by duns and warrants when he
left Charlottesville and had to leave Richmond under a borrowed name. An outsider among the young Virginians, and
constantly reminded of it, with a natural and lifelong craving
for the sympathy of women, he was desolated as a boy by the
death of the mother of one of his friends, the beautiful Mrs.
Stanard of the poem *To Helen*. Then Mrs. Allan also died,
the radiant foster-mother who had stood between Poe and the
feelingless caprices of her husband, and a young man who was

an orphan too might well have felt that the "conqueror worm" was the hero of his tragedy already. For Poe the death of a beautiful woman was always the great theme of verse,—he might almost have remembered the death of his mother also, as he was to watch the long dying of his young wife,—and no man was ever more alone against the world than this "Henri le Rennet" who fled from his creditors in Richmond. Long before Poe came of age he knew the *splendeurs et misères,* the sorrowful juxtapositions of luxury and squalor, that were to make him a preëminent type of the romantic; and who could ever have been surprised that he often seemed nervously strained as a boy, with an ominous look in his eyes of anxiety and sadness? He began to be haunted by nightmares at about the age of fifteen; and, if he broke down a few years later and showed many of the signs of insanity, was this not partially owing to his heredity as well? His sister Rosalie was underwitted, his brother died of consumption and drink, in the manner no doubt of the gay weak feckless father who had long since faded out of the family picture; and Poe's disorders might all have been traced to the desperate existence of his poor little mother, dragging him with her from theatre to theatre as she played her wildly emotional parts. Two or three years of such a life might well have deranged the nerves of an infant,—they might even have deranged Poe's nerves before he was born.

This complex insecurity,—physical, social, financial alike,— explained in large measure the life and the character of Poe, as it also accounted for the nature of much of his writing. He had begun to drink in part because it gave him confidence, as he liked to display his prowess too by assuming the role of the man of the world whose head was full of esoteric knowledge. He might have been, if he was not, the schoolboy in *The Purloined Letter* who won the marbles of all the other boys by observing and measuring the astuteness of his opponents, for having, of course, a mind in a million he also liked to use it because it gave him power over others. For this reason, very largely, he longed to establish a magazine that would make him an intellectual dictator,* an assertion of his superiority that was also in a measure the result of this insecurity of his earlier years. He liked to play for a similar reason the part of a solver of cryptograms, a reader of riddles and ciphers whom no one could baffle, a successful finder of buried treasure and a peerless detector of crimes for whom the official police were mere idiots and infants. For Poe projected a side of himself in Auguste Dupin and Mr. Legrand, the hero of *The Gold Bug* who unravelled the formidable cipher. His analytical faculty was undoubtedly astonishing, and Dickens asked him in later years if he had had dealings with the devil when he outlined in advance the plot of *Barnaby Rudge*. But, much as he loved these exercises, he liked to be known as a wizard too, partly because of the feeling of power it gave him; and this tendency also passed into his tales and appeared in the character of many of his heroes who were persons of ancient lineage and recondite tastes, of vaguely splendid antecedents, strange and profound in their learning and in some way disconnected from the rest of the race. This tendency appeared in the legend that Poe created about his life, in the need that he felt for being a romantic hero, suggested partly by the image of Byron and partly to bolster his self-esteem in the sad and ambiguous position in which as a boy he found himself. Already at college, he talked of going, after the manner of Byron, to Greece, and presently he talked of having been there, and he spoke of his adventures in the Mediterranean and Arabia, which he had penetrated, and the trouble he had had with his passport at St. Petersburg as well. He really disappeared for a while, but the explanation was simple enough. He had enlisted in the army as "Edgar A. Perry," a fact that he wished to conceal at West Point, where enlisted men were looked down upon, while he also wished to account for his withdrawal from college. He had left

---

* "Would it not be glorious, darling, to establish in America the sole, unquestionable aristocracy—that of intellect—to secure its supremacy—to lead and to control it?"—Letter of Poe to Sarah Helen Whitman, at a time when he still had hopes for his magazine, *The Stylus*.

Charlottesville, of course, to see the world. Poe was a lover of hoaxes, as anyone knew who read his tales,—he was like his own Hungarian baron who made "mystification" the study and business of his life,—and he had appropriated some of the adventures of his brother. William Henry Leonard Poe, who appropriated Edgar's poems in turn, had seen something of the world as a midshipman in the navy. This brother had been to Montevideo, probably to the Near East and quite possibly to Russia. For the rest, there was much of the actor in Poe, and perhaps he inherited from his mother and father his faculty of impersonation as of elocution, for which he had won a prize at school and which made him a capital public reader: his recitals, for instance, of *The Raven* towards the end of his life were all but as famous as the acting of Junius Brutus Booth. He had sometimes the air of a stage Virginian, who exaggerated the part a little, because it was not really his by right, and his tales and his poems were full of the imagery of the theatre, mimes and mummers and masquerades, shifting scenery, phantom forms and the "gala night," for example, of *The Conqueror Worm.*

Poe, dismissed from West Point in 1831, informed the superintendent of his next adventure. He was about to start for Paris to obtain through Lafayette an appointment in the army of the Poles for their struggle with Russia. In fact, he went to Baltimore and joined his father's family there, for, having lost favour with the Allans, he had sought out the Poes. He was wearing the black military cloak that made him look like a Spanish brigand, the cloak he continued to wear for the rest of his life; and in Baltimore, where he had published already his second small volume of poems,—the first had appeared in Boston in 1827,—he began his career as a writer of stories also. The Revolutionary quartermaster, his grandfather, General Poe, had won the admiration of Lafayette, and his father had once been a member of the Thespian Club there, but the family had fallen on evil days and Poe's aunt Mrs. Clemm, the sister of his father, supported it as a Baltimore seamstress. She had a young daughter, Virginia, the cousin who later married Poe and who, like his sister Rosalie, remained a child, and she valiantly fought for her sad little household, her bed-ridden mother, her stonecutter son and Henry Poe, who was drinking himself to death. She went the rounds with a market-basket, picking up a child's dress, a loaf of bread, a chicken or a cabbage from her friends, as later in the Fordham cottage, with Poe and Virginia under her wing, she scoured the fields for dandelions and turnips at night. Poe shared the garret of the wretched little house with his drunken dying brother, and there he wrote some of his tales. The *Manuscript Found in a Bottle* was one of the first.

In Baltimore, he fell in with the writers John P. Kennedy and William Wirt, to whom he showed the manuscript of his poem, *Al Aaraaf.* He had written this poem on Sullivan's Is-land, near Charleston, for he had been stationed at Fort Moul-trie there, and he had listened to the "sounding sea" that one heard in his poems and stories later, and observed the palmetto and the myrtle that appeared in *The Gold Bug.* The tulip-trees of Carolina, the live oaks with their streaming moss and Charleston too appeared in some of these tales, and even the house of Usher might have been suggested by the ruinous old mouldering mansions in the Carolina woods. Poe's imagina-tion was peculiarly Southern in flavour and hue,* while his loyalty and faith were always bound up in the South, and he respected the judgment of the Southerners Philip Pendleton Cooke, the poet, and the novelist Beverley Tucker above all others. He went out of his way in after years to defend South-ern men of letters, against the self-sufficiency of the New

* *How* Southern anyone can see who spends an hour, for instance, in the Bonaventure Cemetery at Savannah. Who could forget an alley there, flanked by ancient live-oak trees, with streamers of grey moss overhanging the path, leading down to the moss-covered tomb of a long-dead senator and his daughter, with the waves of the sounding sea breaking behind it? The scene, so quintessentially Southern, is a speak-ing image of the quality of Poe, as, for that matter, are similar scenes in the Magnolia Cemetery, which Poe might well have visited at Charleston.

Englanders, for example, and in general the Southern writers appreciated him and did their best to afford him practical assistance. William Wirt, protesting his "ignorance of modern poetry and modern tastes,"—for his mind had been formed in the post-Revolutionary decades,—was yet most courteous and helpful to this brilliant beginner, and so were John H. B. Latrobe and "Horse Shoe Robinson" Kennedy, who awarded him a prize for his *Tales of the Folio Club*. Somewhat later, the Georgia poet, Thomas Holley Chivers, offered to support Poe altogether. This hero-worshipping Southern physician, the son of a rich plantation-owner, had been publishing poems of his own since 1829, with no "discoverable taint" of Byron or Wordsworth or Coleridge or Shelley, as Poe remarked when he had read and met him. In fact, the "wild Mazeppa of letters,"—Simms's phrase for Chivers,—had a curiously original mind, without taste or discretion, a singular gift of verbal music for which he sacrificed everything else, while achieving remarkable effects with alliteration and rhythm. He "jumbled, tumbled, rumbled, raged and raved,"—as the euphuist Sylvester said of the furies,—coining exotic, sonorous words like the "scoriac" and "Aidenn" of Poe, from whom he borrowed freely in his later poems. But Chivers influenced Poe in turn, as he interested Rossetti and Swinburne and left traces in the poems of Kipling and Vachel Lindsay. He wrote a number of plays as well, one on the Sharpe-Beauchamp murder, the notorious "Kentucky tragedy" of 1825, the theme of Poe's *Politian* and other plays, novels and ballads, the most popular literary theme in America in the thirties.

Chivers was ready to help Poe, as Kennedy and Latrobe had been; for, in spite of the legend that later arose through a natural reaction against the false witness of Griswold, who attacked his honour, Poe found the world in general well-disposed. There were always two persons who defended for one who attacked him. It was his nature, moreover, to struggle, to fight every inch of the way, for he was proud, laborious and devoted. He had had a good name as a student at college,

as a soldier he was called "prompt and faithful," and later, as
an assistant editor, he was described by N. P. Willis as invariably industrious, punctual and patient. He was never by choice
a bohemian, he was far from irresponsible, he made every effort to be practical, in point of fact; and, as he never blamed
others for the "unmerciful disaster" that followed him "faster
and faster" as he sped through life, so neither was he to blame,
though its cause was within him. A neurotic, for various obvious reasons, who was later disordered mentally, when a definite lesion seems to have developed in his brain, he had a
heart-affection too that appeared in this early Baltimore time,
perhaps as a result of the nervous exhaustion of his youth. He
began to break down physically about 1832. There was more
of the tragic in the life of Poe than any sensitive man could
bear, and he took opiates occasionally and drank too much. Was
he not, besides, a victim of the "Imp of the Perverse," like the
hero of the tale that bore this name? When Poe described
perverseness as a primitive, radical sentiment, as one of the
prima mobilia of the human soul, he was picturing a trait of
his own personality,—common enough but neurotic, no doubt,—
that would in any case have wrecked his life. The man who
tells the story has committed a wondrously skilful crime, and
he has no conscience or feeling of guilt about it, and yet from
sheer perversity he is driven to confess the crime precisely
because the confession involves his undoing. Just so, the victim
of the imp of the perverse feels drawn to the brink of the
precipice *because* his reason violently holds him back, because,
instead of the natural desire for well-being, a strongly antagonis-
tical feeling grips him. One saw this wayward motive at work
again and again in the life of Poe,—for example, in his various
connections with magazines. To be a great editor, he said, was
the dream of his life, and he had at one time or another in his
hands a number of the most important magazines. He might
easily have become and remained the greatest editor in the
country had it not been for this imp of the perverse. Poe's

nervous and mental organization would have made havoc of his life in any society, at any moment of time.

Sick or well, he possessed, meanwhile, a literary genius that had had no parallel as yet on the American scene. This genius, moreover, was supremely artistic, as Cooper's, for instance, never was, or even the noble talent of the admirable Bryant, who was also a lover of perfection; for Poe was a craftsman of exquisite skill in prose and verse alike, a conscious master of his methods as well as his effects. Even as a reviewer of books, he affirmed that reviews should be works of art, a point that no writer had thought of in America before, and Hawthorne alone was to rival him in the eighteen-thirties in the art of prose composition and the writing of tales. Irving, of course, was a natural artist, but he had little of the cunning of Poe, while Cooper, a man of genius, was nothing as a craftsman, and Poe was an innovator in verse, a creator of "novel forms of beauty," who influenced poets elsewhere for an age to come. A lover, as he said, of severe precision, "profoundly excited by music," a seeker of the perfect who constantly revised his work, while disdaining all recourse to "poetic licence," he had taken to heart the remark of Bacon that "there is no excellent beauty that hath not some strangeness in the proportion." He had developed variations from the usual metrical patterns, notes that were subtly discordant and wholly unexpected, and, feeling that "the indefinite is an element of the true poesis," he sought "the unknown—the vague—the uncomprehended." His images, instead of creating specific pictures in the mind, evoked a world of sorrowful associations, remote, dim, sinister, melancholy, majestic, his refrains suggested echoes from bottomless gulfs, and when he repeated a word in a rhyme the sound seemed magically altered by the new collocation. One heard in a few of these brief poems a kind of ethereal music like Tennyson's horns of Elfland faintly blowing, though the dream-world of Poe was a wild weird clime indeed. It was haunted by ill angels, vast and formless, "flapping" from their condor wings invisible woe.

Already by 1831, when the third of his little collections was published, Poe had written *To Helen, The City in the Sea, Israfel, The Lake* and others of more than a dozen poems in which he emerged as a new voice in the language. In the end he wrote two score and ten, and perhaps fifteen of these were to bear the stamp that eternity knew as Poe's, the poems in which he had outgrown the spell of Byron, Keats, Coleridge and Shelley and appeared as another member of their family of minds. These poems were as pure as they were unique; and were they not fixed as a constellation in the sky of the human imagination for ever? A hundred years later at least they were certainly to seem so. Meanwhile, the tales that Poe was writing had much in common with them,—they were sometimes even as musical in the beauty of their prose,*—and there one also found dim tarns, wild and dreary landscapes and phantom figures flitting to and fro. Evil things in robes of sorrow presided over some of these tales, with their strange effects of horror, the macabre and the grotesque, a world of the phantasmagoric, suggesting the dreams of an opium-eater and reverberant with Thomas De Quincey's "everlasting farewells." The note of Poe was truly his own,—his tales, like his poems, were original, but they too sprang from a literary mood of the time, and Poe belonged to a family of minds as marked in this other sphere of prose as the family to which he belonged in the sphere of verse. He had something in common with De Quincey, with the German writers Hoffmann and Tieck, with all the contemporary strains of the bizarre and the Gothic (as well as the stately classical strain of Landor), and even with Charles Brockden Brown, the early American story-teller, the lover of melancholy, mystery, the horrible and the dire. Some of his properties, so to speak, were the ordinary properties of the Gothic romance, decaying castles, trances, cataleptic attacks, while *Blackwood's*

---

* E.g.: "Then I came suddenly into still noonday solitudes, where no wind of heaven ever intruded, and where vast meadows of poppies, and slender, lily-looking flowers spread themselves out a weary distance, all silent and motionless forever."—*Adventure of One Hans Pfaall.*

Magazine abounded with stories of a sensational kind that resembled in certain ways the tales of Poe, stories of a man en-
tombed alive, a man who is baked in an oven, a man who goes
to sleep under a church-bell, a manuscript allegedly found in
a madhouse, tales of men who are drowned or hanged and telling how they feel before they die. American authors wrote
similar stories in various American magazines, and several of
Poe's were conventional tales of the time, such as Simms and
Willis, for example, were also writing, with settings in Hun-
gary or Venice or Spain, in sumptuous palaces and vague cha-
teaus, with the usual romantic literary bric-a-brac. If *The Cask
of Amontillado* had been less intense, it might easily have been
mistaken for the work of Willis, as *The Assignation* might have
been written by Simms,—that is to say, if Poe had omitted the
poem in this tale, the miraculous lines *To One in Paradise*.
A few of his more trifling pieces were drawn from French
originals, while he borrowed from Bulwer, Disraeli's *Vivian
Grey* and Macaulay's description of Benares. For Poe was
bathed in the air of his time, and he was a man of a time when
people were living "Gothically" all about him, when they were
building Gothic houses that recalled the school of his childhood in England, with its gates and its pointed windows and
ceilings of oak. Only a step from Baltimore, at Bel Air in Maryland, where the merry Parson Weems had lived with his wife,
the actor Junius Brutus Booth built a Gothic manor-house, with
mullioned windows, dark passages, gables and recesses. Booth,
the Rosicrucian, might have stepped out of the pages of Poe,
who was very much more, however, than a man of his time and
who made something unique of these forms of the moment. In
prose as well as in verse, moreover, he gave the measure of his
mind during these early years in Baltimore. Before he returned
for a while to Richmond in 1835, he had written *Morella* and
the *Manuscript Found in a Bottle*, the *Unparalleled Adventure
of One Hans Pfaall, Silence—a Fable* and other pieces that
revealed the full range of his quality as a teller of tales. Most
of the greater stories he wrote in the fourteen years that still

lay before him were amplifications and variations of these.

Now if one could believe the assertions of Poe, he consciously chose the impressions that formed the substance of his tales and poems, for he appeared to like to think that the essence of his work as well as its form was a fruit of the coldest artifice and the skill of the craftsman. No one could question his skill, indeed, and of course he chose some of his themes; but others, and the most characteristic, rose out of his unconscious mind as naturally and uncontrollably as nightmares, and the personality they revealed apparently offered a clue to Poe's insistence on the power of his conscious thinking. For was it not singular, after all, that he wished to range himself with the fabricators of most of the *Blackwood* tales, whose writing was done in cold blood and wholly produced by the conscious mind because they had no such depths as his to work from? Was he trying to convince himself in all this show of reasoning that his own mind was *not* "tottering upon her throne," like the mind of the neurasthenic Roderick Usher, that his intellect was not only great but master of his moods as well, that Edgar Allan Poe was the captain of his soul? For there was no doubt of the presence of incipient madness in the marvellous imagination that conceived these tales, an imagination all compact of gloom, despair, sepulchral thoughts, grim fantasies and the fear of impending mental decay. There was scarcely even a glimmer of sunlight in this world of sorrow and desolation, of shadow, disaster, horror, revenge and crime, a world overhung with the sable wings of lunacy, perversity, hysteria, of sickness, hypochondria, ruin, dissolution and death. The typical heroes of these tales were victims of neuroses who shared no relationships or interests with the rest of the race, who had forgotten, if they ever possessed, any ties with humankind and whose habits and surroundings reflected and partook of their disorder. They suffered from a morbid acuteness of the senses, they found even the odours of flowers oppressive, while their eyes were tortured by the faintest light: they lived in dark rooms with massive shutters by the gleam of perfumed tapers that threw out only the feeblest and ghastliest of rays. They trembled at the sound of their own voices, they were enamoured of the night and they liked rooms that were closely shrouded in sombre velvet draperies that fell in heavy folds to an ebony floor. They were marked by a nervous irritability, they were unsettled in intellect and their minds were haunted by obsessions, or they meditated crimes, or they were completely possessed by the crimes of others, while they were filled with every kind of abnormal or moonstruck sensation, with affections that were semi-incestuous and vertiginous fears. They were ridden, for example, by a conviction that they were destined to be buried alive and they doubted the fidelity of their closest friends; they spent their days planning a coffin with levers for admitting air and light and springs and ropes that would open the coffin and the vault. Or, as if to escape from all touch of reality, they involved their minds in abstruse studies, fantastic speculations and intricate dreams. Meanwhile, the women of these tales, Madeline, Berenice, Ligeia, Morella and Eleanora were mysteriously stricken and wasted away with maladies that were obscure and fatal.

There were no mornings in the world of Poe, there were only winter afternoons or dull dark soundless days in the autumn of the year, and one sometimes had glimpses of a river or a lake that was saffron or sickly in hue or sullen or livid in the light of a setting sun. Some of the tales were humorous, and these were perhaps the most sinister of all, for one seldom felt any warmth in the humour of Poe, although Dickens was one of his favourite writers and he was genial now and then, as, for instance, in his name for the mummy, "Allamistakeo." There was certainly something engaging in his reference to an Arabian book that was "scarcely known at all, even in Europe," the "Tellmenow Isitsoörnot," and his waddling Dutchmen in *Hans Pfaall* were quite in the manner of Washington Irving, who wrote to Poe sympathetically about his stories. Then his mimicry of the Irish brogue in the sketch of "Sir Pathrick O'Grandison" was no less good-natured than clever, while he was probably right in thinking that his sense of the grotesque was an unmistakable evidence of the artist in him. But his humour was mainly of the sort that makes one shiver, the kind of macabre facetiousness for which nothing is so funny as the horrible and which takes delight in tweaking the nose of a corpse. There was something frightful in the nonchalance with which the characters in these comic tales were flung from the gallery of a theatre into the pit or thrown about until their skulls were broken, while their ears were cut off or their arms were smashed or their sanguinary heads rolled from the tops of steeples into the gutter. They went home in high glee with dislocated necks or they placed corpses in boxes that were supposed to contain champagne with springs to make the corpse rise when the box was opened.

This was the icy facetiousness that goes with the neurotic type, and the tales of Poe were impressive precisely because they were *not* fabrications but involuntary ebullitions of his own sick mind. He shaped his effects with the utmost skill, but these effects had causes over which Poe had very little control indeed, and, while other writers played with the macabre and the grotesque, he lisped his horrors because the horrors came. The unkindness of an unkind fate, death, disease and danger had left their marks in his unconscious mind, along with prenatal injuries, perhaps, and drugs, and the "indefinite sense of wrong" that Longfellow noted in Poe was a whiff of the devil's brew at the bottom of the barrel. Of what nature were the "nightmares" Poe was having at fifteen?—and what were those wild dreams of his later life, dreams so sad and shocking that he could not bear to be left alone and besought Mrs. Clemm to sit near him and stroke his forehead? In all probability were they not those dreams "of a most terrific description" that racked the soul of Arthur Gordon Pym as he lay buried, as it were, in the hold of the ship, in which every species of calamity and horror befell him? Ghastly and ferocious demons smothered him to death between huge pillows, colossal serpents embraced him with shining eyes, and presently limitless deserts spread themselves out, forlorn, before him, and ranks of tall trees with their roots concealed in morasses. The trees waved to and fro their skeleton arms and piercingly cried to the black still waters for mercy. If, indeed, the dreams of Poe were not these actual dreams of Pym, they were certainly similar in kind, as were most of his stories, the story of the dungeon of the Inquisition, of the man who is walled in the vault, of the old man who is murdered for his glittering eye and the madman who gouges out the eye of the cat. The vengeful dwarf burning alive the monarch who had wronged him was an image of some deep desire in the mind of Poe, and the cold lips of the rats that writhed on the throat of the man in the pit had probably sought Poe's lips in one of these nightmares. Had he not shared the sensations, moreover, of the man who was conscious of all the movements of those who bore him to the grave and lowered him within it and left him to his sad and solemn slumbers with the worm? Who can doubt that "wild visions, opium-engendered, flitted, shadow-like" before his eyes, as before the eyes of the narrator of *Ligeia*, visions and images of shrouded bodies, cats with a gallows outlined on them, voices issuing from "distended and motionless jaws" and the tottering figures of pallid tenants of tombs? He had heard the strains of the mad waltzes that echoed in his poems and his stories and seen the wind-blown arrases, tattered and dark, fitfully swaying on the walls of some house of the dead. This child, like De Quincey, had "been in hell," and it was just his personal note, the stamp of actuality, of experience, in fact, that gave the tales of Poe their authority and uniqueness.

"To dream," said the lover in *The Assignation*, "has been the business of my life." So it was with Poe, who wrote the story, and in some of his dreams he carried out the dearest wishes of his heart: he had moments of happiness there that life denied him. He could indulge in the lives of his heroes the kind of material beauty-worship that was beyond his world of shabby lodgings, and his Epicurean imagination found a fulfilment in them that poverty rendered impossible in his own life. There

he could be of ancient family, the child of time-honoured
hereditary halls, descended from a race that was famous for its
mysterious powers, whose parents had provided him at college
with an "outfit and annual establishment" that enabled him
to gratify all his tastes. He could "vie in profuseness of expendi-
ture with the haughtiest heirs of the wealthiest earldoms" and
live in a regal magnificence and a gloomy spendour which the
author of *Vathek* scarcely surpassed at Fonthill; he could be as
fabulously rich, in fact, as Ellison in *The Domain of Arnheim,*
with ten times the treasure and the jewels in the chest of *The
Gold Bug.* He could always have a valet, of course, like the
hero of *The Oval Portrait,* and a personal physician, like Mr.
Bedloe's, devoted solely to his care, and he could be "skilful
in Italian vintages," like the man in *The Cask of Amontillado,*
and a gourmet as famous as Bon-Bon. He could dine as they
dined in the *Maison de Santé* of Doctor Tarr and Professor
Fether, on veal *à la Ste. Menehould* and cauliflowers in *velouté*
sauce, with bottles and baskets and cases of Clos Vougeot, and
his cloak could be, like William Wilson's, "extravagantly
costly," of an inexpressibly "rare description of fur." Then he
could live in a sumptuous house, with windows of crimson-
tinted glass, in drawing-rooms with curtains of crimson and
cloth of gold, and his books could be superbly bound and his
pictures * framed in arabesques and his antique lamps could

* If Poe's taste in painting was like Roderick Usher's it was singularly
"modern": "One of the phantasmagoric conceptions of my friend . . .
may be shadowed forth, although feebly, in words. A small picture
presented the interior of an immensely long and rectangular vault or
tunnel, with low walls, smooth, white, and without interruption or device. Certain accessory points of the design served well to convey the
idea that this excavation lay at an exceeding depth below the surface of
the earth. No outlet was observed in any portion of its vast extent, and
no torch or other artificial source of light was discernible; yet a flood
of intense rays rolled throughout, and bathed the whole in a ghastly and
inappropriate splendour."—*The Fall of the House of Usher.*
One seems to remember seeing this picture at many an exhibition
after about 1910.
In *The Thousand-and-Second Tale of Scheherazade,* Poe has a blue
rat, a sky-blue cow and a pink horse with green wings, after the fashion
of other modern painters.

be filled with perfumed oil. (For the author of the *Philosophy of Composition* was the author of the *Philosophy of Furniture* as well.) If this seemed rather too much in the style of some of the parvenus of 1840, one had to remember that Poe was a reader of Beckford, that his parents had been actors and that he possessed a patrician mind that longed to out-gentleman the gentlemen of Charlottesville and Richmond. Besides, there was something infantile in Poe, as in all the Symbolists who followed him in France and elsewhere.

But, along with this childish materialism, Poe was a lover of spiritual beauty and especially classical beauty and the "glory that was Greece," and occasionally, in his prose and verse, his love and genius crystallized and formed a gem of purest ray serene. The beauty of the little poem *To Helen* was all but matched in a few of the tales by such bits, for example, as the picture of Aphrodite, suggesting a Tanagra figure, in *The Assignation;* * while his fantastic realism, as Dostoievsky called it,† worked like the spell of a wizard over the mind. One absolutely believed the impossible when the art of Poe presented it, so great was the force of his imagination and the skill with which he introduced the trivial and precise details that imparted to the whole effect an air of truth. The behaviour of the cat and kittens in the basket of Hans Pfaall's balloon convinced one that the moon was actually near, especially as the feathers dropped like bullets from the car when the atmosphere had become too rare to sustain them. It was this power of the factual detail that carried one, helpless with terror, to the bot-

* "She stood alone. Her small, bare and silvery feet gleamed in the black mirror of marble beneath her. Her hair, not as yet more than half loosened for the night from its ball-room array, clustered, amid a shower of diamonds, round and round her classical head, in curls like those of the young hyacinth."

† In a preface, 1861, to a Russian translation of three of Poe's tales, calling attention to Poe's mastery of realistic detail.

Poe was translated into Russian and read in Russia long before he was taken up in France. He began to appear in Russian magazines in the late eighteen-thirties.

tom of the hideous gulf in the *Descent into the Maelstrom* and
roped one down with the rats in the Spanish pit. One shared
Poe's nightmares more vividly than one felt one's own.

HAWTHORNE IN SALEM

While Boston and Cambridge were moving forward, Salem,
like most of the other seaports, stricken by the War of 1812,
had lapsed into quietude and decay. Beside its dilapidated
wharves, where grew the fat weeds, the windlass chanty and
the caulker's maul no longer broke the silence. The water-side
streets were no longer thronged with sailors, "all right" for
shore, with their blue jackets and checked shirts, their well-
varnished hats and flowing ribbons, with bundles under their
arms from the cannibal isles, or from India or China. One
seldom heard the lively "Cheerily, men!" while all hands joined
in the chorus. The grass choked the chinks of the cobblestones
over which the drays had clattered. An occasional bark or brig
discharged its hides. One saw some Nova Scotia schooner,
drawn up at Derby's Wharf, unloading a cargo of firewood. A
few idle seafaring men leaned against the posts, or sat on the
planks, in the lee of some shabby warehouse, or lolled in the
long-boats on the strand. But the great days of the port were a
tale that was told, over and over, by the ancient skippers, who
dozed away their mornings at the custom-house, with their
chairs tilted against the wall.

Salem had an immemorial air, the air that gathers about a
town which, having known a splendid hour, shrinks and settles
back while its grandeurs fade. But Salem was old in spirit, aside
from its faded grandeurs. The past that hovered there had
much in common with that of the ancient ports of northern
Europe, where the Gothic fancies of the Middle Ages have not
been dispelled by modern trade. Salem was still Gothic, in a
measure. In its moss-grown, many-gabled houses, panelled with

worm-eaten wood and hung with half-obliterated portraits, dwelt at least the remnants of a race that retained the mental traits of a far-away past. In its isolation from the currents of world-thought and feeling, it seemed to be only a step removed from the age of the Dance of Death. In the mansions of Chestnut Street and Federal Street, one found the traces of a livelier culture, the books that were read in Boston, together with the Oriental spoils brought home by the Salem navigators. But over the quiet lanes and leafy side-streets, where the grave-yards lay, brooded the hush of many generations. Queer old maids with turbaned heads peered from behind the curtains, quaint old simple-minded men hobbled along under the sweep-ing elms, "pixilated" creatures, many of them, as they said at Marblehead,—bewildered by the fairies,—half dead and buried in their houses, or buried in the morbid family pride that flour-ishes where life runs low.

There was vigour enough in Salem, there were plenty of stout merchants and politicians. One saw swarms of boys and little girls, in blue, yellow, green and crimson dresses, bursting from church and school-house, like garden-beds of zinnias or water-colours of Maurice Prendergast. It was only in compari-son with Lynn and Lowell, those near-by towns whose enter-prising burghers, faced with the decline of shipping, had built their factories for internal trade, that Salem seemed somehow grey and sad. The Prescotts, Story, Pickering, Choate and Bow-ditch, the great circle of earlier days, had long since departed. At a stone's-throw from the Essex Institute, one almost heard the silence. One caught the tinkling of the bell at the door of some little cent-shop, even the quiver of the humming-birds darting about the syringa bushes. The rattling of the butcher's cart was the only event of the day for many a household, unless perhaps one of the family hens cackled and laid an egg. Spid-ers abounded in these houses, eluding the vigilant spinster's eye. Indeed, there were so many cobwebs that it might have occurred to a doctor,—some old Salem doctor, as odd as the rest, —to gather the webs together and distil an elixir of life from the dusty compound. In the burying-ground in Charter Street, where the Gothic emblems flourished,—death's-heads, cross-bones, scythes and hour-glasses, such as one found in Dürer's woodcuts,—the office of grave-digger passed from father to son. Just so passed the household legends, behind the bolted doors, grimmer with each generation. Beside the kitchen fires, old serving-women crouched as they turned the spit and darned the stockings, always ready to tell the children stories. Some of them seemed to remember the days of the witches. Their stories were as dusty as the cobwebs.

For Salem, like the whole New England seacoast, bristled with old wives' tales and old men's legends. No need to invent stories there: one heard them in the taverns, from the sailors, from charcoal-burners who looked like wizards, from the good-for-nothings on the water-front. One heard of locked closets in haunted houses where skeletons had been found. One heard of walls that resounded with knocks where there had once been doorways, now bricked up. One heard of poisonous houses and blood-stained houses, old maids who lived in total darkness, misers who wallowed naked in heaps of pine-tree shillings. One even heard of Endicott's dreary times, when the stocks and the pillory were never empty. One heard of the magistrates who awoke each morning to the prospect of cropping an ear or slitting a nostril, stripping and whipping a woman at the tail of a cart, or giving her a stout hemp necklace or a brooch in the form of a scarlet letter. One heard of the grey champion who emerged from nowhere to rebuke the tyrannies of the British king, of children who had sprung from the loins of demons, of the wastrels of Merry Mount and the grizzled saints who had stamped out their light and idle mirth, clipping their curls and love-locks. Would they not have stamped out the sunshine and clipped all the flowers in the forest in order to clear a path for their psalms and sermons? In these quiet towns, where nothing happens—except an occasional murder—to agitate the surface of existence, history is ever-present, lying in visible depths under the unstirred waters; and who could have known in Salem what to believe or not? However it might have been on Chestnut Street, the fringes of Salem society were superstitious. If the ring that Queen Elizabeth gave to Essex had appeared in a collection-box on Sunday, it would not have seemed surprising to some of the people. There were plenty of old souls in the lanes and side-streets who never knew where to draw the line. They half believed the tales they told the children. Were there not hollows in the hills close by where the Devil and his subjects held communion? Were there not ill-famed men in the western mountains who were condemned to wander till the crack of doom? All these tales had their truth, and so did the Indian legends, which the farmers repeated. There was an element of fact behind them. Was there a carbuncle in the Crystal Hills that gleamed like the westering sun, as the Indians said? Or was it the sun itself? There were men still living down in Maine who had never settled the question. Carbuncle or not, they had certainly seen it. At least, they had caught its radiance, far up the valley of the Saco.

Salem was a centre for these legends. The mediæval mind had lingered there, in the absence of recent enterprise; and, while the town as a whole was sufficiently modern, there were odd corners and shadowy households where symbols and realities seemed much the same. The young men and women knew the difference, but sometimes it amused them to ignore it. They did not believe in ghosts, but mesmerism had become the fashion: they let their fancies play on the border-line. They sat up at night and told tales of ghosts, largely in default of mundane gossip. Occasionally, they even thought they saw one. The Hawthornes, who lived in Herbert Street, under the shadow of a family curse, were often troubled by an apparition that seemed to haunt their yard. The only son of the household, Nathaniel Hawthorne, who lived like a ghost himself, haunting a little chamber under the eaves, appearing only at nightfall, could not count the times he had raised his head, or turned towards the window, with a perception that somebody was passing through the gate. He could only perceive the presence with a sidelong glance, by a certain indirection; if he looked straight at the dim thing, behold, it was not there. As no one ever passed through the Hawthornes' gate, it may have been Elizabeth, his sister, who also appeared only when dusk had fallen. In fact, one could live for two years under the same roof with this spectral sister and see her only once. That was the way with the Hawthornes. The father, a Salem skipper, had died of yellow fever, years ago, in far-off Surinam; and no mortal eye had penetrated, or was to penetrate for forty years, the Castle Dismal on the second floor where the mother of the family had taken refuge on the day she heard the news. Her meals were brought up and left outside the door, as they were at Elizabeth's door, and Louisa's door,—at least, as often as not, —and, one flight further up, at Nathaniel's door. When twilight came, one heard the sound of footsteps echoing on the stairs, and a door that must have been opened was certainly shut. Elizabeth went out for a little walk. Then Nathaniel went for a walk, alone, in another direction.

All day long, every day, or almost every day, for twelve years, he had sat in his flag-bottomed chair in his little room, beside the pine table, with a sheet of foolscap spread out before him. He was writing stories that rose in his mind as mushrooms grow in a meadow, where the roots of some old tree are buried under the earth. He had no love of secrecy or darkness, uncanny as he seemed to the handful of neighbours who knew that he existed; he was merely following the household pattern. His family, prominent once, had been almost forgotten, even in Herbert Street. No one came to see him. He had few friends, aside from the circle of his Bowdoin classmates, with whom he had almost ceased to correspond. As a boy, he had often said he was going to sea and would never come back again; and he sometimes remarked to an acquaintance that he thought of disappearing, changing his name, escaping from the orbit of the postman, as if he had not sufficiently disappeared merely by staying at home. He had lapsed into his solitary life, half through a kind of inertia, and half,—he had always known he was going to write,—as if to protect a sensibility that was not yet ready to yield its fruits. His nickname had been Oberon at college, a reference to his shy elusive ways. He had a massive head; his eyes were black and brilliant; he walked with the rolling gait of a sailor; he had a somewhat truculent voice and presence. Standing, he could leap shoulder-high. He liked to look at himself in the upright mirror and make up stories about the image he found reflected there. This image was dark and picturesque, tall and rather imposing. There was something in its aspect that was vaguely foreign.

He felt like a man under a spell, who had somehow put himself into a dungeon and could not find the key to let himself out. He had seated himself by the wayside of life, and a dense growth of shrubbery had sprung up about him, and the bushes had turned into saplings and the saplings into trees. Through the entangling depths he could find no exit. His style, his personality, his habits had been formed as far back as he could remember. At six he had read the *Pilgrim's Progress*. The first book he had bought was the *Faerie Queene*. To see the world in terms of allegory, or in the light of symbols, was second nature with him. At twelve, in a notebook his grandfather had given him, urging him to write out his thoughts,—a few every day,—he had described a child named Betty Tarbox as "flitting among the rosebushes, in and out of the arbour, like a tiny witch,"—phrases that might have occurred in the tales he was writing now. At sixteen, he had written a poem, precisely in the vein of some of these tales, about a young man dying for love of a ghost. He had certainly not acquired from Godwin's novels, however they intensified the taste, the feeling for romantic mystery that had sprung, for him, out of the Salem air. The novels of Scott had only excited further what seemed to be an inborn predilection for the history and the scenery of New England. All he knew was that these habits of mind, already

formed in Salem, had been fostered in Maine, where he had
spent a year, during his boyhood, on a lonely farm in a
border hamlet. He had heard all sorts of stories from the
farmers, tales of the supernatural, tales of ghosts, legends of
the old colonial wars. He had heard the story of Father
Moody of York, who had worn a black veil over his face.
In summer, he had seen the Indians, on the Penobscot river,
in their birch canoes, building their wigwams by the mill-
dams. Round about stood the pine forests, bordering the
northern lakes. He had skated all winter in the moonlight,
alone and silent. He loved the black shadows cast by the
frozen hills.

He might well have been thought uncanny. He was certainly "deep," as the countrypeople said, deep as a night-
scene by Albert Ryder. His mind was bathed in a kind of
chiaroscuro that seemed to be a natural trait; and yet it
was a trait that he cultivated, half by instinct, half by deliberation. He had a painter's delight in tone. He liked to throw
a ghostly glimmer over scenes that he chose because they
were ghostly. It was a taste like Claude Lorrain's for varnish.
He liked to study chimneys in the rain, choked with their
own smoke, or a mountain with its base enveloped in fog
while the summit floated aloft. He liked to see a yellow field
of rye veiled in a morning mist. He liked to think of a
woman in a silvery mantle, screening her face and figure; a
man's face, with a patched eye, turning its profile towards
him; an arm and hand extended from behind a screen; a
smile that seemed to be only a part of a smile, seen through
a covering hand; a sunbeam passing through a cobweb, or
lying in the corner of a dusty floor. Dissolving and vanishing
objects. Trees reflected in a river, reversed and strangely
arrayed and as if transfigured. The effects wrought by moonlight on a wall. Moonlight in a familiar sitting-room, investing every object with an odd remoteness,—one's walking-stick
or a child's shoe or doll,—so that, instead of seeing these
objects, one seemed to remember them through a lapse of

years. Hawthorne could never have said why it was that, after spending an evening in some pleasant room, lighted by a fire of coals, he liked to return and open the door again, and close it and re-open it, peeping back into the ruddy dimness that seemed so like a dream, as if he were enacting a conscious dream. For the rest, he was well aware why he had withdrawn to this little chamber, where there was nothing to measure time but the progress of the shadow across the floor. Somewhere, as it were beneath his feet, a hidden treasure lay, like Goldthwaite's chest, brimming over with jewels and charms, goblets and golden salvers. It was the treasure of his own genius, and it was to find this precious treasure that he had sat at his desk through summer and winter. The snow-flakes pelted against the window-panes, the casement rattled in the December gusts, clouds of dust blew through the open window. Seasons and years rolled by. He had his doubts. Was he tearing down the house of his mind in order to find the treasure? In the end, when the house was destroyed, for all he could say, there might be nothing in the chest but rubbish.

Sometimes, in summer, on a Sunday morning, he stood by the hour behind the curtain, watching the church across the way. The sunrise stole down the steeple, touching the weather-cock and gilding the dial, till the other steeples awoke and began to ring. His fancy played about this conversation carried on by all the bells of Salem. At twilight, he would still be standing there, watching the people on the steps after the second sermon. Then, as dusk set in, with a feeling of unreality, as if his heart and mind had turned to vapour, he ventured into the street. Sometimes, he was out all day, for the sake of observation. He would spend an hour at the museum, looking at the black old portraits that brought back the days of Cotton Mather. These portraits explained the books that he was reading, histories of Maine and Massachusetts, the *History of Haverhill*, Felt's *Annals of Salem*. Or he walked over to Marblehead and Swampscott, where the old salts gathered in the store, in their red baize shirts and oilcloth trousers, enthroned on mackerel barrels. He felt a natural bond with all these Yankees, fishermen, cattle-drovers, sailors, pilots. Some of them could steer with bandaged eyes into any port from Boston to Mount Desert, guided by the sound of the surf on every beach, island or line of rocks. He liked to sit with them in the bar-rooms, alive with curiosity, over a steaming hot whiskey-punch. He studied the coloured prints on the tavern walls. He noted the gateways in the crooked streets, the whales' jaw-bones set like Gothic arches, the bulging windows in the little shop-fronts, filled with needles, fish-hooks, pins and thimbles, gingerbread horses, picture-books and sweetmeats. He stood at the toll-house on the Beverly bridge, watching the procession of carts and sulkies that rolled over the timber ribbon under which the sea ebbed and flowed; or he strolled on to Browne's Hill and traced out the grass-grown hollows, the cellars of Browne's Folly. Occasionally, he spent a day in Boston, haunting the public-houses in Washington Street. He penetrated behind the sober shop-fronts that masked the old Province House. Oftener, setting out at dawn, he rambled over Endicott's Orchard Farm, over the witchcraft ground and Gallows Hill, or perhaps Phillips's Beach, exploring the coast from Marblehead to Gloucester. He would bathe in a cove, overhung with maples and walnuts, pick up shells on the water's edge, skip pebbles on the water and trail the sea-weed after him, draw names and faces in the sand. He would sit on the top of a cliff and watch his shadow, gesturing on the sand far below.

Occupations worthy of a poet who knew the value of reverie. These idle, whimsical movements absorbed his body while his mind pursued its secret operations. One had to be bored in order to think. Passivity was Hawthorne's element, when it was not curiosity. Usually, in the summer, dressed in his blue stuff frock, he undertook a longer expedition, to Maine or the Berkshires, perhaps, or to Martha's Vineyard, or along the Erie canal, as far as Detroit, where the old Connecticut poet, John

Trumbull, was spending his last years. Nothing escaped him then; he had resumed his habit of keeping a notebook. He would stop for commencement at some country college, at Williams, so like his own Bowdoin, and mingle with the sheepish-looking students, half scholar-like, half bumpkin, fidgeting in their black broadcloth coats. He would spend a day at a cattle-fair, among the ruddy, round-paunched country squires who, with their wonderful breadth of fundament, waddled about, whip in hand, discoursing on the points of the sheep and oxen. He fell in with big-bellied blacksmiths, essence-pedlars chattering about their trade, old men sitting at railway stations, selling nuts and gingerbread, oblivious of the rush and roar about them, wood-choppers with their jugs and axes who had lived so long in the forest that their legs seemed to be covered with moss, like tree-trunks, pedlars of tobacco, walking beside their carts,—green carts with gaily painted panels,—conjurors, tombstone-carvers, organ-grinders, travelling surgeon-dentists, the queer confraternity of the road. He would exchange a word with a tavern-keeper, reading his Hebrew Bible, with the aid of a lexicon and an English version. If it was a rainy day, the toddy-stick was in active use and the faces gleamed about the bar-room fire. He would stop at a farm for a glass of milk or linger in the market-place at Pittsfield, among the buck-boards and the farmers' wagons, while the stage-coach discharged its passengers. Opening his notebook in the evening, he jotted down his observations. Why these trivial details? He had seen a tame crow on the peak of a barn. A half-length figure had appeared at a window, with a light shining on the shrouded face. A little boy had passed him on the road, lugging a basket of custard-cups. An intrusive reader, looking over his shoulder, might have wondered why it was worth his while to record such trifling items. To Hawthorne they were anything but trifling. Every one of these notes possessed for him a golden aureole of associations. Traits of New England life, aspects of New England scenery: a stone wall covered with vines and shrubs and elm-trees that had thrust their roots beneath it, a valley like a vast bowl, filled with yellow sunlight as with wine, the effect of the morning sun on dewy grass, sunlight on a sloping swelling landscape beyond a river in the middle distance, an afternoon light on a clump of trees, evening light falling on a lonely figure, perhaps a country doctor on his horse, with his black leather saddle-bags behind him. Dark trees, decaying stumps, a cave in the side of a hill, with the sunlight playing over it. How like the human heart, this cave, with the glancing sun and the flowers about its entrance. One stepped within and found oneself surrounded with a terrible gloom and monsters of divers kinds.

Once, before turning homeward, he pressed on to Franconia Notch. This was the artery over the mountains through which the groaning wagons from the seaports carried the goods of Europe and the Indies to northern New Hampshire and Vermont. There stood the Great Stone Face. One dined on bear's meat in these northern woods, echoing with the notes of horn and bugle. Under some avalanche an ambitious guest, a young story-teller, for example, might have been crushed at Franconia Notch. Who would ever have heard of him then, his history, his plans, his way of life? Or suppose this young writer had frozen to death on the summit of Mount Washington? The mountain would have been a pedestal, worthy of a story-teller's statue. Hawthorne roamed up and down the Connecticut Valley. He fell in with a group of vagabonds, on their way to the camp-meeting at Stamford, a book-pedlar with the usual stock,— a handful of gilded picture-books and ballads, a Life of Franklin, Byron's Minor Poems, Webster's Spelling-book, the New England Primer,—a degenerate Indian with his bow and arrows, willing to turn a penny by shooting at it, an Italian conjuror with a merry damsel attired in all the colours of the rainbow. A travelling puppet-show had joined the troupe. The grave old showman, in his snuff-coloured coat, turned the crank of the organ, and all the little people on the miniature stage broke into lively movement. The blacksmith's hammer fell on the anvil, the tailor plied his needle, the dancers whirled about on their feathery tiptoes, the soldiers wheeled in platoons, the old toper lifted his bottle, the merry-andrew shook his head and capered. Prospero entertaining his island crew! It was a masque of shadows that seemed as real as any other world that Hawthorne lived in. Would it not have been a good idea for a young story-teller to join this group and become an itinerant novelist, like the Oriental story-tellers, reciting his extemporaneous fictions at camp-meetings and cattle-fairs, wherever two or three were gathered together?

Most of Hawthorne's journeys, to be sure, were journeys *autour de sa chambre.* He was never away from Salem long. His notebooks, however, filled along the road with incidents and casual observations, were precious memorabilia. They gave his ideas a local habitation. One saw this in the stories he was writing, sketches of actual life, historical tales and allegories. He thought of these as "twice-told" tales because, in several cases, he had heard them first before he had worked them out himself. How did he feel about his writing? It seemed to him easier to destroy it than to court an indifferent public. He had thrown into the fire the *Seven Tales of My Native Land,* for which he had failed to find a publisher, and he had burned every available copy of his little published novel, *Fanshawe.* There was a devil in his manuscripts. He saw it laughing at him as the sparks flew upward. As for his recent stories,—the annual magazines had begun to accept them, the *Souvenir* and Peter Parley's *Token,*—they seemed to him to have an effect of tameness. They had, he felt, the pale tint of flowers that have blossomed in too retired a shade. If they were read at all, they should be read in the twilight in which they were written. They had been concocted from thin air; but it was this that gave the tales their magic. Some of them were really insubstantial, dim as ghosts basking in the starlight; in others, the apparently insubstantial was a new and original substance. In Tieck's and Hoffmann's Germany, where the Gothic mind had reawakened, in harmony with this mood of spectral Salem, even in Poe's New York, one found similar tales of the

listening dead, of graves and flitting shadows and lovers knock-
ing at each other's tombs. Processions of mourners passed with
measured tread, trailing their garments on the ground. One
saw figures melting in mist; black veils, boys with bandaged
eyes, bridegrooms dressed in shrouds; pools paved with marble and mosaic; images shimmering in water. One heard the
cries of children lost in the woods. Young men slept in the
road-side shade, oblivious of the fates that might have been
theirs if they had been awake; for fortune, crime and love hovered about them.

They were tales like evening moths or butterflies, light as
clouds or flowers of early May, blooming in a woodland solitude. Out of them rose, when they were gathered together, an
opalescent world that was strangely old, yet fresh and unfamiliar; it was like Prospero's island, half terrestrial, half an ethereal fabric. It was a new creation, this world of Hawthorne,
with a past in Merry Mount and the Province House, in
Howe's Masquerade and Esther Dudley, a present in pedlars
and Shakers, in vagabonds and white old maids, in sunny Connecticut valleys and forest hollows, in snowstorms and ambiguous lime-burners, a future in little puckish boys and girls at
play in the flickering sunshine. All very simple, it appeared,
simple as the brightly coloured leaves that drift over a sedgy
stream, only that too often, before one's eyes, the stream sang
its way out of the meadow and carried its bright burden into
the forest, where all grew dark and baleful.

EMILY DICKINSON

The Dickinsons lived in the principal house in Amherst. A
large, square, red-brick mansion that stood behind a hemlock
hedge, with three gates accurately closed, it was a symbol of
rural propriety and all the substantialities of western New
England. Edward Dickinson, the lawyer, had always had his

office in the village, and four times a day, in his broadcloth coat and beaver hat, with a gold-headed cane in his hand, he had passed through one of the gates, going or coming. A thin severe punctilious man who had once been a member of Congress, a friend of Daniel Webster in his youth, a Calvinist of the strictest persuasion, he was a pillar of Amherst College until his death in 1874. The college had been founded, largely by his father, to check the sort of errors that were spreading from Harvard, and he never abated his rigour in the interests of pleasure. He was said to have laughed on one occasion, but usually he was as cold and still as the white marble mantel in his parlour. The story was told in Amherst, however, that once he had rung the church-bell, as if to summon the people to a fire. The whole town came running, for he rang the bell excitedly. He wished to call attention to the sunset.

Next door, behind the hemlock hedge, another ample dwelling stood, suggesting in its style an Italian villa. Here lived the Squire's son Austin, once his partner, who kept open house for the college. While the Dickinson mansion was somewhat forbidding, with the stamp of the Squire's grim ways and his invalid wife, the villa was a centre of Hampshire hospitality that shared its rolling lawns and charming garden. Olmsted had visited there, when he was planning Central Park, to examine the shrubs and trees, the plants and flowers; and distinguished guests at the college commencements and lecturers during the winter season were received and welcomed there as nowhere else. Emerson, Wendell Phillips and Beecher had stayed in this house next door, and Samuel Bowles of the *Springfield Republican* was an intimate friend of all the Dickinsons. The *Republican* was a school for journalists, known far and wide, and travellers,—Dickens and Kingsley among them,—constantly stopped at Springfield in order to have a chat with Samuel Bowles. His paper was a sovereign authority in Amherst, and he often drove over for a call at the villa or the mansion, sometimes bringing manuscripts by well-known authors to show the Dickinson daughters before they were published. His favourite was Emily, who was older than Lavinia, but Emily usually "elfed it" when visitors came. She was always in the act of disappearing. Through the blinds of her western windows, overlooking the garden, she observed the hospitalities of the villa, and snatches of whatever was current in the books and talk of a college town, in the politics and thought of the moment, reached her when the guests had gone away. But even her oldest friends seldom saw her. While sometimes, in the evening, she flitted across the garden, she never left the place by day or night. To have caught a fleeting glimpse of her was something to boast of, and a young girl across the way who watched at night for a light at her window was thrilled if Miss Emily's shadow appeared for a moment. There were nurse-maids who thought she was a witch. They frightened the children by uttering her name, as if there were something malign in Miss Dickinson's queerness.

While her friends seldom saw her, and almost never face to face,—for she spoke from the shadows of the hallway, as they sat in the parlour, or sometimes down the stairs,—they were used to receiving little letters from her. These letters were also peculiar. Miss Dickinson rarely addressed the envelopes. Some other hand, perhaps her sister's, performed this office for her. More often the names of the person and town had been clipped from a printed paper and pasted together, as if it were a sort of violation to expose the strokes of her pen to the touch of the postman. The letters themselves were brief and cryptic, usually only a line or two: "Do you look out to-night?" for example. "The moon rides like a girl through a topaz town." Or "The frogs sing sweet today—they have such pretty, lazy times—how nice to be a frog." Or "Tonight the crimson children are playing in the West." Or "The lawn is full of south and the odours tangle, and I hear today for the first the river in the tree." Now and again, some fine phrase emerged from the silvery spray of words,—"Not what the stars have done, but what they are to do, is what detains the sky." Sometimes her notes had a humorous touch: "Father steps like

Cromwell when he gets the kindlings," or "Mrs. S. gets big-
ger, and rolls down the lane to church like a reverend marble." But her messages often contained no words at all. She
would lower baskets of goodies out of the window to children
waiting below. At times, instead of a letter, she sent a poem,
an odd little fragment of three or four lines, with a box of
chocolate caramels or frosted cakes and a flower or a sprig of
pine on top, heliotrope, perhaps, or an oleander blossom or a
dandelion tied with a scarlet ribbon. Her letters were rhythmical, they scanned like the poems, and they were congested
with images,—every phrase was an image; while the poems
themselves suggested nursery-rhymes or Dr. Watts's hymns,
broken up and filled with a strange new content. They might
have struck unsympathetic readers as a sort of transcendental
baby-talk. It was evident that Miss Dickinson had lost the art
of communication, as the circle of her school-friends understood it. She vibrated towards them, she put forth shy, impal-
pable tentacles, she instantly signalized with a verse or a note
every event in their lives. But she did not speak the language
of the world outside her, and one gathered that she did not
wish to touch it. She was rapt in a private world of sensations
and thoughts. It was even observed that her handwriting went
through three distinct phases and that towards the end the
letters never touched. Each character, separately formed, stood
quite alone.

She had been a recluse since the early sixties, and her family surmised the reason. She had fallen in love with a married man, a Philadelphia clergyman, and had buried herself at
home by way of refuge. When her supposed lover supposedly
pursued her there, her sister dashed across to the house next
door and exclaimed to their brother Austin's wife, "Sue, come!
That man is here. Father and mother are away, and I am
afraid Emily will go away with him." Such was the family
legend, which may have been apocryphal. Undoubtedly, the
clergyman came to see her, but probably only to call. Was he
in love with Emily? Probably not. In any case, she did not

go away. She withdrew from all activities outside the household, and her mind turned in upon itself. She had hitherto been eminently social, or as much so as her little world permitted. Born in 1830, in the red-brick mansion, she had grown up a lively girl who was always a centre of attention. She was a capital mimic. She travestied the young-lady pieces, the "Battle of Prague" and others, which she played on the mahogany piano, and her odd and funny stories enthralled her friends. Later they remembered that she placed bouquets of flowers in the pews of those she liked best, at church. Dancing and card-playing were not allowed in Amherst, but Noah Webster's grand-daughter, who lived there, evaded the prohibition on behalf of her circle. She held "P.O.M." meetings for the Poetry of Motion, and Emily Dickinson excelled in this branch of learning. She joined in picnics and walks over the Amherst hills with groups of boys and girls from the town and the college. They had "sugaring-off" parties and valentine parties, and they often climbed Mount Norwottuck where they found ferns and lady-slippers; and sometimes they met at a brookside in the woods, where the boys went fishing and the girls made chowder. Emily was an ardent botanist. She knew the haunts of all the wild flowers in the region, and sometimes she scrambled alone through the forest, perhaps with her big dog Carlo. She was an expert cook. At home she baked the bread and boiled her father's puddings, but her father was difficult to please. He read "lonely and rigorous books," she said, on Sunday afternoons, fearing that anything else might "joggle the mind"; and Shakespeare, the Bible and Dr. Watts's hymns were the reading that he chose for his daughter. He did not like her to work in the garden, or to make visits without him, and when she was too witty he left the table. At fifteen she could not tell the time: her father supposed he had taught her, but she had not understood him, and she did not dare to ask him again or ask anyone else who might have told him. Now and again, she rebelled. She smashed a plate or a teacup, and her friends and her brother found ways to provide her with books, hiding them in the box-bush that stood beside the front door or on the parlour piano, under the cover. In one way or another, she contrived to read most of the current authors, especially the Brontës and the Brownings, with Hawthorne, Coleridge, Irving, Keats and Ruskin. One of her special favourites was Sir Thomas Browne, and she loved the drollery of Dickens. For the rest, she read Heine in German and Emerson's poems, and Frank B. Sanborn's letters in the *Springfield Republican* kept her in the literary current. She was by no means passive in this house of duty. Once, at a funeral in Hadley, whither she had gone with her father in the family barouche, she ran away for several hours with a young cousin from Worcester and drove back to Amherst in his buggy. At school, she declared her independence. She had been sent as a boarding-pupil to Mary Lyon's seminary, where she had written her themes on the nature of sin. She had listened to lectures on total depravity as if, like most of the other girls, she had meant to be a missionary's wife; but when, one day, Miss Lyon asked all the girls to rise, all who wished to be Christians, Emily alone refused to do so. She had found that she could not share the orthodox faith. Otherwise her life went on, with a few journeys here and there, like that of any country lawyer's daughter. As a young girl, she had visited Boston. She remembered the concerts and Bunker Hill, the Chinese Museum and Mount Auburn; and later, on two occasions, she stayed in Cambridge, to receive some treatment for her eyes. When her father was serving his term in Congress, in 1854, she spent seven weeks in Washington with him. Her father's friends were struck by her charm and her wit. It was on her way home that she stopped at Philadelphia and received the sudden shock that had changed her life.

This was the whole of Miss Dickinson's story, so far as outward events were concerned, when Thomas Wentworth Higginson entered the picture. Higginson had written an appeal in *The Atlantic*, addressed to the rising generation. Remembering the days of *The Dial*, when the hazel wand, waved over New England, had indicated hidden springs of talent in many a country town, he said that to find a "new genius" was an editor's greatest privilege. If any such existed who read *The Atlantic,* let him court the editor,—"draw near him with soft approaches and mild persuasions." Higginson added a number of admonitions: "Charge your style with life . . . Tolerate no superfluities . . . There may be years of crowded passion in a word, and half a life in a sentence." This appeal was anonymous, but many of the Amherst people knew who wrote the articles in *The Atlantic,* for Sanborn's literary gossip kept them posted; and presently Colonel Higginson, who was living in Worcester, received an odd little letter. The letter was unsigned, but the writer sent four poems, and she placed in a separate envelope the signature "Emily Dickinson." She begged this distant friend to be her "master." The poems puzzled Higginson. While he felt a curious power in them, he was not prepared for a "new genius" who broke so many rules as this lady in Amherst, who punctuated with dashes only and seemed to have small use for rhyme and merely wished to know if she was "clear." She did not ask him to publish the poems, and he did not pass them on to the editor, but he wrote her a sympathetic letter that was followed by a long correspondence. She continued to send him poems at intervals, signing her notes "your gnome" and "your scholar," but, although she asked him again if he would be her "preceptor," and he offered her a number of suggestions, she never changed a line or a word to please him. In one note she said, "If I read a book and it makes my whole body so cold no fire can ever warm me, I know that is poetry. If I feel physically as if the top of my head were taken off, I know that is poetry. These are the only ways I know it. Is there any other way?" And once she replied, when he asked her for a photograph, "I had no portrait now, but am small, like the wren; and my hair is bold, like the chestnut burr; and my eyes like the sherry in the glass that the guest leaves." This feminine mystification piqued the colonel. He wrote, "You enshroud yourself in this fiery mist and I cannot reach you, but only rejoice in the rare sparkles of light." When she told him that her companions were the hills and the sundown, he replied that she ought to come to Boston: she would find herself at home at Mrs. Sargent's. At last, in 1870, he went to Amherst. After a brief delay, while he waited in the parlour, he heard a faint footstep in the hallway and a shy, little childlike creature glided in. She carried two day-lilies, which she placed in his hand, saying, in a soft, breathless voice, "These are my introduction," adding in a whisper, "Forgive me if I am frightened. I never see strangers and hardly know what to say." She spoke of her household occupations and said that "people must have puddings," and she added a few detached enigmatic remarks. She seemed to the amiable Higginson as unique and remote as Undine or Mignon or Thekla. But he was disturbed by the tension in the air and was glad he did not live too near this lady. There was something abnormal about her, he felt. He had never met anyone before who drained his nerve-power so much.

At that time, Miss Dickinson was forty years old and had long since withdrawn from the world; and the friends who came to see her sister were used to the "hurrying whiteness" that was always just going through a door. She sometimes swept into the parlour, bowed and touched a hand or two, poised over the flowered Brussels carpet, and vanished like a ghost or an exhalation; but even these appearances had grown rarer and rarer. Only the neighbours' children really saw her. She had given up wearing colours and was always dressed in diaphanous white, with a cameo pin that held the ruching together. She was decisive in manner, anything but frail. Her complexion was velvety white, her lips were red. Her hair was bound with a chestnut-coloured snood, and when it was chilly she wore a little shoulder-cape crocheted with soft white worsted run through with a ribbon. She often had a flower in her hand. She moved about in a sort of reverie, flitting "as quick as a trout" when she was disturbed. (This was one of her sister Lavinia's phrases.) The children knew her "high, surprised voice." They knew her dramatic way of throwing up her hands as she ended one of the stories she liked to tell them. She made them her fellow-conspirators. They followed her upstairs and heard her comments on the guests she had left in the parlour. She would say, with finger on lip, as feminine callers left, "Listen! Hear them kiss, the traitors!" Or, peeping down the stairs, she would say of some man, "Look, dear, his face is as pretty as a cloth pink," or "His face is as handsome and meaningless as the full moon." She remarked, apropos of some scholarly person, "He has the facts, but not the phosphorescence of learning." She said that her own ideal caller was always just going out of sight, and that it made her shiver to hear people talk as if they were "taking all the clothes off their souls." She called herself the "cow-lily," because of the orange lights in her hair and her eyes, and she observed that the housemaid moved about "in a calico sarcophagus." Once she said to her little niece, who was puzzled by her shy ways, "No one could ever punish a Dickinson by shutting her up alone." Meanwhile, her life went on with her flowers and her sister. She had a small conservatory, opening out of the dining-room, a diminutive glass chamber with shelves around it; and there she grouped the ferns and the jasmine, the lilies and the heliotrope and the oxalis plants in their hanging baskets. She had a little watering-pot, with a long slender spout that was like the antenna of an insect, and she sat up all night at times in winter to keep her flowers from freezing. The garden was her special care, and occasionally one saw her at dusk through the gate fluttering about the porch like a moth in the moonlight. When it was damp, she knelt on an old red army blanket that she had thrown on the ground, to reach the flowers. Usually, on summer evenings, she sat for a while with Lavinia on the side piazza, overlooking the flagged path that led to the villa. There stood the giant daphne odora, moved out from the conservatory, and the two small oleanders in their tubs.

Meanwhile, since 1862, Miss Dickinson had been writing poems, although there were very few of her friends who knew it. They all knew the little rhymes she sent them with arbutus buds, but they did not know how seriously she pursued her writing, at night, beside the Franklin stove, in the upstairs corner bedroom, in the light that often glimmered over the snow. From her window she had caught suggestions that gave her a picture, a fancy, an image. Perhaps a boy passed whistling, or a neighbour on her way to church, or a dog with feet "like intermittent plush"; or perhaps she knew that a travelling circus was going to pass in the early morning, and she sat up to watch the "Algerian procession." A dead fly on the window-pane stirred her imagination, and once in the glare of a fire at night she saw a caterpillar measuring a leaf far down in the orchard. She saw the bluebirds darting round "with little dodging feet,"

> *The motions of the dipping birds,*
> *The lightning's jointed road;*

and all these observations went into her verses. She wrote on sheets of note-paper, which she sewed together, rolling and tying the bundles with a thread or a ribbon and tucking them away in the drawers of her bureau; although sometimes the back of an envelope served her as well. But, casual in this, she was anything but casual,—she was a cunning workman,—in her composition. Poetry was her solitaire and, so to speak, her journal, for, like Thoreau in Concord, she watched the motions of her mind, recording its ebbs and flows and the gleams that shot through it; and she laboured over her phrases to make them right. Were they all her own? Were there echoes in them, or anything of the conventional, the rhetorical, the fat? Were they clear, were they exact, were they compact? She liked the common hymn-metres, and the metres of nursery-jingles, which had been deeply ingrained in her mind as a child, and she seemed to take a rebellious joy in violating all their rules, fulfilling the traditional patterns while she also broke them. She was always experimenting with her rhymes and her rhythms, sometimes adding extra syllables to break up their monotony, sometimes deliberately twisting a rhyme, as Emerson did, for the sake of harshness, to escape the mellifluous effect of conventional poems. Many of her pieces were like parodies of hymns, whose gentle glow in her mind had become heat-lightning. For Emily Dickinson's light was quick. It was sudden, sharp and evanescent; and this light was the dry light that is closest to fire.

The visible setting of these poems was the New England countryside, the village, the garden, the household that she knew so well, a scene, the only scene she knew, that she invested with magic, so that the familiar objects become portents and symbols. Here were the hills, the changing seasons, the winter light, the light of spring, the bee, the mouse, the humming-bird, the cricket, the lonely houses off the road, the village inn, the lamp-post that became, in the play of her fancy, sublime or droll; and with what gifts of observation she caught the traits of her birds and insects, of everything that crept or ran or flew,—the snake "unbraiding in the sun," the robin's eyes, "like frightened beads," the umbrella of the bat that was "quaintly halved." She often seemed a little girl, amusing herself with childish whimsies, and, in fact, as the ward of her father, she remained in some ways adolescent; and, as she dressed to the end in the fashion of her early youth, so she retained the imagery of the child in the household. But her whimsies sometimes turned into bold ideas. She saw the mountain, like her father, sitting "in his eternal chair"; her ocean had a "basement," like the house in Amherst, and her wind and snow swept the road like the brooms that she had been taught to use,—the brooms of the breeze swept vale and tree and hill. A journey to the Day of Judgment struck her as a "buggy-ride," and she saw a "schoolroom" in the sky. She domesticated the universe and read her own experience into the motions of nature and the world she observed. The sun rose in the East for her "a ribbon at a time," and the "house-wife in the evening West" came back to "dust the pond." Clouds for her were "millinery," mountains wore bonnets, shawls and sandals, eternity "rambled" with her, like her dog Carlo; the wind had fingers and combed the sky, and March walked boldly up and knocked like a neighbour. Volcanoes purred for her like cats, and she saw the planets "frisking about," her Providence kept a store on the village street, and she thought of death as coming with a broom and a dustpan. The moon slid down the stairs for her "to see who's there," and the grave for her was a little cottage where she could "lay the marble tea." One could not "fold a flood," she said, and "put it in a drawer," but she rolled up the months in moth-balls and laid them away, as she had swept up the heart and put away love; and she saw hope, fear, time, future and past as persons to rally, welcome, play with, flee or tease.

The turns of fancy that marked these poems were sharp and unpredictable, and yet they were singularly natural,—nothing was forced. Miss Dickinson lived in a world of paradox, for, while her eye was microscopic, her imagination dwelt with mysteries and grandeurs. Ribbons and immortality were mingled in her mind, which passed from one to the other with the speed of lightning, though she sometimes took a mischievous pleasure in extravagant combinations of thought, uniting the droll and the sublime, the trivial and the grand. There was in this an element of the characteristic American humour that liked to play with incongruities, and Miss Dickinson maintained in the poems of her later years the fun-loving spirit she had shown as a schoolgirl. To juxtapose the great and the small, in unexpected ways, had been one of her prime amusements as the wit of her circle, and this, like the laconic speech that also marked the Yankee, had remained an essential note of her style as a poet. "Shorter than a snake's delay," her poems were packed with meaning; and, swiftly as her images changed, they were scarcely able to keep the pace with which her mind veered from mood to mood, from faith to mockery, from mysticism to rationalism, through ecstasy, disillusion, anguish, joy. These poems were fairylike in their shimmer and lightness, they moved like bees upon a raft of air; and yet one felt behind them an energy of mind and spirit that only the rarest poets ever possessed. Was not Emily Dickinson's idiom the final proof that she possessed it? Her style, her stamp, her form were completely her own.

Such were the games of solitaire that Miss Dickinson played in the silent room, as lonely as Jane Eyre, in her red-curtained alcove, dreaming over the book with its pictures of the arctic wastes and the rock that stood up in the sea of billow and spray. Miss Dickinson had only this "acre of a rock," and yet what a harvest it yielded of grape and maize. Having but a crumb, she was sovereign of them all, as she said quite truly; for her constant theme was deprivation, the "banquet of abstemiousness," and this sharpened as nothing else her perception of values. When the well's dry, we know the worth of water, and she felt that she knew victory because she knew defeat, she felt that she knew love because she had lost it. Certainly for all she missed she made up in intensity: where others merely glowed, she was incandescent.

HOWELLS

To Howells, living in Cambridge, absorbed in his writing, the dawning age that followed the Civil War was one of peace, prosperity and content. The scandals of public life, the abuses of business were remote from the little world in which he dwelt. Coming from the West, he had found a haven in Cambridge and Boston when the young men who had grown up in this region were most inclined to feel its limitations. Others might hanker for Paris and London: for him the New England capital was all-sufficient. Besides, he had known much more of America than most of the young New England men and had more reason to think it essentially sound. He knew New York and the Hudson river, Ohio and the Mississippi. He had seen Quebec and Montreal. His four years in Europe were incidental. As a child of the Western Reserve, he had shared the old political faith that Emerson and Whitman serenely embodied; and the atmosphere of his family had shaped his mind. His Quaker and Swedenborgian forbears had never questioned the "inner light." He was predisposed to be unaware of evil.

Howells was a happy man. The others were restless and anxious: he was tranquil. Even the Civil War was vaguer in his mind than it was in the minds of Boston men who had seen its woes at close range. In his Venetian consulate, he had caught only rumours of it; and, while he felt responsible for having missed the war, it was like a dream for him, as for some who had fought. Moreover, while most of the other young men were groping for a foothold, Howells had found his vocation and was launched upon it. How could he not have been happy? He was prepared to accept the "true American gospel," that everything was coming right in time. Years later Howells questioned this gospel. He awoke to the evils of his day far more than Henry James or Henry Adams, who had seen these evils at once; and he really faced the problem, which few of his generation faced,—what was a good American to do about them? Howells, happy, was also honest; his moral perception was deep and real. But he was predisposed to trust his country, and he rejoiced in the lull that followed the war. He rejoiced in his work, he rejoiced in his countrypeople, he rejoiced in the noble realities he found about him. Were not the poets and scholars as real as Wall Street? The Cambridge air was kind to the flowers of thought: it carried its burden of pollen from mind to mind. Sufficient unto the day were his misgivings. As the wife said in Tennyson's *Sea Dreams,* "Let all evil sleep." He felt as if the troubles of the world were settled.

In the house he had built on Concord Avenue, with the

Eastlake tiles and the book-lined study, he carried on his work for *The Atlantic*. His travel-papers, reviews and stories were giving place to novels, slight at first, expanded sketches, then gradually more and more ambitious. Meanwhile, he explored New England in the summer season. With his manuscripts and his magazine-proofs, he went for a month or more to the sea or the mountains, to Kennebunkport, Conanicut, Bethlehem, Jaffrey, to the farm boarding-houses and the summer hotels that were rising all over the region. One spring he spent at Lexington, where the fathers of the village, who were proud to have an author in their midst, gave him the town-hall to use as a study. He spent a few days at Campobello, and he passed one summer at Nahant. There he rented an old place with a forsaken garden and a belvedere that overhung the sea, a relic of the romantic days, half ruined, that watched the tides crawl over the shining sand. Once he stayed at Shirley among the Shakers and went to meeting there with the brothers and sisters, dressed in their neat, white kerchiefs and clean, stiff caps and their Quakerish coats and shoes of 1780. One of the brothers wrote mystical tracts, such as Howells's father had also written; another had a system of musical notation, which he employed in hymns of the angelic life. Elder Fraser cultivated his grapevines and blackberries, and others made baskets, palm-leaf hats and rugs. There was much in this Yankee communism that appealed to Howells. It confirmed his belief in equality as the guiding ideal of American life. The Shakers soon began to appear in his stories.

Indeed, the scenes of all these wanderings soon appeared in Howells's stories, the harvest of an all-perceiving eye. At the beaches, he observed the ladies, with their needlework beside them, sitting and talking in rows on the long piazzas. Sometimes they sat in the shelter of a cliff, and one of them read aloud while the others knitted,—*Felix Holt* or *Middlemarch* or the *Evening Transcript*. Occasionally, one of the ladies rose and trailed her shawl behind her, perhaps to pick up a spool that had fallen from her lap. Pursuing the spool, she dropped her scissors and thimble. Then all rose at once and scattered, for the time had come to lie down. While the older ladies were lying down, the young ladies were most in evidence, perhaps on the croquet-ground in front of the hotel or out in the rowboats on the river; for all these summer resorts abounded in loverless maidens, enough to provide a novelist with heroines forever. There were hammocks strung between the birches with young ladies in them, reading novels. They were always doing something to their hair, and all of them seemed to be prepared for what were called "attentions." They were the summer girls of the summer hotels, and it always seemed to be summer in Howells's stories. At the hotels in the mountains, the table-girls were school-teachers, who were adding to their income in vacation, and sometimes, in the afternoon, in their fresh bright dresses, they played the piano in the parlour. The clerks were usually college boys, and often young men from the hill-towns, with their girls in the buggies beside them, drove over for supper. Now and then, a landscape-painter appeared with his easel and colours,—he was making studies of goldenrod and granite and spread them about in the parlour for the guests to see. The great event of the day was the hop in the evening. When a Boston family arrived, or a bride and groom, the plot began to thicken. The waitresses straightened their hair, the ladies looked up from their knitting, and everyone knew that something was about to happen. What happened was a Howells story. It had to occur before it was written, but the chances were that, next summer, the young ladies in their hammocks were reading this. For the chances were that Howells had seen what happened. It might have been invisible to others, or nothing more than a breath or a ripple, the sort of thing that novelists seldom noticed. To Howells, who noticed everything and who seemed to be ubiquitous, this "nothing" that happened—for others— was the best of all. That he made something out of this nothing was the marvel of his mind and art; and moreover the something in question was highly important. It was love, in its

American phases, love in the American form; and what, for American readers, was more important?

Sometimes, in his wanderings, Howells stopped at Hartford, a halfway house on the road to New York where Mark Twain was living. Howells had first met Clemens in Boston. He had reviewed *The Innocents Abroad* and Clemens had called to thank him; and since then the two ex-printers, both of whom had pilot forbears and who had much else in common in their Western boyhood, had struck up a lasting friendship. Later they wrote a play together,—or, rather, they tried to do so,—on the story of Colonel Sellers from *The Gilded Age*. Mark Twain knew that Colonel Sellers was the only strong figure in the book, and he wished to give this figure a separate existence. It was to help him in this that he called upon Howells, a far more skilful craftsman than himself. In the end, he succeeded alone with his play, when Howells found that he could not work with Clemens,—a proof of the independence of Howells's talent. It was as if Vermeer had tried to work with Rubens, as if Jane Austen and Henry Fielding had attempted to write a novel together. But the incident was important for both these writers. While it threw Mark Twain back on his own resources, Howells had not wasted his energy. At this very moment, he was writing plays himself, and the failure of his attempts to work with Clemens undoubtedly cleared his mind. One only understands oneself by learning what one cannot do. Howells tried his hand at plays, as if to make sure of his proper form before he committed himself to novel-writing. He had tested himself, just so, as a poet and critic, and he carried on all these lines to the end of his life. He knew they were minor lines, but he was competent in them all, and no doubt his experience with them enriched his mind. As for his plays, they were comedies, and the best were farces. Like his own Maxwell, in *The Story of a Play,* he disliked the theatre as much as he liked the drama. The conditions of the stage were repugnant to him, and this showed that Howells was not a playwright born; but he had a gift for private theatricals,—dramatic chamber-music, as one might call them. In *The Elevator, The Register, The Parlour-Car, The Sleeping-Car,* he exploited the possibilities of these inventions. One overheard conversations through registers, and strange things happened when elevators refused to budge between the sixth and seventh floors. Parlour-cars and sleeping-cars lent themselves to situations. In after years, Howells's farces recalled a moment of history when all these modern toys were excitingly new.

Howells's friendship with Mark Twain had various repercussions, for each served the other as a foil. Each became better aware of his quality in contrast with the other mind, as always happens when men of high talent meet. They defined themselves in this relation, and, while both were pliable up to a point, each learned something from the other. Mark Twain confirmed Howells's American consciousness, which might otherwise have been overborne by Boston; and his scorn of all things European precluded any danger that Howells would follow the course of Henry James. On the other hand, Mark Twain deferred to Howells in matters of form and style. In this he profited greatly, for his feeling for aesthetic values was uncertain and weak. Howells's delicate taste and skill checked his genius of improvisation, which was always running wild in absurd caprices. But Mark Twain also fell a victim to Howells's limitations, for he seldom questioned the right of his friend to censor and alter his work.

These curious limitations of Howells, his tendency to the namby-pamby, his prudery and his timorous over-niceness, were partly temperamental and partly due to circumstances, his editorship, his marriage, the place and the moment. With a taste for the "cleanly respectabilities," he had avoided "abhorrent contacts," * while still a reporter in Columbus, the contacts with police-stations, saloon-keepers and ward-politicians who represented the seamy side of life. He had a morbid horror of the sordid and ugly; and this squeamishness had

* Howells, *Years of My Youth.*

grown on the tender-minded Howells with his life in Venice
and later in Cambridge and Boston. In Venice, alone with his
wife, he had known few men; and, in fact, Mrs. Howells
was more and more a nervous invalid who required, if she did
not exact, his continual devotion. He wrote much more for her
than for anyone else, and his mind was unconsciously governed by her distaste for all that was disagreeable and unpleasant. He had whimsically complained to Norton that he
suffered from "too much female society"; and, for all his literary friendships, he was never thrown closely with men. To
see the world through the eyes of women, to humour them,
to share their interests, to avoid whatever shocked their prepossessions, this was an instinct and a tendency in Howells
that his life on *The Atlantic* had confirmed. He had been an
editor before he began to write novels, and his mind was further shaped by this ordeal; for the new age of readers was
mainly an age of women readers, and his mind was naturally
in harmony with this obvious condition. As an outsider, as
one who revered *The Atlantic* and was anxious to forward its
interests, he was eager to be so. Thus the editorial habit, with
its feeling for the prospective reader, determined the novelist's mind as it were in advance.

All this qualified Howells's realism. His view of life was
severely limited, although he was scarcely aware of these limitations. "Nuns fret not at their convent's narrow room"; and
there was something nunlike in Howells's Quakerish innocence
cence and simplicity of heart. A deeply truthful nature, both
honest and courageous, he shared the romantic American
worship of women. This did not prevent him from deriding
their foibles, but to accept their "sex-piety," as the editor Ful-
kerson called it, was second nature with him as a man and
a writer. His mind was bathed in a feminine atmosphere;
the air of his stories was sometimes close; he was singularly
preoccupied with domestic matters, and he had a tendency
to fuss, to make too much of trifles, that was also characteristic of Henry James. The tendency to fuss had always been a

New England trait, and the decay of its larger public interests had revived in the Yankee mind this spinsterish habit. Howells was obliged to reflect it, but he often seemed to humour the trait. He lent himself to the point of view of people who magnified scruples and quibbles into problems of conscience, who thought for days about some peccadillo that a larger mind would settle and dismiss at once. Could a young man offer himself in the waiting-room of a railway station? Was it not wicked to go driving with a girl one did not "quite respect"? Misunderstandings over such trifles abounded in Howells's weaker novels, and often formed the substance of the story. In some of his moral-obstacle races, the obstacles were cobwebs that a breath of common sense would have blown away.

Howells's mind, for all this, was large, alert, observant and witty, and the world that appeared in his novels was a revelation. For here was the real American scene, reflected in a burnished mirror, as no American eye had ever perceived it. This was not the romanticized scene of Cooper, or Hawthorne's crepuscular world, or the rudely drawn reality of Mrs. Stowe, still less the distorted scene of the ordinary novels, those formless artificial sentimental inventions that passed, in 1870, as reflections of life. There were no heroes or heroines here "dying" for each other, no turgid flights of fancy or exaggerations, but a manifold assemblage of Yankees, New Yorkers, Southerners, Westerners, all in their habits as they were, going about their business in the morning sunlight. Aware as Howells was of Europe, which often appeared in these novels, he saw his people in terms of themselves and their country, moving in their own orbit, under their own American sky, in all the actuality of their daily existence; for he had followed Emerson's counsel, not seeking the great, the remote, the romantic, but sitting at the feet of the low and familiar. His work was an ample reply to those for whom America was not sufficiently rich and complex in its types to provide a novelist with subject-matter. In range and variety, his portrait-gallery was second to none; and so truthfully drawn were all his people that every reader exclaimed at once, Yes, this is right, how well I know them! They all assumed flesh and blood at once. For Howells's eye for detail in their costume and appearance was as subtle as his knowledge of their motives. And how natural were his conversations, what an ear he had for shades of distinction in tone between regions and classes, the rustic and the urban, the Western, the Virginian, three or four kinds of Bostonians and the people of Maine. Add to this Howells's style, so limpid and precise, so animated, gay, adroit and fresh, and one could understand the joy with which his American readers acclaimed this panorama of their charms and their foibles.

While New England, for a number of years, was Howells's central *mise-en-scène,* his mind from the first was continental. If he had a purpose, this was to reconcile sections and classes in a broadly democratic feeling for life; and, in order to bring them together, he often presented his people as travellers, who meet in hotels, in stations, on steamboats, on trains. One gathered from his novels that Americans were always moving, always going or coming, abroad or at home; and, in fact, in this respect, these novels reflected the post-war years and Howells's own habit as a constant tourist. In one of his tales, the girl was married in a storage-warehouse. She had been meeting the young man there for years, for the families had been twenty times "in and out of storage." But how, except as travellers, in a country so diversified, could Howells have assembled so many varieties of people? Where could Kitty Ellison of Eriecreek, New York, have met Mr. Arbuton of Boston except on a Saint Lawrence riverboat? Where, save on the "Aroostook," could Lydia Blood have fallen in with Staniford and Dunham? Only in Venice could Lily Mayhew have told an Austrian officer that her home was in Patmos, New York; and only in a station or a summer hotel could the South have encountered the West in the casual natural fashion of Howells's novels. Accordingly, for settings, he liked these fortuitous meeting-places, where his fellow-Americans gathered on a neutral ground; and he shared all their pleasure in the bustle of travel, in the chaos of docks and wharves, in the rattle of baggage, in the jolting of stages and coaches, in the views from the trains. How charming, as one sped past, the sight of a woodcutter's shanty, losing itself among the shadows in a solitude of the hills! How amusing to sit in a waiting-room and establish fanciful relations with people whom one saw for half a minute! Howells delighted in these adventures, in the hissing and coughing of locomotives under the flaring gas-jets of a station at night, in the odour of paint and carpet that prevailed on the steamboats, in the tinkle of the ice-water pitchers, in the cinders on the trains, in the Negro waiters, the porters, the conductors, the drummers, whom he viewed with all of Whitman's benevolent eye. What joy, as he conveyed it, to receive your stateroom-key an hour before departure on the Albany night-boat, well knowing it would be light enough until you reached West Point to see the best scenery on the river. How pleasant, on a summer evening, on the Nantasket boat, as you sat on your camp-stool on the deck, to feel the air freshening, while you watched the gay life of the harbour, while the islands of the bay waxed and waned and Boston slowly vanished in the hazy distance. Was there ever such upholstery and music as one found on the Fall River boat! Such gorgeously carpeted cabins, such a glitter of glass, such a multitude of plush chairs and sofas! Or such mirrors as one found in the great hotels in Portland and Boston, such tessellated floors and marble mantels, such acres of Brussels carpet and glossy paint, so many varnished tables and fluted pillars! Howells's people moved about their world in the perpetual presence of these mild marvels, with a chorus of customs officials and condescending hotel-clerks, stewardesses, cabin-boys and consuls.

This was the "young country" that Europeans talked about, and the moon that overlooked it was of lucent honey. In the foreground of every American landscape one saw a bridal pair, at Mount Desert or Niagara, on the Florida keys; and Howells was an accomplice of all the lovers. Was not this country a larger Arcady? It struck him so, at moments, in the presence of all these shepherdesses and shepherds. Wherever he looked there were brides and brides, charmingly dressed, with ravishing toilets. How small their gloves were, how high the heels of their little boots, over which the snowy skirts electrically fluttered! Howells was a born match-maker; he delighted in a pretty woman; he had an eye for every touch of style, and he liked to show how naturally the simplest American village girl assumed the grace and elegance of the world of fashion. All his "young ladies" were "stylish," wherever they came from, whether the Lapham girls or Helen Harkness, with her vividly birdlike mobility, or Lydia, from South Bradfield, where the village seamstress had studied the paper patterns and *Harper's Bazaar,* while she observed the costumes of the summer boarders; and Howells shrewdly noted the trifles of behaviour that so often carried the day in his game of love. A girl ran up the steps of a house with the loop of her train in her hand, or she wore the special "light hat" that settled the question, or she poked with her parasol a shaving on the pavement which the young man was holding with his foot. She changed the bow at her throat from scarlet to crimson, or perhaps she laughed at everything, not because she was amused but because she was happy. She always knew just how she looked; she always knew, like Howells, what she was doing. The parents often stood in awe of these phantoms of delight, deferring to their knowledge of the world; and Howells shared all their tender solicitude for them. He loved to see them piloted into safe harbours. With what distress he hovered over Helen Harkness, when she lost father, house and money and helplessly floundered in Boston to keep afloat. With what anxious care he followed Egeria, in *The Undiscovered Country,* drifting about the roads with the visionary doctor, until she found a haven with the Vardley Shakers,—and he liked to picture Lydia as the idol of the ship, with its pride and chivalrous sentiment revolving round her. When Lydia boards the "Aroostook," what pleasure the fatherly captain takes in making her feel at home in the little white cabin, with the rug that his wife has hooked and the gim-cracks left by the girls and all as snug and tidy as a farm-house kitchen.

Howells's world was a paradise of lovers, though the centre of his picture was not love. He was in reaction against the old romancers who saw love in a monstrous disproportion to the other relations of life. But his earlier novels especially abounded in love-scenes,—love in a blueberry-patch, in a sailboat, a row-boat,—and some of these were exquisitely felt. Such was the scene in *The Undiscovered Country* when the journalist Ford and Egeria, on opposite sides of the grapevine, find each other. No word of love passes between them, and yet, across the screen of vines, as they catch occasional glimpses through the leaves and the tendrils, they establish a perfect understanding. Howells excelled in these idyllic moments, and it was not from any fault of his if a life of endless holidays did not lie beyond them. He knew how often marriages failed,—in *A Modern Instance* he pictured a failure,—but, if he had had his way, the course of love would always have run smooth. Romeo would have saved his Juliet, and somehow Hamlet would have re-gained Ophelia. In fact, his people were usually happy. His nature obliged him to see them so, as he naturally saw human beings as decent and honest. His world was one of mutual trust, and Dr. Boynton's faith in people, when this Alcott who never found his Concord set forth on the road without a penny, confident that doors would open for him, was reflected in Howells's general view of life. His Dr. Ellisons abounded in self-respecting candour, his Kittys never imagined themselves misprized for anything but a fault. His policemen were kind and obliging; and if, in his New England, you went out for a walk, and the rain overtook you in the country, you could borrow a waterproof at the nearest schoolhouse. You could leave the waterproof with the station-master, knowing that the stage-driver would safely return it.

Howells's Americans were all a natural family, and family loyalty was his favourite theme. His novels were full of loyal

households, the Maverings and the Coreys, the Gaylords, the
Laphams, and Howells delighted in testing the bonds that held
them together, conjugal, maternal, paternal and filial. With
what pleasure he showed how Dan Mavering, the young man
in *April Hopes,* awoke to his father's intellectual interests. How
proud the Laphams were of one another, the more they
plumbed the probity in each. Howells grieved over the inequal-
ities that kept his worthy people apart, and he liked to show
how trifling their differences were. Staniford quickly penetrated beneath Lydia's rustic phrases. Mr. Corey was ready to
find that the bull-headed Lapham was the soul of honour.
Howells resented only those who broke this law of trust that
bound his Americans together,—the arrogant, the vulgar, the
pretentious. He liked to show how far from vulgar the apparently vulgar could be, how the poetry of Lapham's paint
redeemed him; but he could not abide presumption, pretension
or sham. Profoundly anti-aristocratic, he treated his real patricians, the Bellinghams and the Coreys, with understanding;
but he was merciless to those who presumed on their caste.
With what cold scorn he pictured Mr. Arbuton, the little
Boston prig in *A Chance Acquaintance,* who slighted the
charming imaginative Western girl! This was the young man
who felt that he honoured the farm in Quebec by saying it was
just like Normandy and expected the cows to be grateful.
With what zest Basil March rallied his wife, who was a bitter
aristocrat at heart, when she took for a foreign nobleman the
haughty commercial traveller with the stare that seemed to
suggest a long descent. It was notable that Howells's black-
guards were often newspapermen, like Bittredge, in *The Ken-
tons,* and Bartley Hubbard, who broke his law of mutual trust
with their prying disregard of human dignity and rights. Like
Henry James and Henry Adams, he detested these glib young
journalists who represented the new publicity. As an old news-
paperman, he disliked to see this new type pushing aside the
journalist with a feeling for letters.

As Howells advanced, his more serious novels reflected, one by one, the changing conditions and phases of American life. *The Undiscovered Country* described the rise of spiritualism at the time when Mrs. Eddy was settling in Boston, the queer streets where the mediums lived, with "Madam" on their doorplates, and the air was full of astral manifestations. Egeria and Dr. Boynton were types of the moment, as Marcia Gaylord was in *A Modern Instance;* for the growth of divorce was another sign of the times. *The Rise of Silas Lapham* was the best of all the pictures of the new self-made millionaires, and *A Woman's Reason* presented another type of the eighties, the girl setting out to make a living in open competition with the world of men. Through decade after decade, Howells followed the life of the nation, and he caught so many of its phases that as a social historian he had no equal. No doubt, he was most at home in domestic relations. His portraits of women perhaps were the best of all, and he aroused a passion of protest with his realistic record of their foibles and their instinct for manœuvre. An age of "feminization" was not prepared for this particular aspect of the Howells mirror, for these women with their strategic headaches, these mothers who feed on their daughters, who carry on a system of strikes and lock-outs and whose cabins, when they travel, are smugglers' dens. But Howells's portrait-gallery was varied and large. He knew the town and the village, the farm and the city, the factory, the business-office and the lumber-camp, the artisan, the idler, the preacher, the teacher; and he pictured artists and editors, shop-girls and students, American scholars in Italy, professors at home, religious impostors, philanthropists, helpless parents, manufacturers, scientists, journalists, country squires, hotel-keepers, lawyers, sterile dilettanti, the hare-brained villager and the village fool. All these people were admirably real, and they recalled in later times a prosperous, buoyant American age when everyone "got on" and most were happy. If there were other stories, these were true also; and Howells himself told some of the other stories. His vision darkened as he advanced in life. But, while he lacked a certain intensity, his writing never lost the charm of a truthful, candid, cheerful, hopeful temper. Howells was the most winning of American writers.

JOHN MUIR

John Muir visited in 1879 one of the wildest of the states, the "battle-born" Nevada, admitted during the Civil War and already strewn with grey and time-worn ruins. On every hand dead mining towns stood forlorn amid broken walls, with their chimney-stacks, furnaces and machinery half buried in sand, towns in which coyotes wandered now through the sage-brush in the streets where churches and hotels had flourished ten years before. John Muir had already seen the California mining camps. A few survivors whom he found in the washed-out gulches had shown him around the old Calaveras diggings, but he had been tracing the channels of pre-glacial rivers and the mines were only picturesque for him. He saw the Sierra gold-region as a "rose-purple zone" consisting of low tawny waving foothills, roughened with brush and trees and outcropping masses of slate, coloured grey and occasionally red with lichens. Muir, a naturalist, was also a writer whose first paper in the *Overland Monthly* had aroused immediate interest in 1872. It described an unusual snow-storm in the Yosemite valley.

John Muir had arrived in San Francisco in April, 1868, with a wish to go, as he said, "anywhere that's wild," and he presently set out for the Yosemite on foot, camping along the way, ignoring the roads. It was the blossoming time of the year over the lowlands and the coast-range, and the valley of the San Joaquin was drenched with sunshine, one vast level flower-bed, a lake of colour, perfume and light, with the meadow-larks and the streams singing together. Muir wandered enchanted through this glorious garden in long wavering curves, knowing by his map that the Yosemite lay to the east. There, during the last few years, two or three settlers had wintered and one of them had even planted an orchard in the valley. Muir, at last arriving there, found employment as a shepherd for a while. He was to spend many years in the heart of the Sierras.

A few weeks before this, he had finished his "thousand-mile walk to the Gulf," a botanical excursion from Louisville through the Southern states, not the first of his expeditions, for he knew the Northern wildernesses, but one that took him to Florida and even to Cuba. Pushing southward through deep woods, by the leafiest and least trodden ways, with a small rubber satchel and a plant-press, he had followed the course of the migrating birds, finding Kentucky, as Audubon had found it, the most favoured province of all for the lover of wild life. In the great bedroom of the open night, he slept in this paradise of oaks, with its rapid streams and flower-bordered canyons, travelling only with a loaf of bread, living for weeks on crusts and water, wandering as free as the wind in forests and bogs. He had little to fear from the bands of guerrillas roaming the Cumberland mountains, long accustomed to plunder in the recent war, who thought nothing of murdering a traveller for a handful of coppers. As for plants, he had looked for them even in the Chicago streets, finding a few between the paving-stones, and he discovered rare varieties in the river-lands of Georgia, where William Bartram had botanized long before him. Penniless when he reached Savannah, he built a shelter of rushes and moss and camped in the Bonaventure cemetery, the old forest graveyard, spending five nights among the tombs, which suggested so many of the poems of Poe, under the silver streamers waving from the live-oaks. He searched the swamps and pine-barrens of Florida and the creeks with water as black as ink, watching the pelicans fill their baskets and the herons, blue as the sky, winnowing the warm air on quiet wings. Other lonely old white herons drowsed between tides in their favourite oaks, curtained by long skeins of Spanish moss. Once he dined on venison and milk, after a ramble through the flowery woods, with a former Confederate officer who had become a planter; then, sailing to Cuba for a month, he gathered shells and plants in the sun-flower bogs and wild gardens along the shore. He longed to go on to South America, visit the basin of the Orinoco and float the whole length of the Amazon on raft or skiff, a dream that Mark Twain had shared a few years before him. Then his imagination turned to California and its wonders and he sailed thither by way of Panama.

In the Yosemite, Muir's first task was to watch over sheep in the pastures near by, then he was employed to build and run a saw-mill; but, able as he was to live on three dollars a month, he was not obliged to sacrifice much of his freedom. He put up a little shanty of sugar-pine shingles that stood near the foot of the lower Yosemite fall, digging a ditch for a stream from the creek that passed through the cabin and gave him society and music as well as water. For it fell enough to ripple and sing in low sweet tones that made delightful company, especially at night. There was a floor of rough slabs and a bed suspended from the rafters, while ferns climbed over the window by the writing-table. It all cost less than four dollars: it was cheaper than the hut where Thoreau had lived in a similar spirit at Walden. Muir roved by day through the trackless forest crossing the pathways of ancient glaciers, tracing mountain streams through lily-gardens, learning the habits of the squirrels and the birds in the redwood groves and among the rocks, camping for the night at the foot of some wild cascade. With resinous firewood from a storm-beaten thicket, he boiled the water for his tea, sleeping in chambers as snug as a chipmunk's nest, well-ventilated and full of spicy odours, enchanted in the wilderness of shattered crags, ridges and peaks, botanizing, geologizing, sketching and writing in his notebooks. During his first year he explored much of the Divide between the Tuolumne and the Merced basins, while he climbed Mount Dana and Mount Hoffman and penetrated the Bloody Canyon to Mono Lake. In winter, with its wondrous storms, snowbound in his cabin he ranged through Humboldt and Agassiz by the cozy fire, through Lyell, Tyndall, Darwin and Emerson's essays, considering his discoveries of the summer in the light of their minds. He had become convinced that a vast ice-mantle had once covered all this mountain region, grinding and sculpturing it into the forms that one saw today as it followed rock-cleavages and faults in its slow descent. This was the "glacial erosion" theory of the origin of the valley which he presently expounded in articles in Greeley's *Tribune,* the first of all his writings for publication,* a theory that was scouted by Josiah Whitney, who conducted the survey of the valley, along with his assistant, Clarence King. Whitney and King rejected the views of "that shepherd,"—who was right,—believing that the valley originated in a cataclysm. Muir even found living glaciers in the Sierras that were unknown before 1871. In the autumn of that year he discovered the Black Mountain glacier in a shadowy amphitheatre between two peaks. He had never expected to find an active glacier as far to the south as this in the land of sunshine.

Thus began the explorations that he carried on for forty years in the mountains of California, in Nevada, in Alaska, recorded in books that were published later, many of them after his death, but largely compiled from his journals of these earlier days. Towards the end of his life, as a student of trees, he visited Australia and Africa and realized his early dream of the forests of Brazil by sailing for a thousand miles on the Amazon river. Meanwhile, for ten years he wandered alone among mountains and storms, exploring all day long in the high Sierras, setting out as a rule before daylight with a bundle of bread tied to his belt and striding away with his notebook in the bracing air. Going to the woods was like going home for him, and it even pleased and amused him to sleep on rocks, curled like a squirrel round a boulder, when he could not find a fragrant bed of fir-plumes, and he was as happy as Daniel Boone in his sunny forest garden in these calm vast measureless mountain days. He lived without animal flesh, for he never carried a gun with him and even left the rattlesnakes un-

* 1871.

molested, rejoicing in the glorious landscapes about him, the serene assemblage of ice-born peaks and the great domes and ridges that shone below them. In their wide-sweeping belts and beds covered and dotted with forests and groves, the moraines that looked so barren were full of life, composed in a wild harmony, moreover, and the lakes scattered on the table-lands, linked together by shining streams, glowed for him like pleasant human faces. He bathed in the floods of light, watching the sun-bursts over the peaks and the radiance of noon on ledge and cliff, with the pure blue bell-like sky brooding over all. In the forests, ponds and meadows in the hollows, there were always new crystals and plants for him, arctic daisies, lilies higher than his head, and to him the rocks seemed talkative and friendly, with warm blood gushing through their granite flesh. He never tired of the valley itself, a paradise for him that made even the loss of Eden seem unimportant, with its groves of pine and oak strewn over the grasslands and the river flashing in the sun as it swept between them. But he found no one to share his feeling about the trees until Emerson visited the Yosemite in 1871. The silver firs and the suger-pines filled Emerson at once with delight and awe, and, riding up to the saw-mill on horseback, he was immensely interested too in Muir's collection of Sierra plants and sketches. Together they rode out to the Mariposa grove, and Emerson seemed to be pleased when Muir, who was thirty-three years old, proposed an immeasurable camping-trip in the depths of the mountains. Muir pictured the fire he would build in the woods, the beautiful fragrant sequoia flame and the great trees transfigured in the purple light, while the stars looked down between the mighty domes, but Emerson, already old, was a child in the hands of his friends and their indoor philosophy held him to the hotels and trails. It was Emerson's afternoon of life, but Muir remembered later that no one before him had properly seen the valley, while Emerson, happy in his visit to this mountain tabernacle, found Muir the right man in the right place.

For the better part of six years Muir lived in the Yosemite.

He often scrambled about the brink or went for a ramble along the walls, which were sculptured into an endless variety of spires and gables, of battlements and mural precipices, all trembling with the thunder tones of the falling water, cascades so airy and so light beside the cliffs over which they poured that even while their voices filled the valley they seemed like wisps of smoke or floating clouds. Sometimes he made discoveries, as when he first found Shadow Lake, hidden in the glorious wildness like unmined gold. He spoke of this charming lake only to a few friends, fearing it might come to be trampled like the Yosemite valley, and, visiting it year after year, he never found traces of humanity there beyond the remains of a camp-fire and the thigh-bones of a deer. The Indians had broken these to get at the marrow. Occasionally an Indian would suddenly appear, standing silent and grim before him, as motionless and weather-stained as an old tree-stump, with that wonderful art of walking unseen and escaping observation which his people had slowly acquired in their forest life. Once he was startled by a group of queer hairy muffled creatures that came shuffling and stumbling towards him out of the woods, with a boneless wallowing motion like that of bears. They were Mono Indians wrapped in blankets made of the skins of sage-rabbits with dirt on their faces that was fairly stratified: old and thick enough to have almost a geological meaning, it was divided into sections by furrows that resembled the cleavage-joints of rocks. Strangely blurred, with a worn abraded look that suggested exposure in a castaway condition for ages, they were travelling to the Yosemite to gather acorns.

Often Muir was out in storms. He made rather a point of being so, for even at the opening of the winter season, when he hastened down to his valley den, it was not to "hole up" and sleep the white months away. He was abroad all night at times and every day as well, wading, climbing, sauntering amid calms and gales, when the snow-laden summits were swept by a wild norther and the snow-dust on the exposed slopes, caught by the winds and tossed into the sky, was borne from peak to peak in resplendent banners. He had seen these snow-banners nearly a mile in length, and once, when the whole Yosemite fall was torn into gauzy shreds and blown horizontally along the face of the cliffs, he saw the peaks of the Merced group waving banners against the sky, as regular in form and as firm as if woven of silk. He found himself once enjoying an avalanche-ride. After a heavy snowfall he had set out early to climb by a side canyon to the top of a ridge when he was swished down of a sudden to the foot of the canyon. It happened as if by enchantment, and Elijah's flight in a chariot of fire could scarcely have been more exciting than this flight in a milky way of snow-stars. Once when he was out exploring a tributary valley of the Yuba river he was overtaken by a Sierra windstorm and found himself, as it were, blown on through the midst of its passionate music and motion across many a glen from ridge to ridge. In order to have a wider view, it occurred to him to climb one of the trees and get his ear close to the music of the topmost needles, and, choosing a tall Douglas spruce, he mounted about a hundred feet while the tree swirled round and round and rocked in the torrent. He clung to the lithe, bushy top, braced like a bobolink on a reed, while his eye roved over the excited waving forest, watching the light that also ran in ripples and swelling undulations across the wild sea of pines from one ridge to another. The shafts of the trees were brown and purple, tinged with yellow here and there, with masses of grey, chocolate and vivid crimson, and he listened to the click of leaf on leaf, the deep bass of the branches and the tense vibrations of the pine-needles, whistling and hissing. He kept his lofty perch for hours, frequently closing his eyes to enjoy by itself the water-like flow of the wind or to feast on the delicious fragrance streaming past him.

In later years, extending his travels, Muir went on a rambling mountain journey of eighteen hundred miles across Nevada. He reconnoitred Utah and studied the northwestern states, and he made several trips to Alaska, beginning in 1874, espe-

cially to see the stupendous glaciers there, pushing as far as the
Arctic ocean, on one of these expeditions, visiting northeastern
Siberia and the Aleutian chain. He had spent years in the
Sierras studying the action of ancient glaciers that had created
new landscapes with their tremendous pressure, and, aside from
this interest, he found sea-voyages inspiring as a change, with
water hills and dales in motion instead of the permanent waves
of the rocks. Alaska was a wonderful country for a lover of pure
wildness. There one could travel thousands of miles without
seeing any mark of man save some little aboriginal village now
and then, or the faint smoke of a camp-fire, and Muir was
determined to get into the heart of it,—trusting to his usual
good luck,—with his bag of hard-tack. He spent weeks of rapturous speculation canoeing through the intricate channels of the
coast, between the small islands of grey granite, closely observing the Stickeen Indians, the Chilcats and the Chilcoots,
sharing their dinners of salmon and the fat of a deer. For des-
sert they boiled with seal-grease the hips of wild roses. Muir
was almost too happy to get any sleep in Glacier Bay, where
the thunder of the icebergs rolled through the solemn stillness.
Some of the bergs were purplish by day and some were of pure
blue crystal throughout, while all of them had azure caves and
rifts of ineffable beauty in which exquisite tones of light pulsed
and shimmered. New bergs were constantly born from the ice-
cliffs, falling from the sides or top or emerging with a grand
commotion from below, springing up with tremendous voice
and gestures, while tons of water poured down their sides and
they plunged and rose again and again before they settled in
perfect equipoise. On dark nights when the winds were blowing
and the waves were phosphorescent the glaciers stretched
through the gloom with an unearthly splendour. The luminous
torrents streamed from their sides like long robes of light and
they roared in awful harmony with the waves and the wind.
Deep called unto deep and glacier to glacier all over the wonderful bay. Muir witnessed unheard-of auroras in Alaska also.
Magnificent upright bars of light appeared in bright prismatic

colours and swiftly marched in close succession along the northern sky. On another occasion a silver bow, colourless and stead-
fast, majestically spanned an inlet between two peaks, as intense in its solemn white splendour as if all the stars had been
raked together and fused and welded to make this celestial
bridge. More than once Muir was in peril of his life in these
regions, canoeing on ice-floes, caught in the midst of charging
bergs or scrambling over glaciers enveloped in grey flying
clouds and crossing crevasses hidden under the snow. But he
felt that, as compared with death from some shabby lowland
accident, it would be a blessing to meet one's fate on a glacier
or a mountain.

All this was in the later years when Muir had become a
public man, the father, as the newspapers called him, of the
national parks, who had seen the great California trees, the
oldest and largest of living things, blasted for commercial ends
by dynamite. He awakened the nation to the importance of
saving them. Meanwhile, he had taken up fruit-ranching not
far from San Francisco, where he shut himself up in a room
in a hotel to write, leaving the ranch from time to time to
compose from his journals the series of books that did not begin
to appear till he was almost sixty. In these he conveyed an
exhilaration that was often ecstatic, like Thoreau's, and like no
other American nature-writer's, and he resembled Thoreau
again as a lover of all things wild who did not "mould in," as
he said, with the rest of the race. It pleased him to discover
that even wild wool was finer than tame, that the wool growing on the mountain sheep in northern California was more
delicate in texture than ordinary cultivated wool. If there had
been a war of races between the bears and civilized man, he
would have been tempted, he said, to side with the beasts, for
he had a certain disdain of humanity that sprang from his
native Calvinism and preferred the "less vertical" creatures,
at least at moments. "Rough as the rocks," as he said of himself, "and about the same colour," congenial with mountains,
glaciers, snows and storms, he often wrote well of animals too,

detesting the anthropocentric notion that the world was especially made for the uses of man. Every crystal, bird and plant controverted this and proclaimed that it was made for itself, and its uses, alone, yet man's enormous conceit went unchallenged. Muir detested equally the notion of the behaviourists that animals were merely "machines in fur and feathers," for he had been deeply impressed by their intelligence and courage, by the fresh mountain vigour and valour of the Douglas squirrel of which he wrote and the loyalty, constancy and prowess of the dog Stickeen. This was the small black beast of most uncertain origin that followed him week after week through the flying snow on one especially perilous Alaskan journey. Nor could Muir praise the deer enough, at home as they were the continent over, whether in the Florida savannahs or the Canada woods, roaming over the northern tundras, crossing canyons and roaring streams, adding beauty moreover to every landscape.

EDWIN ARLINGTON ROBINSON

With Henry Adams, the New England mind seemed to have come full circle. It had passed through its springtime, its summer and Indian summer, and Edwin Arlington Robinson was not the only Yankee who saw

> A dreary, cold, unwholesome day,
>   Racked overhead,
> As if the world were turning the wrong way,
>   And the sun dead.

Had Charles Francis Adams's "ice-age" reappeared in this vigorous region, which had produced such abundant fruits of the spirit? The fatalism of Henry Adams was surely ten times darker than Calvin's fatalism had ever been. Was the tale of the Adamses symbolic? One thought of old John Adams, under his apple-tree at Quincy, rejoicing in the prospects of his "Christian Sparta"; and one thought of his great-grandson invoking Nirvana under the sickly shoot of Buddha's bo-tree. How much had waxed and waned in these four generations! Brooks Adams had only to look homeward to find an illustration that seemed to prove the truth of his theory of cycles.

Edwin Arlington Robinson personified winter. Abandoning New England, he had carried to New York an aura of blight, desolation, decay and defeat. His view of the world was wintry, —so was his life,—and his style and his personality were bleak and bare. Had there ever been a poet who loved life less or found so little joy in the turning of the seasons? In the down-east phrase, Robinson was "master chilly." There was something starved and cold about him, as if his clothes were too scanty and his blood was too thin, as if the Maine wind had invaded his marrow. He was like the stranger in his *Tasker Norcross* who confessed that he had "never yet been warm." Taciturn, shy as an owl, diffident, lonely, he could only establish relations with others by drinking; yet everyone confided in him, for he was the most sympathetic of men, as winning as he was aloof, and completely unworldly. Helpless in practical matters, naturally forlorn, he had the will to write but not to live; and he suffered himself to be rescued again and again and reverted again and again to a life in the shadow. Abjuring the "octopus of superficial self-respect," he haunted mean streets and sordid houses, for the only success that he recognized was failure in the eyes of men, and he saw even this as distorted and thwarted. He had become vaguely known as the "poet in the subway," in days when few were aware that he wrote or existed; for he had a post, in New York, in the newly-built underground railway, checking the loads of material that were dumped at the mouths. There, all day, in his long black coat and broad-brimmed hat, he paced the damp dark tunnel, with its odour of gases. If he saw a light at the end of the tunnel, it was usually choked with mephitic mist: it was not so much a light as a murky glimmer. And this was like the light in Robinson's poems. He seemed to share at moments the old Emersonian faith, which he variously called the "gleam" and the "vision." But, in him, this faith was only a dim conjecture. More often he looked out upon "dark tideless floods of nothingness," where men escaped from their dungeons only to drown.

Robinson brought to the "Town Down the River" a view of life that was formed in "Tilbury Town." He saw New York as he had seen Gardiner, Maine, in his youth in this moribund port on the Kennebec river. Gardiner, which had once been a thriving shipping-centre, had gone the way of other New England towns, and Robinson, whose father had been a prosperous timber-merchant, had witnessed in his own household the decay of the region. The family fortune, such as it was, had vanished, and Robinson's brothers had fallen on evil days; and Gardiner abounded in men who had once been important and who had no life any longer to shape to their code. Their minds had been formed for a large way of living. They had set the tone for their neighbours and headed their clans. But they had no clans to lead now, and the making of laws was not for them: they were left with the "dusty ruins of their fathers' dreams." They had lost their confidence, as the years went by, and they crept away into their houses and grew queerer and queerer. Eccentricities multiplied on humbler levels also, and misery walked patch-clad through the streets. There was never a more wintry world, as Robinson saw it. The sun rose dull there. Brown weeds grew through the floors of houses. Torn curtains flapped in broken windows. The trees were leafless, a ghostly band in cold array, and the thin leaves skipped on the stones with a freezing whisper. The streets were swept by an icy wind from the river, and the water was black under the piles of the docks. Spring never came there. At best, a late autumnal glimmer lingered by the river-side and warmed the bones of aging men. There were Archibalds and Isaacs on some of the farms, ripe and sweet as the cider they kept in their cellars; there were good old uncles who were good old liars; there were admirable doctors of billiards, "fallen from on high." But these were few beside the lonely men who wandered through the scene, disconsolate shadows. There were outcasts, in broken shoes, sleeping in doorways on Water Street, who had once driven their span of horses; there were skirt-crazed old reprobates, misers and spendthrifts; there were men who had been wrecked by kinks, horrors who had never lived, ruins ridden by fear and killed by terror. There were creepers among catacombs, "whose occupation was to die," there were respected citizens who blew their brains out; and one saw them straggling through the town, stumbling over frozen ruts, in the cold white shine of a dreary day. In short, this population was a whole *Spoon River Anthology*, acting out its epitaphs in the world of the living.

Such was Robinson's picture of Gardiner, where he had seen his future life as a "long and foggy voyage;" and through the cold fog, wherever he went, he saw the old familiar faces. Sometimes the derelicts of Gardiner appeared in New York, and "queer fellows" drifted all over the city. But why were they derelicts? Why were they queer?—and were they not, in any case, more interesting than men who were called successes? They interested Robinson more, as they interested many another young man who was living in New York at that moment and who found a spokesman in Robinson, then or later. Robinson was always drawn to them. Most of his Gardiner friends had been square pegs in round holes, a doctor, for example, who had lost his standing, a disreputable tinsmith, an outcast named Wash Benjamin who kept a mistress down the road. As long as the town did not respect them, they were likely to find a friend in him,—and not because he felt himself a failure. He had no interest in success; and he was quite content when a single suitcase contained all his possessions, including his books. Nor did his kindness explain it, kind as he was: he made an intimate friend of a lighthouse-keeper largely because he had had a foot wrenched off. He had, he said, a little of the hobo in him; and he sought, by a natural impulse, the despised and rejected, the lost, the maladjusted and the lonely because, in his time and his place, he was a poet. Who were the successful men, on the whole, in a world of business? One might have asked Sinclair Lewis, who was young just then, and who was so soon to reply with *Main Street* and *Babbitt*. Whether in New York, in Gardiner or in Gopher Prairie, the "bitch-goddess Success" repelled the young. It was noisome to the sensitive, as it had never been before: even for Horatio Alger it had lacked the glamour that failure as a symbol had for them. When Henry van Dyke was a great man and Veblen was a nobody, the Veblens had for the young an extraordinary charm; and one saw in every "queer fellow" a genius *in posse,* if not *in esse,*—one knew that if they were geniuses they had to be queer. To be adjusted to such a world, yet not to be a Babbitt, implied an all but unprecedented force of soul; and, as people had ceased to look for heroes and the young could scarcely believe they existed, they regarded maladjustment as a sign of grace. Five times out of ten, in fact, it was so. Most of Robinson's "lost" souls possessed some spirituality, and it was just for this reason that they were "lost." The people who were queer were the people who were real. Such was Robinson's message for an age of rebels.

Now, of course, there was nothing new in this. The founders of all the religions had known where to look for their apostles; and Hawthorne, in his *Feathertop,* had pictured the successful man who had not been able to pass through the eye of the needle. That successful men could not pass through it, neither Christ nor Hawthorne said; but a poet in a day like Robinson's could not dwell on exceptions. Poets had seldom dwelt on these exceptions, well knowing that successful men can look after themselves. In a day when success was the only visible goddess, a poet could only point out that it signified failure; and Robinson's successful men were Feathertops in every case, whited sepulchres full of dead men's bones. This, and its natural corollary, was the whole of his teaching. In all his long psychological poems, he stripped the emperors of their clothes,—

what was false within always betrayed them; while he turned
the tables on conventional opinion by showing goodness and
genius walking in tatters. It was the Fernando Nashes and the
Captain Craigs, the castaways who "went begging" that really
"went giving"; and this, the oldest of morals for poets, had never
ceased to be new. The novelty had always lain in the local
application. Hawthorne had applied it, and Robinson applied
it, each in his own place and time; and Robinson thus revealed
a fact which Americans had almost forgotten, that poetry is
always opportune. Emerson had restated this fact two generations before him, and only Emily Dickinson had revealed it
since, in the line of the Yankee tradition; and Robinson carried
on their line,—he was their natural heir,—just as he carried on
the line of Hawthorne. If, moreover, the Yankee tradition
seemed to be tapering off with him, this was characteristic of
the moment. The scene that he pictured was moribund, and
the Emersonian gleam that often appeared in his poems was
shrouded and dim. He could not share the old assurance that
life was part of a purposeful plan, much as he wished to share
it and almost did so. A sad man in a withered world, he could
not believe in the triumph of life, and the best of his real
successes were scarred by their failure. They, too, all too often,
were sterile fruit for the button-moulder, children of the abyss,
impotent and vain.

In later years, after the first world-war, when poets talked of
a "renaissance," Robinson was called its prime precursor. At a
time when American poetry had reached its lowest ebb, he,
in his obscurity, was real and vital; and the "irony and pity"
with which he regarded his victims of fate struck the new note
of the novelists as well as the poets. His probing, questioning,
doubting mind was the mind of the new generation; and his
portraits, even his sonnets, were novels in little. His longer
psychological poems continued the line of Howells and James;
and his technical development foreshadowed the poets that
were coming. He had cast off early the influence of Aldrich,
which dominated the magazine-verse of the moment, although,

as if to train his hand, he had written his villanelles and ballades. He had reacted against this facile jingling. He had sought for the spoken phrase, for the neat and plain; and, if his style was too prosaic, if it was too bare and cold, it was hard, it was clear and it was honest. Here again Robinson was in the line of Emerson, who liked "dry light and hard clouds, hard expressions and hard manners." Robinson eschewed the nebulous, the blurred and the vague, as he abhorred the fatuous and the stereotyped. In short, in a poetical world of baker's bread and confectionery, Robinson brought forth real bread again.

It might have been foreseen that, after this return to nature, American poetry was destined for a liberation. The "renaissance" that soon occurred was the result of various causes, and Robinson was only one of these. But his austere integrity and his tragic feeling were more than a little influential and his style cleared the ground for other growths; and the time was approaching when no one who was concerned for poetry looked for this year's birds in last year's nests. Robinson, a traditional poet, carried on the New England tradition, together with the classical tradition that lay behind it; but "last year's nests" in poetry, as the new poets saw them, were the nests of the romantic mind in its hour of decay. Romanticism had given birth to a verbal fatty degeneration that revealed the degeneration of the life it sprang from, in a world whose actual deity was the goddess Success; and younger minds reacted against such phrases as "reverence for life" and "quest for beauty," because of their sense of the false and the hollow behind them. The older poets, in all good faith, had used these phrases because they meant them. They really reverenced life, they sought for beauty; while the recent poets, the magazine-poets, used them merely because the older poets had used them. They did not reverence life,—they only said so; and they sought for the pretty and the charming but not for beauty. The passions they claimed were not real passions; their heartbreaks never broke their hearts. They took in vain a language that had once been great.

In short, they were "phonographs," as Amy Lowell presently said, or, as she might have said, ventriloquists, for their voice was not their own, it was alien to them, and they were either ordinary children of Mammon or wistful sentimentalists without strength. What had become of the great old life? What had become of the great old language? The bitch-goddess had them in her toils, and the "great words" had gone down with the great life-patterns.* It was no use to talk to the young about "sacred" and "glorious" things, especially when the war had traduced them further; and the more sacred one felt they were, the more one felt it was obscene to use the words or even think about them. The younger writers, growing up in this dying phase of the old society, knew that Robinson was right. Success in this civilization was inevitably failure, although failure might be success. The more honest these younger writers were, the less they believed in the world they lived in,—they were all rebels at the outset,—and the better they expressed their minds, the surer they were to express them in terms for which Robinson had prepared the way. For just as he had swept the house for all that was truthful and loyal in living, he had swept it for plain speaking, veracity and candour. As for poetry, he had broken up the "roof of heaven,"—the cotton-batting roof it had become,—and the "new forms" followed as a matter of course. The free verse, the new rhythms, the imagism, the realism, the characteristic forms of the coming decades,—and especially the classicism that was salient also,—expressed new states of mind and new ideas of which Robinson was one of the prophets.

---

* "It is advertising that has been the death of words.
  The word 'Personal' now on an envelope means 'impersonal;'
  'Important,' 'unimportant.'
  'The Finest,' 'The Best,' 'The Purest'—what do they mean now?
  Something somebody wants to sell.
  We are a nation of word-killers: *hero, veteran, tragedy,*—
  Watch the great words go down."
          —Edna St. Vincent Millay, *Conversation at Midnight.*

AMY LOWELL

In 1915 it looked as if New England had withered and floated away from the rest of the nation. It was a Wickford Point, sadly adrift from realities, whom there were few to love and less to praise. Its force seemed to have spent itself, it followed random impulses without the repressions that were natural when the force was focussed; it was like a clock that was running down, and those who loved it saw in it a vanity of effort, together with a certain "sadness of predestined failure." * Where was New England in New England? Was it not like Chekhov's Cherry Orchard, where there was nothing left but to put up the shutters, turn the key in the lock and go away?

Those who felt this did not know the writers, in whom the prescient saw other signs of the times. For the Yankees were writing again with talent and vigour; and did this suggest that New England was really exhausted? Had they ever ceased to write with vigour? Had they ever ceased to write in the New England way? The clock of Wickford Point went on ticking; and the new Yankee writers, appearances notwithstanding, remained in the New England tradition which they seemed to flout. They sometimes thought they were outside it, they sometimes wished to be outside it, but unconsciously they were within it, which was more important; and was it not part of their tradition that they should flout tradition, even as the greatest of the Yankees had flouted it before them? That one

* "I can see that Wickford Point was like a floating island that once had been solidly attached to the mainland. I can see it being severed from realities when I was still very young, and drifting off, a self-contained entity, into a misty sea . . .

"The whole place was like a clock which was running down, an amazing sort of clock, now devoid of weights or springs or hands, yet ticking on through some ancient impetus on its own momentum. Always when you thought it was going to stop, it would continue ticking."
—John P. Marquand, *Wickford Point.*

should flout tradition was the first of laws for Emerson's heirs. Rebellion was of the essence of the Yankee tradition, which was always concerned for fresh affirmations of life; and the most obvious thing about the new rebels was that they rebelled in the Yankee way. If they derided New England, if they disliked a standardized world, if they opposed the rigidities of the times and the mores, were they not repeating the pattern of 1840, when the young had been rebels at the outset? They all ran true to type in one fashion or another. To invent a "new way of being alive," the motive of E. E. Cummings, was a new way of being Thoreau at Walden; and no one ever vibrated to the "iron string" more than this terrible child, who wrote on the lintels of his doorpost, Whim. The author of *The Enormous Room* was an Ellery Channing with genius; and to turn one's back on banalities, with Edna Millay's force of feeling, was not remote from Margaret Fuller's plan. Amy Lowell played a role that had many a Boston precedent; and Robert Frost revived, for a new generation, the part of the poet-seer of Emerson's day. These writers represented a high degree of intensity, and all the moves of their game were buoyant and fresh; but they were all tarred with the brush of the Yankee tradition. One saw this in the doggedness with which they pursued their careers; and they proved that the Yankee mind was still alive.

Amy Lowell's force of will, the secret of her success and failure, was her most markedly racial characteristic. For this was the Yankee will, and she won her victories by it, and she largely failed by this will in her life as a poet. Too much of her poetry sprang from the will, not the poet. But there was no doubt about the will. She was a Lowell and a Lawrence, and she liked to run things, whether fleets of clipper-ships or colleges or towns; and, having the taste, she had the capacity, as dozens of the Lowells had,—she ran right well whatever she chose to run. She was a born promoter, as masterful as her forbears were, and the shrewdest of salesmen also, like the old China traders; and, seeing that America was giving birth to a first-rate product, she put her shoulder to the wheel and pushed it on the market. The product was American poetry, which was plainly on the rise again and which she handled like any other "big business." Was it good, bad or indifferent? What did it matter? It was good in bulk, and that was the point. It was another form of Standard Oil; and Miss Lowell set out to put it "on the map," as others had put salvation or woman's suffrage. Agassiz, in just this wholesale fashion, had put natural science on the American map; and this required perception, in his case as in hers. For Miss Lowell had perception, just as her grandfather's cousin had had it when he saw that American poetry was on the rise and wrote his *Fable for Critics* in the eighteen-forties. What scorn she felt for those who did not have it!—for the "caged warblers" and "phonograph" poets who thought they still lived in Victorian times, for those whose work was not their own but echoes, for those who cowered in ivory towers and never looked out of the window, for those who praised the glories of old New England and could not see the genius of Masters and Sandburg. She scorned Henry Adams, who had thrown up the sponge. She scorned Henry James and other "traitors." She scorned the lady-painters and performers of Chopin, with their "ghastly nights on cracked hotel-pianos." She was arrogant enough to impress occasional English observers, who were full of admiration for her because she reminded them of their own dear betters. She ran ocean liners and terrorized their orchestras by telling them to stop their outrageous noise; and she whizzed over the face of the earth in her claret-coloured motor, reorganizing hotels where she spent the night. Like Eliot's Cousin Nancy, she "strode across the hills and broke them"; and, if she was not bearded, she was full of oaths; and her bed had eighteen pillows, and she had ten thousand black cigars and seven megatherian sheep-dogs that mauled and all but murdered her visitors. This Daniela Webster was also an actress, whose earliest idol was Duse, and all her dramatic flair, with her verve and her gusto, went into the great pitched battle that she waged for the poets. She fought in the front rank, when occasion called for her, or, as less often happened, behind the lines, where she mustered her majors and colonels, her generals and lieutenants.

For literary soldiership, or literary statesmanship, America had never seen Miss Lowell's equal. Literary politicians had always abounded, but she was the prime minister of the republic of poets; and under her control this republic rose from the status of Haiti and became an imperial republic of the calibre of France. The poets had reason to thank their stars that they had a Lowell behind them, for whom editors and publishers were factory-hands and office-boys. Her telephone had the force of a gun: one could hear this going off at the other end of Texas. But the Texans and Nebraskans and the people of St. Paul crowded the window-ledges of their halls to hear her; and the map on which she had put poetry started and trembled under her feet,—the map of poetry blossomed in purple and red. She touched a fuse wherever she went, and fire-works rose in the air; and there were no set-pieces more brilliant than hers, no Catherine-wheels or girandoles or fountains. There was no still, small voice in Amy Lowell. Her bombs exploded with a bang and came down in a shower of stars; and she whizzed and she whirred, and she rustled and rumbled, and she glistened and sparkled and blazed and blared. If, at the end, it seemed like the Fourth of July, it was a famous victory, none the less, though the fields and the trees were littered with the sticks and the debris, with charred frames and burnt-out cases.

Besides, much more was left than people felt on the morning after. Miss Lowell was a pyrotechnist, but some of her scenic effects were permanent; and when she was not permanent she was salutary. Her theory of "externality" was undoubtedly fallacious, and much of her work was factitious, the fruit of the will. As if poetry could ever be "external"! Yet her actual externality was good for the moment. It was a challenge to internality at a time when the "internal" poets were so often sentimental, derivative and soft. When the *fond* was so corrupt and weak, the way to sting it into life was to assert that nothing was important but the *forme;* and all the new poets made much of technique,—they sometimes talked as if nothing else mattered. And what, in the end, did this matter?—though the end perhaps might be long in coming. The poets of the further future were to gain by this immediate future, in which the false remnants of the past were trampled out of sight and in which all manner of new forms were placed at their disposal when they developed the *fond* that was equally worthy. The world could always wait for its poets, and this was a time for tuning the instruments; and the free verse and polyphonic prose which Miss Lowell adapted and popularized provided a whole new orchestra for the poets who were coming. How good this audacity was after so much futile indirectness. After so much weltering in borrowed souls, how good it was to "live in the eye alone." How good was imagism to sharpen the perceptions, and all this zest for seeing, reporting, recording, this joy in the visible world, this picture-making, after so much wreathing and writhing and fainting in coils. How good this "religion of art," the note of the epoch, after so many woolly abstractions and impotent emotions, so many blurred conceptions and mouldy morals,—this technical virtuosity, so clean and fresh, this feeling for orchestral colour and verbal music, and this all but morbid fear of the obvious also. These poets reacted against bad technique by making technique an end in itself. What of it! The poets of the future would redress the balance. And they rightly threw out of the window the old New England classics, with all their Miltonic ideals and all their Victorian nature-worship. No need to fear that they would not come back. Were the Yankees really in danger of losing their ethos? If the classics went out by the window, they were sure to return by the door when the noble mind had outlived the abuse of its virtues. The new generation started with Poe, the first favourite of Frost as of Robinson, with Emily Dickinson's novel perceptions and Whitman, who had discarded the past. The new generation was also redressing a balance.

As a writer as well as a propagandist, Miss Lowell was part of all this movement, so similar in France and England in its causes and effects. For the whole Western world was undergoing the same changes, and Boston was a centre of this world, —as it had been in the eighteen-forties. It had never ceased to be a centre, despite the croakers and despite the dry-rot; and in the darkest hour of Boston and Cambridge world-influences had emanated from these twin cities in the persons of William James and Mrs. Eddy. For all the reactionary forces that opposed new culture, they were still hungry for new culture; and Amy Lowell was as hungry for the culture of this morning as an Omaha woman's club was hungry for the culture of the day before last. She made the Omaha woman's club hungry for it,—and she begged it and borrowed it, stole it, invented it, like all the writer-conquerors, with a high hand and a high heart and the enterprise of a merchant-adventurer. No doubt, her externality reflected her own extroversion. It was an escape as well from a troubled psyche, for Miss Lowell's inner life knew no repose. She had solved none of her vital problems, and she remained the conventional child that expressed itself in the first of her volumes of poems. Indeed, she was never a poet, properly speaking,—the poet in her never struggled through,—so she seized on the outsides of things as her only chance of effectuality, and her dramatic instinct achieved the rest. She had awakened suddenly to modern painting and music, and she pillaged them as she pillaged the Boston museums where she had played as a child. Among her treasures she was always the child, a Gargantuan child with the avidity of a khan or a brigand; and she pillaged books,—she tore the entrails out of them,—and she used in the composition of her rockets and pin-wheels the *alchimie du verbe* of Rimbaud, Verhaeren, Mallarmé and various others. She wrote free verse after Debussy's piano-pieces; she stole the show at aquariums, with their "swirling, looping patterns of fish"; and every place she read about and every place she visited,—whether Mexico, China, Peru, Saint Louis or Charleston,—left in her hand some scrap of a rhythm or a picture. She found a mine in Keats, whom she admired for his fearlessness, straightforwardness, directness, for all he had in common with herself; but everything served her purpose that gave her a little gold or brass, a beam of sandalwood or a bolt of silk, a flag, a trumpet, a tuba or a box of spices. And she toiled over her poems from midnight till dawn, not as one to whom the muses whispered, but as one who had to wrestle with them and force them to their knees in the sweat of her brow.

Well, was it all for show? Was it merely a night of the Fourth of July? Was it only a parade and swagger of Boston fashion? There was surely enough of the material in Miss Lowell's talent, too much noise, too much excitement; and yet how much remained that was new and crisp, what vividness of colour, what joy of action. One could say much for externals that enlivened the senses; and, when one had given up to time the bric-a-brac, the petals of Chinese flowers whose roots were somewhere else around the planet, one came back to Miss Lowell's story-telling. She was a story-teller, if not a poet, who had studied her art in Chaucer, in Keats and in Browning, and who, in some of her best tales, followed Miss Jewett and Miss Wilkins, when she was not touched by Robert Frost. Perhaps this deep Yankee in her was to live the longest, the Yankee whose tales in *East Wind* and the ballad of *Evelyn Ray* refurbished this old New England *genre* with a note of her own that was wholly fresh. Her colours here were browns and greys, but some of her blues and reds were fast; and, among other pieces, *Can Grande's Castle,* with its cinematographic style, remained her most characteristic. Perhaps its excess of vivacity wore one out. It was charged with enough electricity to burn one's hand off: it was like a third rail, it was like a power-line, and one had to touch the wires with circumspection. But there Amy Lowell exulted in her strength; and her feeling for ships and battles, for barbarism and heroism, for pageantry, pomp, dash and fanfaronade, for the theatre of history and the clash of peoples boiled up and bubbled over with a splendid brio.

She was Lady Hamilton, she was Nelson, she was Commodore Perry in Japan, with his sailor-chanties; and no New England writer since the great days of Prescott and Motley had given the world such brilliant historical scenes.

Essays and Sketches

ESSAYS

AND SKETCHES

JOHN BUTLER YEATS

MY MEMORY of John Butler Yeats goes back to 1908, to a little gas-lit bedroom in the old Grand Union Hotel, whither I had been taken to meet the "father of the poet." At that time, the Irish Literary Revival was at its height, and there were no names more glamorous than Yeats and Synge. The "father of the poet," with his air of a benevolent sage, looked the part to perfection, looked it and spoke it indeed so perfectly that he shone for us at first only with innumerable reflected lights. He had come to America for a fortnight; he was to stay for thirteen years. He was to experience between the ages of sixty-nine and eighty-three a second career as affluent as his first had been. How soon it was to be forgotten that he was anyone's father! In that early time,—it was natural enough,—he pulled for us all the strings of association. If he had not seen Shelley plain, he had been as an art-student a commensal of Samuel Butler and William Morris; he had been one of the first Whitmanians,—Whitman sent him his affectionate remembrance in a letter of 1872; for forty years he had agreed with York Powell and disagreed with Edward Dowden; he had known the father of Wilde and the mother of Shaw. All these recollections he poured out in a stream of enchanting anecdotes. He was lost for us at first in the light of his own talk.

His earlier career, to be sure, had been wanting in no element of the illuminative, when it was not the paradoxical. It was the career, as rumour told us, of genius in solution, or at least not too forbiddingly crystallized, the career of being human to such a tune that two generations of Irish poets and artists had grown up literally under its wing. The story of Yeats's Dublin studio is to be found in Katharine Tynan's autobiography and I do not know how many other books, just as the record of his influence is to be found in his elder son's *Reveries over Childhood and Youth*. Never, surely, had a man been more the cause of a more various wit in others, and this without prejudice to his having been the Gilbert Stuart of a stirring age in his nation's history. He had painted all the distinguished, the interesting, the charming men and women of his time, painted them with such insight and such grace that his gathered work constitutes of itself,—remote as it must have been from any suggestion of the public, the official,—a sort of National Portrait Gallery. He would not paint the dull, if only, it might seem, because it was they who wished to pay him for the trouble; it was the angel of impecuniosity, as he once remarked, that had given him his freedom, a sensitive angel, no doubt, whose protection he wished not to jeopardize. His studio was thus closed only to clients,—he would fly to escape from a lucrative commission, which meant that there would not be good talk during the sittings, the good talk that implied a current of sympathy. Nor was this merely petulant: he could paint only those whom he saw, and he could see only those whom he admired. He painted, as Swinburne criticized, for "the noble pleasure of praising." In this, as in so many other respects, his fashion was that of the ancients; and one cannot but think that his pride, and all this multiform expression of his pride, must have had its effect in the rebirth of the Irish spirit.

Such questions could hardly have interested Yeats himself. "Your artist and poet, unless he becomes a rhetorician," he wrote in one of his last essays, "is a solitary and self-immersed in his own thoughts and has no desire to impress other people."

It was thus that we were to see him, a true solitary himself, and never more so than when he most suggested (to those who did not know him) the autocrat of the dinner-table. But as time went on, his interest in painting in a measure dropped away, and I remember the final self-portrait that stood on his easel for thirteen years and that he left at the end still unfinished. Again and again he would rise from his chair and add a stroke or two with his old zest, but he never seemed able to finish it and one thought of it more and more in the light of Balzac's story of the *Chef-d'-œuvre inconnu.* It was another case like Washington Allston's last picture,—he could neither complete the work nor let it go. When he first arrived in New York, the impulse to paint was still strong; in the early days at Petitpas' he always had a sketch-book in his pocket and would draw as he talked; to the end his letters, even his briefest notes, were usually adorned with a little pen-and-ink impression, of himself, as a rule, and not too hasty to fix some humorous or ironic "state of the soul." I imagine, however, that few of the portraits he did here were as good as those he had done at home, perhaps because his sitters were not initiated into the secret, which must have been legendary in Dublin, that unless his pictures were carried off, discreetly but forcibly, at the right moment, he was sure to overpaint and spoil them. His son speaks of his having painted a pond somewhere in Ireland: "He began it in spring and painted all through the year, the picture changing with the seasons, and gave it up unfinished when he painted the snow upon the heath-covered banks." Everyone discovered this trait sooner or later, but in New York it was usually later: it was not the open secret it might have been if his American sitters had been able to compare notes. And besides, who could escape from his presence?—like Socrates, he was a flute-player more wonderful than Marsyas, who charmed us with the voice only. His art suffered in consequence, for he required the co-operation of a practical and resolute sitter. He should have painted only men without ears.

It was at Petitpas' that his star rose for us,—the French *table-*

d'hôte in Twenty-ninth Street. He had found his way to that
friendly house within a year of his arrival and was not to
leave it again; and there he had his Indian summer of the
mind, a Jovian old age with few visible counterparts in a country where age as well as youth obeyed the counsel of Mr.
Rockefeller—not to talk but to saw wood. For his play of conversation he required no such preliminaries as Sarah Battle,—
there was no rigour in Yeats's game; yet one condition he would
not forgo,—a clear abundant light. He disliked the duplicity of
the candle-lit American dinner-table; he wished to follow the
expressions of his interlocutors and would recall the luminous
mahogany tables of old that reflected the dazzling chandelier
and brightened the faces from below as they were brightened
from above. The lights were high in Twenty-ninth Street,—
witness John Sloan's portrait-group, "Yeats at Petitpas'," or even
George Bellows's murky lithograph of the same subject. It was
really characteristic, this desire, for it signified that our philosopher could not have loved art so much had he not loved
human nature more. Once he spoke of a friend of his in
Dublin, a judge who had retired from the bench. When someone asked this judge what remained in his mind, what had
most deeply impressed him, during his fifty years in the crim-
inal courts, his answer was, "The goodness of human nature."
The grand old Yeats, who also loved his species, quoted this
with a smile of agreement, for, although he did not take an
easy view of life, he felt that a seasoned magistrate knew
whereof he spoke.

His own conversation was all of human nature. It flowed
with every sort of engaging contradiction, with a wisdom that
was by turns cheerful and tragic and a folly that was always
somehow wise. W. B. Yeats tells us that when he was a boy
his father would choose to read to him the "less abstract" poets;
he preferred Keats to Shelley and the first half of *Prometheus
Unbound* to the second half. During the last few years the
metaphysical habit grew upon him, and, as he had a terminol-
ogy all his own, it was sometimes difficult to follow him. Yet

even then, as he distinguished between "feeling" and "emotion," for example, or "brains" and "intellect," one discerned his point without, so to say, perceiving it,—nothing annoyed him so much as to be pressed for a definition. Besides, his point never failed to bury itself in one's mind: one would find oneself puzzling it out years afterward. He had lost some of his mischievousness, so that he would no longer maintain, for instance, that even English tailors are inferior, but he still wove about his thought the airiest web of images. He would say of the difference between a photograph and a painted portrait that the photograph was like the description of a ball given by a jaded, bored old chaperon who had spent the evening in an armchair, the painting like the description given by a pretty girl who had thoroughly enjoyed herself. He would say that there were three kinds of criticism, constructive, appreciative and destructive, and illustrate the three kinds by the mother who is constructive when she is teaching her little boy to keep his hands out of his pockets, appreciative when she is adding the last touches to her daughter's dress in front of the looking-glass before the ball, destructive when she is talking after the ball about Mrs. Robinson's daughter. He continued in a similar vein once about American art and letters, saying that exacting criticism was what they needed. He explained this in some such words as these: "Criticism should be exacting, as a mother is about her daughter's party-gown. She never dreams of comparing her girl with the girl over the way; it is understood that no other woman's daughter is to be thought of with her own. But, as the girl turns this way or that, so that her frock may have the last inspection, the mother's eye is severe as no other is, watching for any infelicity in the hang of the dress and any possible way of improving it by the change of a bow or a ribbon. So it is the kindest critic that is the hardest to please."

He had the wisdom of the heart, so rare in New York, along with the other wisdoms, if such exist; and I recall how benignly he lingered over the words, "The Emmet cradle is never empty."

Then how tenderly he smiled over the phrase in one of Darwin's letters, "A nice soft woman on a sofa." Once he spoke of the ladies of Manchester who had known De Quincey's mother, lamenting his wild ways: "Thomas De Quincey, what is he! A waif and a stray! And to think that his mother moved in the best county society and had her feet planted on the Rock of Ages!" He would picture the Puritan minister "sitting in company with the father of the family in a sort of horrid conspiracy to poison life at its sources." He would tell of some Irish peasant who, describing a well-dressed man, added that he "fell away in the breeches." Or he would call up some picture from the past, as of John Richard Green, for instance, in the days when he was known as a brilliant man who had done nothing and was expected to do nothing,—of Green, in some drawing-room, surrounded by admirers, and remarking in a high chant: "All women seek to combine two mutually incompatible positions, the position of perfect strength and the position of perfect weakness." When I spoke of the painter Watts, he said, "Watts, ah, yes. His literature was bad,"—which seemed to hit the nail on the head; and he told many stories about George Moore, whom he had known for years in Dublin. This was the Moore who, as Susan Mitchell said, did not kiss and tell but told and did not kiss. He would say, if you met him in the street, that he was on his way to buy his housekeeper a smarter pair of corsets. He would say that, at an evening party, he could go into the cloak-room and find any lady's cloak at once. He could pick it out by its smell. He told Yeats how he had shocked his pious old-maid cousins, with whom he was dining in the country. When one of them asked, "George, why have you never married?" he replied, "Because, dear Mary, I prefer adultery." Yeats always spoke of Moore as "the elderly old blackguard in Ely Place."

He had forgotten nothing that revealed human nature at its most singular, touching, absurd, above all its most characteristic. He could forgive anything but rhetoric, legality, emotionality and gregariousness,—these were his four abominations. He had

had reason in his own country to deplore the folly of the oratorical mind; and regarding legality his opinion was much the same as St. Paul's, that it was the "strength of sin": perhaps he was the more certain of this because he had begun life as a lawyer himself. As for his dislike of the emotional and the gregarious, it may have been a result of certain American experiences: I know that his opinion of Whitman changed entirely after he had lived here for a while. Having admired him for years, he turned against the "emotional bard," remarking in one of his letters: "The Sacred Nine have not heard his name even to this day." Nor was he free from reservations in regard to the Celtic Revival. I remember his horror, for instance, when a rather gushing lady accused him of having had some commerce with leprechauns. The truth is that he was at bottom an old-fashioned Anglo-Irish country gentleman, redolent of the classics, a sceptic of the eighteenth-century tradition, who had also drunk in his youth at the spring of "political economy" and John Stuart Mill; and upon this foundation had been superadded, to the confusion of the simple, the doctrines of Rossetti in painting, of Morris in economics and of Irish nationalism in the political sphere. It was a combination that made for an infinite, if a somewhat bewildering, wit,—a wit, moreover, that drew the line on the other side of the banshee. For in this he most gravely believed. There was no sign of incredulity in the voice with which he read me a letter describing the death of his brother-in-law in Sligo. The banshee had wailed about the house, as I recall, from midnight on, and the old man died as the sun was rising.

"Idleness and conversation" was Yeats's formula for the good life. Like the "Be hard" or the "Carefully cultivate your faults" of other sages, this was a stumbling-block to the foolish, among whom Yeats counted the population of Belfast and those who have "leather" faces and pursue the dollar. Who could forget his praise of "that idleness which is so diligent, idleness, the teeming mother of the arts"? The "sacred duty of idleness" was Yeats's special message to the harried and hurried Americans.

It reminded me of Thoreau's saying, "Nothing can be more useful to a man than a determination not to be hurried." Yeats, in preaching idleness, was consistent. He told me how his son "Willie," the poet, had stayed in bed all day as a young man. His friends and the family remonstrated: why should Willie lie in bed when he was well in his twenties and the family was so poor? He ought to be up and doing. But Yeats said no. Something perhaps was brewing in Willie's mind; and what, in fact, was brewing as he lay in bed? Willie was composing *The Wanderings of Oisin,*—there was a reward for a father's forbearance. And "idleness" in his own case signified an activity of the mind and the feelings that knew no check in eighty-three years; for, if his painting had lapsed, he wrote his first play at seventy-eight and he was experimenting in poetry to the last week of his life. His "high-bred amicability," to quote Goethe's phrase about Molière, was a veritable school of manners, of the natural in manners; and he was always quick to draw out the least articulate of his companions. How many must have blessed him who had never known, until they talked with him, that they too had something to say! But what seems most fortunate now is that his exile turned him more and more to writing,—his three books were all written in America. For years he had been urged to write his reminiscences,— York Powell, as one discovers in the latter's correspondence, suggested it a generation before; and his *Recollections of Samuel Butler* shows us what the book would have been. But what does it matter? He drew his own portrait in every line he wrote. Had the *Pensées* of Pascal taken their final shape, we should have had only the same Pascal, plus the mortar of "rhetoric"; and it is all the more characteristic that in Yeats's record we should miss the connecting links he so cheerfully ignored in life.

From his essays and his letters the thought drifts up, as Ezra Pound said, "as easily as a cloud in the heavens, and as clear-cut as clouds on bright days." In the letters his conversation lives again; in the essays we find it recollected, as it were, in tranquillity, soberer than his wont was, if only because more studied. Yet everywhere the effect is of a pure spontaneity. He will mention "the most deliciously uninteresting young girl I ever met, her perfect aplomb in selfishness was a perpetual surprise and pleasure." He will say that a "perfectly disinterested, an absolutely unselfish love of making mischief, mischief for its own dear sake, is an Irish characteristic." He will press to the depths and return with this:

"Except for one or two, I have never had a happy day," said the magnificently fortunate Goethe. The never-dying aches of the probe of pain are in every bosom: only while others resort to some kind of laudanum the poets let these work, finding in them the root of happiness, the only sort which, though it be twin with sorrow, is without a fleck on its purity.

He will recur to those leading ideas—that "desire and not emotion is the substance of art," that "character is the self-evolved enemy of personality," that "in obeying rules, the highest even, we shall never forget that in so doing we are not alive"—which underlay all his other thoughts and expressed his own "certitude of belief." His mind was of such a perfect candour that the printed page reproduces it like a sensitive-plate; we hear him talking as we read, we see him bend and smile.

No doubt the novelty of his American experience, the sharp contrast with everything he had previously known, led him thus to define his point of view. His essays on "The Modern Woman" and "Back to the Home" are markedly the fruit of such a reaction: in the presence of our chaos the disparate elements in his own mind, in his life, in his memory, came together and he rose above them in harmonious flight. So we may say that America had its share in the making of him. It was his energy, he said, a month before he died, that kept him in his adventurous exile; but he also stayed because he liked us. That was a compliment, and one we shall not forget.

LLEWELYN POWYS

It was in 1921 that I first saw Llewelyn Powys, in the New York office of *The Freeman*. He had just come from Africa, where, for five years, he had managed a sheep and cattle ranch on the shore of Lake Elmenteita. One of a group of brothers and sisters who were all but prodigiously gifted, with two great English poets among their forbears,—John Donne and William Cowper,—he was already at work on the sketches of African life that soon announced a master of English prose. With his bright curly hair and weathered features and his deep-set eyes that were used to the glare of the sun, with his rough grey woollen coat and sprig of holly, he had an old-country look that suggested some shaggy god in exile, an Apollo playing the shepherd in a far-away land.

When, later, he used to walk to Westport, by the Wolf Pit Road and Nash's Pond,—for he was a notable wayfarer and he often stayed at Norwalk,—he gave me this impression still more strongly. He was at home in the country, and only there. Well as he knew cities, and many of them, from London to Jerusalem and San Francisco, he had nothing whatever in common with their tone and temper. Men who had forgotten how to hunt or to grow corn or catch wild fowl were mechanical dolls to this lover of life, who preferred farm labourers or gypsies. One could scarcely imagine him reading a newspaper,—his style is untouched by newspaperese; and his speech was full of rustic saws and rhymes. But even in his rusticity there was something strange, a vague hint of the prehistoric that clung to his personality, with the ripeness of his culture and the sweetness of his courtesy. If the day was cold, he sometimes wore the old plaid shawl that had once belonged to the poet Edward FitzGerald, the friend of his great-uncle, "old Donne." Cold or not, the day seemed always May-day. He had contrived to find a little knot of field flowers where no other eye had seen them by the road, and he had brought spring with him in his hand. But this spring, in his talk and presence, recalled the pagan rites of Druids and the ancient earth-worship of the flint-men. It was not the spring of modern poets, or even of Herrick or Shakespeare, although Powys repeats their note in many essays. It evoked the first May-poles in the dawn of England, the smell of goats, the chants of the diviners in days when men whose bones lie under barrows, mad in their zest for living, adored the sun.

At that time, no one knew Llewelyn Powys as the formidable pagan thinker he later became. He had not yet published *The Cradle of God*, that wonderful meditation on the biblical story, so grave and often sublime, perhaps the most deeply reasoned of all his writings. While few true believers have embraced the story with any such poetic understanding, he follows Ecclesiastes there as elsewhere: "For the living know that they shall die, but the dead know not anything." In half a dozen other books, he reiterates this with a splendid eloquence. "Brief as a rainbow your dream also will be. There is no clemency, no reprieve, no escape; no, not for the strongest heart deep mortised in life." There is no existence save that of the senses, no acceptable state of consciousness aside from this, and the senses die with the beasts of the field,—such is the burden of his thinking. One doubts if there has been a writer since Robert Burton and Sir Thomas Browne in whom the contrast of life and death has inspired more magnificent periods. But why this passion of negation? It suggested an immense vitality incomparably menaced, and that this was the case one saw in his beautiful essays in autobiography, especially *Skin for Skin* and *Black Laughter*. In more than one sense, FitzGerald's mantle fell upon his shoulders, for Omar's "phantom Caravan" never included a mighty hunter with a keener sense than his of the "bird of time." But he himself said, "I cannot reconcile myself to the lack of gusto" that FitzGerald displayed in his quatrains, their wan Pre-Raphaelite sadness; and his own gusto, his thirst for life, was beyond all measure virile and eager. When such a man for thirty years dwells in the constant presence of death, he may well find the light sweet and rejoice that his eyes behold the sun. When every hour of every day has been snatched from the hand of fate, the things of the hour and the day are beyond all price. It is true that in some minds, in these conditions, the super-sensual world becomes all-important; and perhaps for most men, under any conditions, a philosophy of the senses is insufficient. But most of the pessimists,—for Powys was a pessimist,—are so because they find life nugatory, whereas merely to breathe for him was a daily rapture.

It might not be difficult, running through Powys's various books, to trace the natural history of his view of life. In the Swiss sanitarium, which he describes in *Skin for Skin,* he first became convinced that "nothing mattered." To possess the present, to see, to hear, to taste, to touch, this was enough for a young man who believed that he was dying and who could almost feel his nostrils, mouth and ear-holes bunged with potter's clay. His African adventure accentuated this animal faith. "Kill! kill! kill!" was the rhythm of existence there, "hand against hide, claw against horn, beak against fur." In the trees moulting vultures waited, and the jackal and hyena prowled at night. Every game-path and open glen was "frequented by silent-footed shadows on their eternal quest for blood," and life was "a perpetual pursuit, a perpetual flight." There chance was the only law, and the past was nothing, the future nothing. All nature seemed to cry, "Seize the moment;" and Llewelyn Powys's writings show us with what superb and reckless courage a man can hold this faith and act upon it. No one ever lived more dangerously, and few indeed are the modern writers who have drawn such a harvest of joy from their moment of life. As sensitive as a hare in the brush or a dace switching his tail in some English river, he threw the huntsman off the scent and eluded the fisherman's hook, while snuffing the sun-soaked earth and exulting in wind and water. His astonishing gift of metaphor and the richness of his lan-

guage were proofs of this alertness of the senses; and with what
zest he absorbed new places and new atmospheres, how expert
he was in describing new sensations! There are wonderful passages in his travel-writings about Africa and the Rocky Mountains, Palestine, Switzerland and Capri: one feels as if these
places had never been seen before, so startling are the reports
of his "rabble senses." What reader can ever forget, for instance, the chapter in *Black Laughter* in which the "man of
God" appears in his hut at night?—the witch-doctor's cry outside, with "all the lunatic misery of the debased outraged soul
of the African Negro," the motionless form that invades the
room with its odour of rotting blood and flesh and the foot-
prints stamped in the dust of the threshold, visible with the
rising sun, one a foot with toes, the other a foot with claws.
No palate was ever more sensitive than Powys's to the wine of
life, however the wine might be mingled at moments with gall.

Wherever Llewelyn Powys lived, his mind always turned towards England, the homeland that haunted him like a passion.
Under the stars in the African jungle, poring over Robert Burton, whose rhythms left long traces in his style,—a style that is
often archaic and always rare in texture,—he dreamed of English gardens. In New York, in the clattering streets, he would
see the cuckoo perched singing on the top of Sandsfoot Castle.
He could always regain serenity, he says in one of his essays,
by thinking of the playground of his childhood, the pear-trees
of Montacute vicarage. High as his fever might be, the memory
of this enchanted ground quieted his pulse in a moment; and
his pictures of England suggest the eye of the convalescent, as
if the world had been reborn for him. They are full of an all
but miraculous freshness. He has told us with what delight,
returning home, after his exile in Switzerland, when all his
sensibilities had been sharpened by illness, he absorbed the
sights and sounds of the Somerset meadows, how he came to
know every lane and bypath, the character of each field-gate,
the gap in every hedge, the alder-shaded pools and grass-strewn
bartons. Scrambling about the high chalk cliffs with the rain

lashing against his face, he studied every rock and ledge of curlews, marvelling over the gleaming pebbles, the cries of the gulls at dawn and the old stone circles of the Druids. Through all his later years he kept his astonishing sensitivity. Indeed, he perceived more acutely than ever the homestead and the farm-wain, the glittering dew on spider's web and burdock, the bark-ing of foxes at twilight and every common earthy odour, the smell of the fur of water-rats and of horses' backs hot in the sun. He could tell you the sound of a hare drinking in some dreamy meadow where owls with clutching pounces floated from tree to tree. England for Powys was still a mirage-world, quiver-ing with yellow sunshine and hay-field grasses. It inspired in him that "heightened awareness of the poetry of existence" which he never ceased to praise as the true religion.

Beneath this sensuous England there were other Englands that left their deposit in his mind. One feels in his pages depth upon depth of historic experience, a life of the heart and the soul as well as the instincts that carried one back to the men of the old stone circles. I have said that a hint of the prehistoric clung to his personality. Was it because he retained some trace of every epoch, or because his interior world knew nothing of time? A deeply compassionate nature, he was indif-ferent to secular interests. "We should grow less involved in society," he says in *Damnable Opinions*, "and more deeply in-volved in existence." His chosen companions were those for whom "existence" was incomparably more engrossing than the things of the world, the fisherman, peasants and shepherds for whom time has no reality and who live, as he wished to live, in the fugitive moment. Deeply akin as he was to these earth-bound natures, he shared their poetry and wisdom. But let no one suppose that Llewelyn Powys was merely another nature-writer, eloquent, observant and persuasive. He had something to say to this age of despair and darkness, an age in which writers in all the tongues of Babel repeat that life is futile and worse than nothing. It may be that only a man who had to fight for existence could prize it and exult in it as he did, beating his forehead upon the grass in jubilant acquiescence and uttering daily paeans to the earth and the sun. All the more should we cherish his will and his courage and the noble and beautiful art that permits us to share them.

THE MISEDUCATION OF HENRY ADAMS

The readers of *The Education of Henry Adams* are as numerous as the stars of the Milky Way, yet few seem to have been troubled by the burden of this book, by Adams's belief that he had missed his destiny. He went through the world with the air of a deposed emperor, not quite knowing who had deposed him, or from what; his life, as he says somewhere, had been a broken arch, and this was surely because the artist's instinct in him had not had proper scope.

There is a curious passage in one of John Adams's letters of 1782 that throws light on the enigma of this later Adams. "I must study politics and war," the old President wrote to his wife, "that my sons may have liberty to study mathematics and philosophy, geography, natural history and naval architecture, in order to give their children a right to study painting, poetry, music, architecture, statuary, tapestry and porcelain." The life of art, in short, in the logic of the Adams mind and family, was scheduled,—one can use no other word,—to emerge in the third generation. And the life of art emerged, with a certain difference. It was not his own line alone that John Adams had in mind in this prognostication. He had in mind, as always, the nation of which he was one of the founders. He saw this nation labouring for humane ends: by the third generation the machinery of society was to be in good running order and men were to begin really to live, free to devote themselves securely to the ideal activities of the spirit. The tragic testimony of Henry Adams, looking back a century and a quarter later, was that this machinery, instead of subsiding into its place as the servant of human beings, had become the soulless master, and that man had lost forever his grip on the rudder of his own destiny. Samuel Butler's nightmare! How much objective truth was there in this conception? Part of it, at least, was subjective. Henry Adams knew that something had gone amiss with his own career. He saw in himself a patrician born too late in a world too old for patricians. But he never clearly saw, what we can see, that he was by nature an artist, who,—partly because he was also an Adams, sprung from a family in which, as he noted, two tendencies predominated, family pride and a tendency towards politics,—was prevented by a conspiracy of circumstances from finding his own soul.

It is all very well to say that Henry Adams actually was an artist. An imposing list of books came from his pen. But how much of the true elements of creativity is there in those voluminous historical studies that occupied the best years of his life? Even if we had never read them, we could find a certain answer to this question in his own retrospective view of these professional labours. "I care more for one chapter, or any dozen pages, of *Esther* than for the whole history, including maps and indices," he writes in 1891; "so much more, indeed, that I would not let anyone read the story for fear the reader should profane it." That is not the word of the born historian, the way of Motley and Parkman, for example, or George Bancroft, who wrote their poems and their novels first, and turned to history as their vital interest. *Esther*, slight as it is, was the work that was "precious" to Adams, the work that was written in his "heart's blood," and this alone suggests that it was only partially the instinct of the artist, the instinct that animates the great historians, that led Adams into these toilsome paths. The family conscience also had its word: his ancestors had made this history, the least he could do was to write about it. His real disposition he revealed elsewhere. Who has failed to observe his constant interest in Swinburne, a man of his own caste,—one can hardly ignore that,—who had flouted all the Victorian respectabilities and made himself the symbol of a hedonistic an-

archy? Or that constant preoccupation with the life of the artist,
regarded so oddly from the outside, with so much of the mere
collector's passion, that interest in the processes of workmanship
which the *Life of George Cabot Lodge* exhibits, that passion
for the age of cathedral-building, that restless desire to try his
hand at fiction and poetry, which always remained the desire
of an amateur? Here was the buried artist in Henry Adams,
who looked at art ever askance and strangely, with a touch of
that "otherwise-mindedness" which his brother Charles Francis
ascribed to himself. For surely it is not without significance that
he published both his novels anonymously, that he had his
name as the author printed not on the title-page but only on
the fly-leaf of the life of Lodge,—a trifle, but not without meaning,—that he issued *Mont-Saint-Michel and Chartres* pri-
vately, as well as the *Memoirs of Marau Taaroa,* that he destroyed his diaries and notes and recalled and destroyed as
many as he could of the letters he had written, that he refused
to publish the *Education* and wrote it in the third person.
As we see, he was "otherwise-minded" all the time. All the
time, but once! And that once, that episode of his life in the
South Seas, in 1891, with John La Farge, reveals the inner
Adams, the true Henry Adams, as all his previous life had
never revealed it.

For what a change came over this "dull dog," as President
Hayes called him, dull for all his brilliant intellect, ruled by
caution and the family conscience, for whom the Jay Goulds
had blotted out the sun, when, with an artist for his sole companion, a "spectacled and animated prism," he escaped from his
"eternity of hares and rabbits," of empty politics and emptier
society, escaped from the harness of his caste to the velvet-
green mountains of Tahiti, streaked by their long white threads
of waterfalls, where the ferns grew thick on the dripping banks
and the sea glowed blue through the lace-work of pandanus
leaves, where the palm-trees rustled in the strong gusts and he
learned how to feel the subtle and various charm in the colour
and light of every hour, the violets and masses of purple and

the broad bands of orange and green in the sunsets. La Farge taught him this, as La Farge taught him to understand years later the stained glass at Chartres; but had there ever been an apter pupil than this man who, in his youth, had "learned" the Dresden Gallery by heart? What if he could, after it was all over, write in his old vein to Senator Lodge, "As financial investments, none of the Pacific islands, except the Sandwiches, are worth touching. They are not worth any one of the West Indies, if you lumped them all together." The retired man of affairs whom "motion alone amuses" could still have his say; but this was not Adams's vein in writing to the women who understood him. The ice that bound his soul had melted in this man who found himself for once in a social setting which broke his inhibitions and revealed the tender feelings that lay beneath them, where he took to his water-colours, mixing his colours by the dozen, and laid one deep wash over another, struggling to follow La Farge, feeling as he had felt as a boy about going fishing, "as though I might get a bite tomorrow," where he sat in his native house, receiving and making visits, watching the sea and sky that made him so desperately homesick, for what he could hardly say, writing disquisitions on Tahitian legends and folk-songs, coaxing the queen of the islands to write her memoirs, fancying himself a kind of king of Babylon who had loved a Tahitian girl in the days of great warriors and splendid lovers and immortalized her in verse. There, in the South Seas, he had met for once an aristocracy that made his own caste of no account, that made him feel like "the son of a camel-driver degraded to the position of stable-boy in Spokane West Centre." And there he had found a communistic system, where private property was unknown or disregarded; rather a pleasant system, as he noted,—"On the whole, it suited me better than our own." There, in short, he ceased to be "otherwise-minded"; and, for the rest of his life, this man who had passed his climacteric gave himself, otherwise-minded or not, with all the energy an elderly man can muster, to the world of art and poetry.

Who can pretend to elucidate all the motives that lay behind his earlier diffidence? He had not been able to bring himself to believe in the free role of the artist; in spite of an irrepressible aspiration, he had had too much native Yankee caution, too much of the pride of prudence. "One findeth rarely," as Meister Eckhart said, "that people come to great things except they first go somewhat astray"; and Adams had never been willing to take this chance. He would rather have died, as he wrote in his early twenties, than "make one of that butterfly party which New Yorkers seem to consider their literary world," than to do what the men did who wrote in *The Atlantic Monthly*, *Putnam's* and *Harper's*. Such risks as that involved, and such associations, he felt were beneath his dignity, he whose joy was always the study of art and who, in the midst of his desert of politics, wished only that he might "quietly slide into the literary set." Was ever a man more outwardly cold-blooded in his attitude to the literary life? "The question," he writes to his pupil, Henry Cabot Lodge, "the question is whether the historico-literary line is practically worth following, not whether it will amuse or improve you. Can you make it pay? either in money, reputation, or any other solid value . . . I think you will see at once that this profession does pay. No one has done better and won more in any business or pursuit, than has been acquired by men like Prescott, Motley, Frank Parkman, Bancroft, and so on in historical writing . . . Boston is running dry of literary authorities. Anyone who has the ability can enthrone himself here as a species of literary lion with ease, for there is no rival to contest the throne. With it comes social dignity, European reputation, and a foreign mission to close." How is that for a counsel of perfection, that counsel of "doing better" and "winning more" which is worthy of a Yankee tradesman,—a counsel that involves the life of art, the life that a real artist would gladly pursue naked in a tub, or mounted like St. Simeon on a pillar, if any question of "contesting thrones," of "social dignity" and "foreign missions," stood between him and his private *altitudo*?

The marvel is that, having had such thoughts, he could ever have written a paragraph worth reading.

Better even than the *Education,* the letters exchanged during the Civil War between his father, his brother and himself reveal the beginning of this division of interests. One easily perceives between the lines Henry Adams's natural inclination. "You tired of this life!" his brother writes from the seat of the war. "You more and more callous and indifferent about your own fortunes! Pray how old are you and what has been your career? . . . How am I throwing myself away? Isn't a century's work of my ancestors worth a struggle to preserve?" One sees there all the contempt of the "red-blood" for the "mollycoddle,"—the railway magnate of the future is rebuking this skulker among the tombs of the Old World who, in the midst of his country's struggle for existence, can speak of "Young England, Young Europe, of which I am by tastes and education a part." Henry Adams, serving in the London legation, is plainly at the crossing of the ways: his instinct drives him towards the life of thought, and all he requires is a little corroboration. We see him depressed, irresolute, at bay; and no wonder, since, craving this corroboration of his deepest self, his principle of growth, he finds himself subjected every day to influences of the most powerful kind that run directly counter to his desire. Every day, in fact, he is reminded that he is a son and grandson of the Adamses, and that the political fortunes of America are at stake.

A strange inner drama these pages reveal. In this hour of crisis we see the family pattern stamped for good on the wax of Henry Adams's malleable youth. "Your family is large," his brother Charles writes to his father, the minister to England, pleading for permission to enlist in the Union army; "your family is large and it seems to me almost disgraceful that in after years we should have it to say that of them all not one at this day stood in arms for that government with which our family history is so closely connected." How, in the nature of things, could Henry Adams, whatever his preoccupations were, fail to share this acute sense of patriotic responsibility? With his brother writing in this strain from home, his father was as constantly reminding him that the Adamses were statesmen by divine right and that all his sons must uphold the family tradition. "It may be my predilection that biases my judgment," the minister says, in words that have since become famous, "but I think I see in my father the only picture of a full-grown statesman that the history of the United States has yet produced. By this I mean that in him were united more of all the elements necessary to complete the character than in any other man." And thereupon, a true connoisseur of statesmen, he launches into that elaborate comparison of John Quincy Adams with all the other builders of the Republic,—a comparison with which we of a later time cannot but agree, so great is the distinction of this man, as corresponding, in his own sphere, the sphere of the *genus* statesman, with the highest and purest type of the classical artist,—ending with these words: "In my opinion no man who has lived in America has so thoroughly constructed a foundation for his public life as your grandfather."

This was the daily object-lesson that was held up before Henry Adams's eyes. It may have been true that America needed artists and thinkers, but no one ever mentioned this to him; and America certainly needed men of action, it needed statesmen, more perhaps than ever. It needed, in short, Adamses! The Adamses had surely made America, and the time had come for the Adamses to save it; and so, "It worries me all the time," we find Henry Adams writing soon, "to be leading this thoroughly useless life abroad while you are acting such grand parts at home." And "Great will be the responsibility," his father writes to his soldier-brother, "that devolves upon you!" How could they ever have known, these Adamses, in the days of the Civil War, that the sun of their race was setting, that America in the coming generations was to have no manner of use for classical statesmen, who felt themselves appointed to guide their country? Had not Charles Francis Adams, before their eyes, by the force and skill of a diplomacy that had kept England from uniting with the South, shown that they were as securely in the saddle as ever their fathers had been? How then could Henry Adams plan to live the "irresponsible" life of thought and art, he whose race and its peculiar role had been so magnificently vindicated? An Adams he was, an Adams he must remain. "Let us have order and discipline and firm ranks," he writes to his brother, "among the soldiers of the Massachusetts school." And again: "The nation has been dragged by this infernal cotton, that had better have been burning in Hell, far away from its true course, and its worst passions and tastes have been developed by a forced and bloated growth. It will depend on the generation to which you and I belong, whether the country is to be brought back to its true course and the New England element is to carry the victory." To the Adamses, America must still yield the helm!

We remember how, in his autobiography, the younger Charles Francis Adams tells us that, emerging from the war, he found the railway system "the most developing force and largest field of the day" and determined to attach himself to it. There was the centre of power of the new age, and Charles Francis Adams approached this centre in the spirit of his father; he prepared himself for the task of railroad-building as for a learned profession, he "constructed a foundation" for his active life as laboriously as his grandfather had done. But railroad-building was not statesmanship; and America was not the same America. Intellectual and moral force no longer counted; the nation had ceased to have a "true course," or any course at all; the nation was out of hand; the *genus* statesman had become extinct, and Charles Francis Adams, looking cynically backward in his old age, perceiving the vanity of his family's dream, perceiving that the reality of power had long been held by men whom he despised, felt only one regret, that he too had not accumulated, as he might so well have done (with a little less learning and "foundation"), "one of those vast fortunes of the present day rising up into the tens and scores of millions,—what is vulgarly known as 'money to burn.'" And as for the tender-minded Henry Adams, overborne by another pride than that of the artist,—what work did America offer him? Obliged to adapt himself to the Adams pattern, to become, if not a statesman, the nearest possible equivalent of a statesman, he accepted the role of the political historian. Not for long, to be sure; he has amply told us in the *Education* how distasteful he found this role. We remember how, in *Democracy,* Mrs. Lightfoot Lee goes to Washington in search of "the mysterious gem which must lie hidden somewhere in politics ... What she wanted," our author says, "was Power." It was in search of this mysterious gem, this same phantom Power, that Henry Adams also, resigning from Harvard, went to Washington ("I gravitate to a capital," he wrote, "by a primary law of nature"), following the ancestral trail, only to pass the rest of his life as a bewildered spectator of the "degradation of the democratic dogma." And there, among the dying embers of the old political traditions of the Republic, among the ghosts of his fathers, a ghost himself, as he said, "dead as a mummy," living in "spectre-like silence," this man who had repressed so many of his natural instincts, in order to conform to an obsolete model, amused himself constructing one of the bleakest philosophies of life that has ever crossed the human mind.

Philosophies are confessions; our spiritual needs shape and determine their forms. This is plainly true of Adams's philosophy. That "the universe has steadily become more complex and less reducible to a central control" is a proposition that may have its objective validity. But if, for the term "the universe," one substitutes the term "the United States," as Henry Adams himself conceived this term, we can see that it surely has a subjective bearing. Again, it is certainly more than arguable that "the American man is a failure." But when these possible truths are held as Henry Adams held them, not as interpretations of a moment in history, but as final pronouncements on destiny, then we ask ourselves, What sort of life has this man lived who utters them? For we know that the world is reborn every day,—not for us, perhaps, but for someone else,— that every day some child comes into the world who is going to create new life, and that not till another million years have passed can any man say, with any more finality than cynics have always said it, that humanity is a failure. We may ourselves be pessimists of pessimists, dwellers in all the dungeons in the air; but our reason tells us this. What Henry Adams meant,—for these words clearly say nothing else,—was that *he* had failed (as he himself asserted), because he could not control *his* universe, because, in a word, his energies had been dissipated, and his deepest instinct had never come into its own. John Quincy Adams had flouted Emerson for his "wandering" of mind; the Adams tradition had always prevented his grandson from feeling that there was any ultimate dignity, any justification, at least, to be compared with the true Adams role, in the role of the artist and thinker. What else could have lain behind that diffidence with which he presented all the books he wrote? For surely he had no fear of public opinion, or, what is more general perhaps with American writers who are truly conscientious, no feeling that his work was inadequate. He was all too eager to maintain, at the cost of what he most desired, the habits of mind and feeling of what he called, without a touch of irony,—he who possessed, in regard to so many other worldly considerations, such a genius for ironic depreciation,—his "class and breed"; and that is what the artist cannot do, whatever his class may be. He dreamed himself back into the great age when art was the central activity of man; with fascinated eyes he saw and remembered in Swinburne another Anglo-Saxon, an aristocrat like himself, who had thrown himself into the creative life with all the abandon of a Dionysus. But when he wrote himself, it was somehow different. He wrote with his head turned, as it were, the other way.

SIDNEY LANIER

The austere monastic Father Tabb was an unreconstructed Southerner. He could never be persuaded to travel north of Mason and Dixon's line, though he outlived his friend Lanier by a full generation. The son of a Virginia planter, born near Richmond, he began to publish his poems in 1877, and seven of these he inscribed to Lanier, whose language and thought he echoed at times, dry as he was where his friend was so vaporous and lush. No two poets were more unlike,—the clear, brief, hard, sharp, desiccated Tabb and Lanier, so spongy, so vague, so loose and soft, so diffuse and so tortured where the other was laconic and simple, though Tabb was over-ingenious also, for his wit was occasionally a little forced, while generally his poems were delicate and firm in texture. Admiring his fellow-Virginian Poe, he had taken to heart the admonition in *The Poetic Principle* against long poems, and, ceasing to experiment with forms in which he had never succeeded, he worked at the quatrains and epigrams in which he excelled. A fastidious craftsman in miniature verse, he recalled at times the contemporaries of Herrick, whom he read apparently only in a cursory way, and he also suggested Emily Dickinson in his closely packed lines on flowers and birds, although he was quite without her magnetism. Fine as his little poems were, *Fern-Song,* for instance, and *Evolution,* he lacked a certain intensity and magic, yet it seemed not unlikely that he might outlast Lanier. For, original as Lanier was, this admirable spirit, the friend of Tabb, struck one in later times as more important in the role of a personage and thinker than he was as a poet.

But, pale, dark, slender, nervous and eager, with a passionate belief in his mission in the world, Lanier was the ideal of the bard to many in his time, a realization of the hero as poet of whom Carlyle had written, with an overflowing romantic sense of life. Brought up in a strict Presbyterian household at a time when the Calvinist faith was stronger in the South than it was in eastern New England, Lanier was in grain as much of a Puritan as Emerson ever had been, while he shared belatedly the New England delight in Carlyle. As much as the Concordians of the Transcendental age, he had felt the power of the German romantic writers, and before the war destroyed his plan he dreamed of studying at Heidelberg religious philosophy, literature, poetry and music. His novel *Tiger Lilies* was all compact of Novalis and Richter. He made translations from Herder and Heine while passing through other phases of thought that characterized him as a Southerner of the pre-war years, especially those fantasies of the age of chivalry that he never quite outgrew and that were nourished in his boyhood by Froissart and Scott. Thinking of himself as a knight and minstrel, he imagined that the new Confederate nation would embody all that was finest in the chivalric life, and later his prose and verse abounded in figures of paladin and paynim, the tournament and the battle-axe and cross-bow. He drew from Froissart's Chronicles the story of *The Jacquerie*, the long poem on which he worked off and on, and among the several books that he edited for boys were simplifications of Malory, Froissart and Percy.

With these tokens and tastes of the older South, Lanier combined more recent notes that gave him distinctly the character of a voice of his age, in some respects an important voice of the nation as well as the South with a faith in America as a whole that suggested Whitman's. Interested at all times in science, he read Darwin, Tyndall and Huxley with care and accepted the evolutionary creed of the new generation, studying biology and chemistry too, mineralogy, botany and the physics of sound, the scientific aspect of the music he loved above all. When he wrote his book on prosody he called it *The Science of English Verse* in the mood of a moment when science was triumphantly advancing, when historians were talking of historical science and scientific method and Christian Science was the name of a new religion. Aware of economic problems and deeply concerned for the South, he studied its social conditions with his usual zest, collecting statistics about cotton and cattle and gathering clippings from country papers that gave him the neighbourhood news of the Georgian farmers. Eager for their welfare, he wished to keep closely in touch with the actualities of small-farm Southern living, struck as he was by the rise of the small farmer since the war and convinced that the South of the future required small farming. With the nation as well as the section in mind, he felt that the Republic needed large farms in order to achieve its "mighty works," but that it needed the small farm too to foster manhood and self-reliance, the farming that was not a business but a way of life. Let the Northwest have its great farms, the heirs of the old plantations of the South, but let the Southeast have its counter-balance with small farms and a village life developed as it might be, with village orchestras, libraries, theatres and schools. In order to prosper, the Southern farmers must cease to plant cotton for ever and ever and diversify their crops with corn and wheat. This was the thought that underlay Lanier's first long poem *Corn* and some of his dialect verses of the Georgia crackers.

Lanier was one of the earliest Southerners to use the phrase the "New South," to the problems of which he devoted much shrewd thinking, after brooding over the abandoned farms and deserted Georgian hills that bared to the sun, as he wrote, their seamy breasts. He had seen how the over-production of cotton had bankrupted the region while the farmers continued to produce it, and he wrote *Corn* near his birthplace Macon among the corn-fields there, feeling that their growth assured the salvation of the state. Then, fighting King Cotton in the South, he fought the greater evil Trade, which he saw supplanting all that was human in the country, destroying in the interests of capitalism the ancient prestige of the farming life, a change that Melville and Whitman were also deploring. As much as Melville, Lanier detested the "hell-coloured smoke of the factories" and the business and industrial regime that had risen since the war, side by side with an unheard-of political corruption, and as early as 1870, in his Confederate Memorial address, he attacked the "boisterous god" of the century, Trade. It was the idol of an age, as he said, that was not grand but adroit, not strong but supple, not large but keen; and, fearful of cities along with trade,—the "terrible towns" of *The Waving of the Corn,*—he rebuked in *The Symphony* the growing capitalist system. He spoke with contempt of the "flimsy houses" that were built on the "shifting sands" of trade, while he satirized the new business world in a lighter poem *The Hard Times in Elfland,* which Santa Claus, now pale and thin, had been obliged to mortgage. A "stock-thief" had ruined him, he had had to give up everything,—even his reindeer,—and plod through the snow on foot, for the smooth-tongued railroad man had come to his house with a project that suited the nineteenth century better than the reindeer. This was to build a Grand Trunk railway through to earth's last terminus, touching at every chimney-top, an elevated railway, of course, that presently failed. It was trade that had overthrown chivalry, and Lanier saw chivalry rising again, with its scorn of the small advantage, to overthrow trade; for his criterion was vaguely mediæval. But, aside from the spirit in which he attacked the rising power of the business world,— a spirit that in certain ways resembled Ruskin's,—the attack in itself made him a voice of his age, with Whitman, Bellamy, Howells and Henry George.

What made Lanier, for the rest, important, especially for the South, even more than his poems, was his feeling about them, the sense of the high vocation of the poet and the dignity of poetry in a region where it had been previously regarded as a pastime. It was this that made him a symbol and example for Southern writers in times to come who had never been affected seriously by Poe or by Timrod, poets who had reacted earlier against this Southern attitude by similarly dwell-

ing on the "science of English verse." No regional group of
American poets has studied prosody indeed as the Southern
poets were to study it for four generations, from Poe to Allen
Tate and John Crowe Ransom, and one might be excused for
supposing that this was due in part at least to the relatively
late development of poetry in the South. That poetry was an
accomplishment merely was a view that prevailed below the
Potomac years after the appearance of real poets destroyed it
in the North, and this way of taking it seriously was com-
pensatory perhaps.

Lanier was important as well in attempting to turn the attention of poetry to the actual problems of his troubled world
and time. He was an original poet, moreover, whether a good
or a bad one, not just another Victorian like Timrod or Hayne,
and in this he had something in common with Whitman, who
shared his feeling for science too and especially his lofty conception of the poet's role. His poet was one who leads the

> *timid time*
> *And sings up cowards with commanding rhyme,—*

another phrase for Whitman's "literatus,"—while both were
striving in different ways for new and freer forms of verse
and Lanier's experiments were almost as bold as Whitman's.
In this respect they were unlike the other American post-war
poets, who were more than commonly conventional and artificial. Lanier suggested now and then the range and sweep of
Whitman, and he too was a passionate lover of the American
soil; for this ex-Confederate blockade-runner, whose sectional
feeling was both deep and wise, expressed as whole-souled a
feeling for the nation as Whitman. Lanier, discovering Whitman in 1878, delighted in the "bigness and bravery" of his
"ways and thoughts" and his "strong and beautiful rhythms,"
as he wrote the poet, so different from those of the "plentiful
mannikins" who generally spoke for American verse and whom
he scorned himself as much as Whitman. Later, in his lec-

tures on *The English Novel,* he turned against the poet, taking too seriously some of his earlier phrases, saying that he mistook the body for the soul, offended by Whitman's animality and his rude display of physical health, which filled him with all the resentment and distaste of the consumptive. Lanier was tender-minded, to use the expression of William James, in spite of his protestations of a love of science, and he hated the naturalism of Zola too and said he could blot from the face of the earth the novels of Richardson, Fielding, Sterne and Smollett. Seeing in Lanier a beautiful spirit, Whitman surmised that he himself was far too rough a dish for so delicate a palate. As for Lanier's "extreme sense of the melodic," his "over-tuning of the ear," he felt it detracted seriously from the value of his work.

Lanier himself had said in a letter that poetry for him was a "tangent" merely into which he shot at times from his true line, music, and this partly explained the weakness of his work, which seemed somehow abortive in later times and all but unreadable in spite of its largeness of feeling. Its "lavishness and looseness of adjectives," the fault Lanier found in the poems of Hayne, its diffuseness and vagueness and lack of finality and precision were all in part attributable to an over-dependence on his sense of music, which he called the "characteristic art-form of the modern time." So, while in a way he invented a style, it was therefore not a good style, it was seldom or never natural, direct or simple, and it abounded in errors of taste and verbal effects that were constantly forced and suggested a kind of archaism that was false and hollow. This was the result of his early reading of the oldest English poets along with the isolation of his formative years: indeed he never sufficiently lived within the literary current of his time to learn what a writer could and should not do. His language, too often over-wrought, was sometimes silly or namby-pamby, with too much of the mawkish adolescent in the quality of the feeling, and there were elements in his writing as well of the high-flown Southern oratorical style and the

feverish exaltation of tuberculosis. Yet, good or bad, his poems
were new, or some of them at least, where most of his American contemporaries were shadows and echoes, in all that
made them poets aside from their themes, and there was much
that was moving and beautiful especially in *The Marshes of
Glynn*, with its intimate and special report of the Southern
scene.

POE AS A CRITIC

FOR ALL the unsavoury traits of Rufus Griswold, his anthology of American poetry was historically important, and its popularity was a proof, the first decisive proof perhaps, that Americans were aware of the possession of a literature of their own.
With no excessive nationalism, with a calm and simple pride
of country, Griswold told the poets in his preface that the
time had come for certain obvious things,—they should begin to appreciate their own majestic scenery and the glory and
interest of American history and life. Griswold's anthology represented a consciousness, more or less mature, that America
was coming intellectually into its own, and the same consciousness governed Poe, whose criticism indicated a similar point
in the development of the American mind.

Griswold had never suggested that poets should confine
themselves to American themes,—as various jingo writers were
already insisting,—he had merely wished to stress their intrinsic importance; nor was Poe this sort of nationalist either,—
he said it was a purely political question where a poet found
his subject-matter. But Poe professed "*that* nationality which
defends our own literature, sustains our own men of letters,
upholds our own dignity and depends upon our own resources"; and he believed that American literature had at last
reached a condition where it was ready, as he said, for criticism. We had survived, Poe remarked, the "first licentious

hours of a hobbledehoy braggadocio and swagger," and this
was the time for critical standards, a rigorous "plain speaking"
and a serious effort to uphold the dignity of genius. Poe set
out, on the one hand, to check the prevalent spirit of puffery,
which had thriven with impunity hitherto,—so that most American writers were overrated,—while he attacked, on the other
hand, the "sin of indiscriminate censure," the other swing of
the pendulum of a clock that had never been regulated. It did
not do, in a civilized land, to run amuck, Poe observed, and, as
all our poets were *not* Miltons, so some of our poets were not
drivellers either,—Willis, for instance, was "not *quite* an ass,"
and Bryant, for another example, was "not *all* a fool." Poe
undertook, in other words, to introduce discrimination and
regulate the clock of American letters.

This was the work that he had begun on the *Southern Literary Messenger* in Richmond, the work he continued in Philadelphia and was to continue in New York, for he had a sys-
tematic interest in American literature and American authors:
he was planning to write a critical history of them. With his
intellectual clarity and his genius for analysis, he had no fear
of literary god or devil,—full as he was no doubt of other fears,
—but he took a little pleasure in arousing fear in others, for of
course there was a cruel streak in Poe. Then sometimes in his
criticism one found a note of special pleading, as if its spring
of energy was a wish to prove that the work of Poe alone was
true and pure, but this was understandable too, for many a
writer of genius has appreciated greatness only of his own kind.
How salutary, for the rest, were the critical writings of Poe, on
the whole, at a time when ordinary criticism was corrupt or
feeble, when the practices of small provincial papers were common in the largest towns and New York was ridden by shabby
little coteries and cliques. Poe had appeared at a moment when
literature had gathered a certain momentum and was ready for
ideas and directions, when writing in the United States was
just on the brink of its greatest hour, a moment that was more
pregnant, in fact, than any later for seventy years. Moreover,

he wrote with authority as well as discernment, and his gospel
was the gospel of art in an artless age,—he dwelt on the need
of craftsmanship, deliberation, conscious skill, in season and
out of season, when all the seasons were right for this. For Poe
was even acutely aware of his own mental processes,—he had
reached by a "route obscure and lonely" the principles and the
secrets of his writing,—and his essays abounded in perceptions
that testified again and again to the rigour of his literary conscience and his practical knowledge. He had his obsessions,
undoubtedly, the obsession of plagiarism, for one, the obsession
of the value of brevity and the "short poem," but, always ex-
celling in definitions, in the clear exposition of general ideas,
he was able to lift the humblest themes into the air of the universal.

Was Poe a great critic, then? Scarcely, in spite of a few fine
essays in the realm of literary theory or on single authors,
Bryant, Mrs. Browning, Dickens, Hawthorne. The paper on
Hawthorne was superb and the general essays were of permanent interest, though mainly as throwing light on Poe himself;
and yet his range was narrow and his judgment was erratic, in
spite of all his power of discrimination. While he praised to
the skies the *Orion* of Richard Hengist Horne, he referred to
Æschylus as "shallow," and, all too free with the word "im-
mortal," he said that George P. Morris would live forever by
virtue of his songs. If one had taken Poe's word, there was no
difference in stature between the Yankee Emerson and the
Yankee John Neal; and, mentioning Emerson's "occasional
poems in which beauty is apparent *by flashes*," he spoke of
the "unquestionable genius" of Richard Adams Locke. Here
was a "poet of high order," while "William Wallace of Kentucky" was also "among our men of genius," and, as for the
"fair authoresses" who won the extravagant praise of Poe, his
papers on them were scarcely more than "surreptitious valen-
tines." * There were, alas, unhappy reasons for Poe's description of the verses of "Estelle" as "inexpressibly beautiful" and

* Edward Dahlberg, *Do These Bones Live.*

so on; but he was a free agent when he said that Mrs. Amelia Welby had "all the passion of Mrs. Norton," with a "nicer ear" and "equal art." He took the fashionable poetesses *au grand sérieux,* in this resembling critics of a later day, when qualities that were totally different had become the vogue,—and critics who were excellent but not the superior critics who fully partake in their time without prizing its fashions.

Many another distinguished writer shared these tastes of the moment with Poe,—for example, his admiration of the Davidson sisters, the two young poetesses of Plattsburg who died of consumption before they were twenty and who corresponded in their way to the fashionable heroine of the thirties and forties. Lucretia, who was the first to die, had written in a darkened room, to the music of an Æolian harp in the window, her Persian visions, in the manner of Moore, and her poems about Circassian maids, with their wild and romantic descriptions of the bulbul and the rose. One might have seen her, in steel engravings, perhaps in *Godey's Lady's Book,* with the long black ringlets on her shoulder, beside her mother on the window-seat, with clasped hands, in the moonlight, gazing across the waters of Lake Champlain. The story of Lucretia's death touched Samuel F. B. Morse, who was visiting in Albany when he read her poems, and he edited them with a memoir under the title *Amir Khan,* while in England the poet laureate Southey wrote another memoir of her. Southey compared Lucretia to Chatterton, and Mrs. Southey wrote a sonnet addressed to Mrs. Davidson, Lucretia's mother, also a poetess and also consumptive, like the younger daughter Margaret, whose poems, in turn, were collected by Washington Irving. The memoir that Irving wrote appealed to the young historian Prescott as the story of Eugénie de Guerin was soon to appeal to a multitude of literary Frenchmen. "What a little flower of paradise!" Prescott exclaimed in one of his letters,—she recalled to him the rose of Malherbe that "lived for the space of a morning." Was it surprising that Poe found "wonderful" and "thrilling,"—with this young girl's "bursts of the truest poetic fire,"—a literary case that stirred minds of the strength and distinction of Prescott, Washington Irving, Southey and Morse? What determines, in a given age, the meaning of a given mood?—the prestige of certain themes at certain times?—the power of peculiar images and situations to evoke, to affect, to inspire, to touch, to move? A young woman dying of consumption had played a part in Irving's life that was almost as decisive perhaps as it played in Poe's; and this, one might say, was a typical reality of the moment. One can say with assurance at least that Poe was quite in the tone of the time in presenting "the death of a beautiful woman" as the most poetic of all themes.

Poe was not a great critic, for he was too much in the tone of his time, though this did not limit him at all in his poems or his stories. He had no feeling for other times or types, and therefore he saw nothing in perspective, but just because he dwelt so much on the art of composition he was a valuable critic for the moment, for the place. He wrote about literature as an art when this was the one thing necessary, at an hour of triumphant democracy when a multitude had begun to write who had never known the discipline of the cultivated few. It was an hour of budding energies that needed to be moulded and pressed into form, and even men of education and writers of genius, like Fenimore Cooper, were slovenly, careless and hasty in the thirties and forties. Poe was not above discussing questions of grammar and punctuation, and he spoke with the authority of a master on the craft of writing; yet his influence, great for a decade or more, was to pass away completely,—Poe was to leave no followers behind him.

This was a curious fact of the future, and because the eclipse of Poe coincided with the rise of the New England authors it was sometimes supposed that the latter were to blame for his eclipse. Some of the Yankees did not like Poe, and Poe disliked certain of the Yankees with something more than a Southerner's disesteem, while he went out of his way to insult an audience in Boston, affirming that he had acted of malice prepense. As

Whistler said of the town of Lowell, Poe simply "wouldn't be born" in Boston,—he could never pardon "Frogpondium" for giving him birth; and, admiring the poet Lowell and Haw-thorne, he detested the Transcendentalists, whom he ridiculed as the "merest nobodies" on every occasion. He laughed at their "Irish philosopher called Furrier" and their "great moment of Progress," though he shared their deep respect for Coleridge and knew the writings of the brothers Schlegel, who had both been published in Philadelphia. It was not for personal reasons, however, that Poe was submerged in this contest of forces. The Transcendentalists and their heirs won the day in American letters because the main stream of American feeling ran through them, and Poe was outside of this main stream that reached full flood in Whitman and left him in an eddy of his own. He attacked the New Englanders on the score of the "heresy of the didactic"; but was Whitman ever didactic? He was broadly humane; and so were the Transcendentalists, who may have been unjust to Poe, but only because they demanded of poetry a human substance that he lacked. Poe himself had never shared the developing mood of the American tradition, which his fellow-Virginian at Monticello had done so much to shape, and as he never shared it he could not guide it. So American literature flowed past Poe, without dislodging him indeed, but without ever being diverted or seriously affected by his presence. Nothing could have proved more clearly the toughness and reality of the American tradition than the patent fact that Poe *was* outside it. He was even outside the main stream of the human tradition. When he said of poetry that "unless incidentally, it has no concern whatever either with duty or with truth," he denied the testimony of the greatest poets of Greece, Rome, Italy, France and England. Were not the elements he disavowed the source of the animating passions of all the major poets from Homer down? The passion for liberty, the love of honour, loyality, religious exaltation, the springs of the noble actions that poets have praised,—it was precisely these that Poe omitted in the theory and the practice of his verse. But who, of all the American poets, was ever to give more pleasure, and who excelled him in the "rhythmical creation of beauty"? By these criteria he wished to be, and should be, judged.

A NOTE ON MARK TWAIN

MARK TWAIN revealed in *Roughing It* a masterly grasp of an American scene, and his tale of Buck Fanshawe was one of a number in which he consciously reproduced the story-telling manner of Jim Gillis and similar frontiersmen. Others, written then or later, were the story of the Jumping Frog, the Jaybird and Acorn story of *A Tramp Abroad* and the stories of Jim Blaine and his grandfather's ram and Dick Baker's cat, which he tried to tell exactly as he had heard them. Later he developed this art in *Huckleberry Finn*. Meanwhile, he wrote in *Roughing It* about the Sandwich Islands, for, to report on the sugar-industry, he had gone to Honolulu, a town that suggested, vividly indeed, New England. The streets were lines of white frame houses with picket fences and green blinds and the little white wooden churches that one found in Vermont. In the dwellings of the missionaries, the traders, the whalers, smothered in tropical vines and flowers, one found the same objects that one found in Nantucket or New Bedford,—sea-shells carved with biblical texts, whales' teeth with full-rigged ships, glass paper-weights with miniature pictures of rural snow-storms. The Hawaiian king sat on a barrel fishing on the wharf. Charles Warren Stoddard had visited the islands two years before Mark Twain with feelings and a point of view that were totally different, for Stoddard was charmed precisely by the pagan elements that shocked this "brevet Presbyterian," as he called himself. Mark Twain spoke up for the Protestant missionaries, the "devoted old Puritan knights" who had broken the tyranny of the chiefs over the people, while, relishing the voices of the island girls, so liquid, free and joyous, he found their native dances "strange and unpleasant."

This little touch of prudery recurred in other books in which Mark Twain was to record his impressions of travel; he could not contain his fury, for instance, at one of Titian's Venuses, which he called the "vilest," the "obscenest" picture in the world. He described this lady as "Titian's beast" because of the position of one of her hands, for he was a very prudish man, "demonstrably more prudish than Howells," in the view of one who has read his unpublished papers. He had grown up in a different world from Stoddard's or Bret Harte's, children of cultivated families who had come from the East with its liberal traditional standards of the old European culture. Mark Twain was the true frontiersman, like David Crockett, in an earlier day, who was shocked by the mild goings-on in the theatre in Philadelphia* and "blushingly retired," in a phrase of the time, as Natty Bumppo would have done and many another grave American woodsman. One and all had absorbed the atmosphere of the evangelical Protestant sects that were strictest in their taboos in the sexual sphere, the simple old frontier religion that dominated Mark Twain's mind long after he had consciously ceased to accept its creed. His favourite poems were *The Burial of Moses* and *From Greenland's Icy Mountains,* he was always drawn to ministers, though he liked to shock them, and his delight in Robert Ingersoll, whose writings he "devoured," was a measure of the depth of his early religious faith. Like the popularity of Paine's *Age of Reason* and Volney's *Ruins* on the frontier, decades after these books were obsolete elsewhere, it

---

* "We started for the theatre, and found a very full house . . . What a pity it is that these theatres are not so contrived that everybody could go; but the fact is, backwoodsman as I am, I have heard some things in them that was a leetle too tough for good women and modest men . . . Folks pretend to say that high people don't mind these things. Well, it may be that they are better acquainted with vice than we plain folks."—*Col. Crockett's Tour to the North and Down East,* 1835. What David Crockett heard in Philadelphia in 1835 must have been very mild indeed.

bore witness to the presence and pressure of the old religion and the "limitless fire and brimstone" that he recalled. He had shared this to the point where, at the age of twenty-three, he regarded himself as a "lost and ruined sinner," * and his mind retained the impress of it, like untold thousands of American minds that had lost their belief in its dogmas and in heaven and hell. The sabbath and the Sunday school constantly recurred in his stories and jokes, with the old celestial imagery of harps, haloes and hymn-books, reflecting the culture of the frontier,—almost exclusively biblical,—where the Holy Land was always and everywhere a subject of interest.†

The stamp of this old religious faith went very deep in Mark Twain, and how much was not the fatalism of his later thinking a result of the predestinationism he had heard as a child? His contempt for the "damned human race" had largely a Calvinist origin too, his notion that God made man "because he was disappointed in the monkey," and Mark Twain's first important book, *The Innocents Abroad,* was a singularly complete expression of the frontier culture. While the "innocents" had seen much of Europe,—France, Italy, Spain and Constantinople,—they had "cared nothing much" about it, as Mark Twain observed, and it was the Holy Land that brought out their enthusiasm,—the "pet feature" of the excursion, he said, was the "pilgrimage part." In Italy Mark Twain himself marvelled over the great railway stations, the smoothness of the road-beds of the railways, the magnificent turnpikes, hard, level, straight as a line, as white as snow,—which pleased him because he understood them, as he frankly said,—while, convinced of the superiority of his own country in everything else, he confronted the European scene in the mood of a "de-

* See the letter to his sister Mollie, June 18, 1858, written at the time of the death of his brother Henry.—Mark Twain's *Letters,* I, 39-40.
† Even at Virginia City this interest flourished. Mark Twain lectured twice there on the Holy Land after his return from the voyage of *The Innocents Abroad.* One might multiply examples indefinitely. James Whitcomb Riley wrote a few years later that at Rossville, Michigan, the Holy Land was the subject in most request for a lecture.

bunker." For he was the "man from Missouri" who had to be "shown" there. With his fellow-travellers, as he described them, he "galloped through the Louvre," he observed that Lake Como would seem only a "bedizened little courtier" in the august presence of Tahoe, the Sierra lake, and this ex-Mississippi pilot remarked that the Arno, a "historical creek," would need to have water pumped into it to become a river. Thus Mark Twain galloped through Europe too, as well as through the Louvre, feeling the need of a "tourist for breakfast" when he saw how the travellers' books had deceived him—until he came to Palestine, which was another story. Like the other pilgrims he was all excitement over the Sea of Galilee, Samaria, Nazareth, Tabor and the mouth of the Jordan. The Holy Land was the "grand feature of the expedition," he said. The taste of the frontier triumphed in *The Innocents Abroad*.

Mark Twain's intention in this book was to see the old world with his own eyes, not as other and earlier American tourists had seen it, to tell what he had seen, not what he had read. The guides in Italy were delighted, he found, to secure an American party because they were usually so full of emotion and wonder, expressing a delight and admiration that he could have envied when it was real but that struck him as too often conventional, sentimental and false. He tried to be honest about his feelings, he tried to distinguish, both then and later, between his own and those he had borrowed from others, and he once remarked that he had visited Niagara Falls fifteen times before he got his imagined Falls "gauged to the actuality." Only then could he "begin to sanely and wholesomely wonder at them for what they were, not what I had expected them to be." * In his efforts to "get a natural focus" on things that he observed, he struck the first note perhaps of the tourist mind

* *Following the Equator.* See, in the same book, his remarks about the Taj Mahal. He could not "keep down," he said, his enthusiasms and emotions about it, although he knew they were not his but belonged to the writers whom he had absorbed. In order to find out what his own genuine feelings were, he carefully itemized his indebtednesses to the descriptions of others.

that flourished in American writers fifty years later, when they
were determined not to be fooled by "culture," but he also
resembled too many of them in throwing out the baby with
the bath, in rejecting the "truths" of culture along with the
"shams." Really believing, as he later wrote, that a "chromo"
was as good as a "Raphael,"—or equally important, at least, to
civilization,—that the "august opera" was no better than the
hurdy-gurdy, he attacked the legitimate claims of culture along
with its illegitimate claims, as equally a "superstition . . . im-
posed upon the world." So, teaching writers to be honest in
their vision, he also sanctioned the bad taste, the provincial-
ism and philistinism and ignorance of the American masses.

Yet just in this, oddly enough, Mark Twain performed an
essential role, distressing as this was at the moment to cultivated
people. Had not Emerson looked to the "rank rebel party," the
Western Jacksonians and their heirs, to root out the "dilettantism" of American culture? He hoped these berserkers would
have their way that the "new" might start with greater promise,
the "genuine growths" of the American mind that had begun
to appear already in the Western stump-orators, for instance,
and David Crockett. Thus Emerson had written in 1843; and
was not Mark Twain, the "Vandal abroad," as he called himself in an early lecture, precisely the kind of berserker that
Emerson had hoped for? Did not Mark Twain, in his negative
way, do almost as much as Walt Whitman had done to clear
the path for an American culture of the future, as the Vandals
of old prepared the way for another new culture in the north
of Europe because they were insensitive to the Mediterranean
culture? For ignorance and incomprehension are the womb and
the cradle, as often as not, in which new states of mind are conceived and sheltered, new cultural variations, new human types.
Ignorance, *not* independence, was Mark Twain's contribution,
in *The Innocents Abroad,* to the growth of an American culture, for if he had been prepared for Europe as he was prepared
for the Holy Land would he not have been moved there too
to the conventional raptures? As Huck Finn said in *Tom Saw-*

yer Abroad,* "There ain't anything that is so interesting to look at as a place that a book has talked about," and the Bible had aroused Mark Twain's interest in the "holy places," † whereas he had inherited the immunity from Europe of the settlers who had crossed the Alleghenies and who shared the feeling of the later "isolationists" in advance. If he had inherited the feeling for Europe of the usual good little Boston boy,—quite comparable to the Westerner's feeling for the lands of the Bible,— would he have shown the independence of Emerson, the author of *English Traits,* or the author of the *French and Italian Notebooks,* Hawthorne? Not so, to judge by the conventional thrills, the appropriate tourist's emotions that Mark Twain actually registered at Versailles and at Milan; for, in spite of all his efforts to be "honest," Mark Twain's impressions were stereotyped as Emerson's and Hawthorne's seldom were, and *English Traits* and Hawthorne's *Notebooks* were both independent and mature beside the infantilities and banalities of *The Innocents Abroad.* But Mark Twain's active ignorance was nevertheless on the side of growth at a moment when the national feeling was awakening in letters and when the "best people," as an English traveller observed in a novel of Howells, talked with admiration "only" of Paris and Rome. If this defiant Americanism encouraged the Philistine frame of mind and the frontier fashion of regarding "history" as "bunk," it also destroyed the subservience of Americans to the local ideals of the motherlands,—it broke the umbilical cord that attached them to Europe. This was an indispensable step in the process of building ideals that were not derivative but native and in time universal.

Thus Mark Twain with his fathomless naivety prepared the ground, as Whitman did, for a new and unique American art of letters, in a negative way with *The Innocents Abroad,* in a

* It was symptomatic that Tom Sawyer's "abroad" in this story of Mark Twain's later life did not include Europe at all. It was an old-fashioned Western Sunday school "scholar's" romantic dream of the biblical "land of Egypt."

† Mark Twain carried a Bible with him on the tour of *The Innocents Abroad.*

positive way with the Western writings in which he contributed to establish and foster this art. For *Huckleberry Finn,* with *Tom Sawyer* and the first part of *Life on the Mississippi,*— books that were all composed before 1885,—were germs of a new American literature with a broader base in the national mind than the writers of New England had possessed, fine as they were. As the literary centre of gravity of the country shifted slowly westward and the Western writers in time came into their own, one found traces of Mark Twain in their rhythms, in their vision, in their choice of themes, in their mode of seeing and recording what they heard and saw. *Huckleberry Finn* with its panorama of river-towns and river-folk was the school of many a later Western writer: the imaginative world of Sherwood Anderson was largely based upon it and the style of Ernest Hemingway owed much to it as well. By his recreation of the frontier life in the great central continental Mississippi valley, by his skill in recapturing its speech and its turns of mind,—the accent and the manner of the world he had known as a child,—Mark Twain preëmpted for later writers a realm that was theirs by right of birth but might never have been theirs for literature if he had not cleared the way.

A Chilmark Miscellany
was designed by Rudolph Ruzicka and
is set in his Fairfield type.